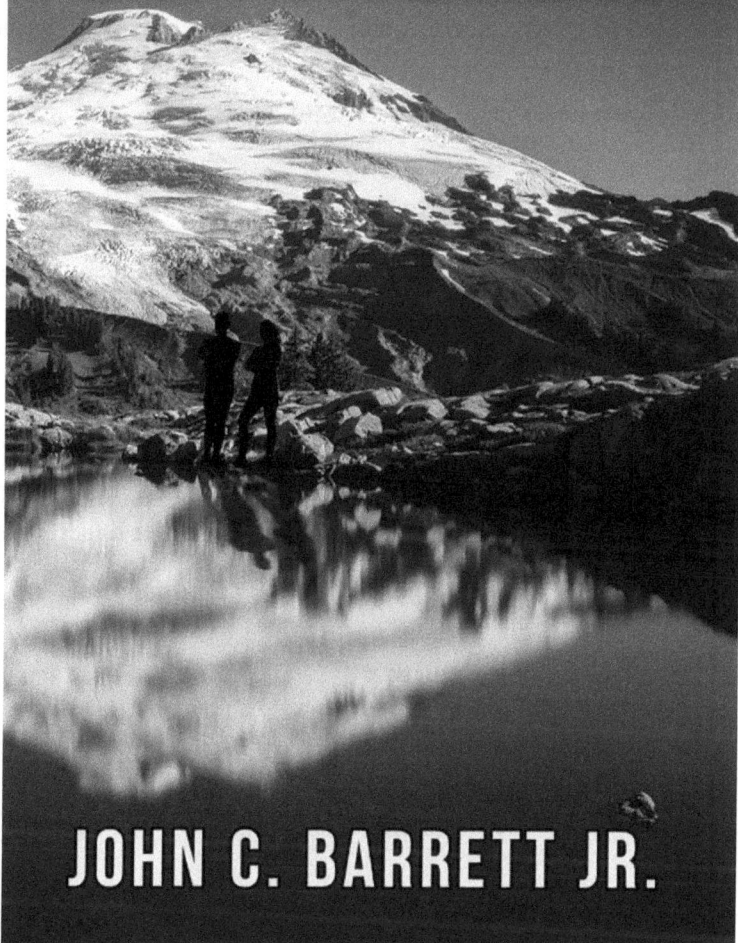

SOS-LIFE ENHANCEMENT

JOHN C. BARRETT JR.

DISCOVERING THE REAL YOU?

SOS Life Enhancement
Let us help you climb your mountain
Copyright © 2015 Dr. John C. Barrett Jr. PH-D
Published by SOS Publications West Plains, Missouri U.S.A. Printed in
U.S.A.

Dr. John C. Barrett Jr. is the coordinator of Support outreach Services =
SOS. Dr. Barrett is dedicated to publishing books on helping you help
yourself. It is our hope that this book will help you discover truths for
your own life and help you meet the needs of others.

Support Outreach Services (SOS) LLC West Plains, MO 65775
(417) 204-8022
www.sosselfhelpbooks.info

ISBN-13: 978-0692434628
ISBN-10: 0692434623

Cover Design: Lisa Narodowski – WiredNDesign Book Design: Lisa
Narodowski – WiredNDesign

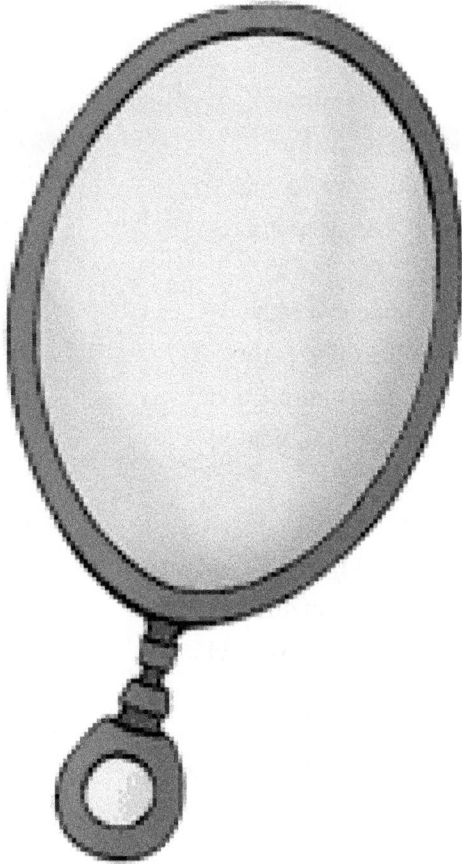

The Mirror of Life

DISCOVERING THE REAL YOU?

Catherine Pulsifer, (c) 2012

Life is but a mirror,
Looking back at us.
Everything we do each day,
Should lead us to impress.

And sometimes when we need,
To see life differently.
We have that mirror to help us,
Change our view gently.

The eyes of everyone,
Also reflect back.
Mirrors come in different ways,
To show us what we lack.

But most importantly,
Don't forget to always look.
Be your best
And life will look after the rest.

What we see and what we do
Are reflections of what is true
Don't let your mirror reflect the things
That you do not want to come true.

Instead each day set your goals
Strive to complete, it is good for your soul.
Give life all you've got
Never look in the mirror and stop.

Dedication

I dedicate this book to my mom, Lorene Hopkins Barrett

DISCOVERING THE REAL YOU?

Table of Contents

Preface: Opens the doors to SOS Life Enhancement 9-13

The Function of the Brain
Steps 1- 6: Identifying Your Behaviors
Steps 7 – 10 Modifying Your Behaviors

CHAPTERS 1 - 10

PREFACE

SOS Life Enhancement
Opens the doors to mental & personal well-being

The basic premise in this book contends that there is a need for support and, in some cases personal support, a person's need for help and the ability to help others. We start with the need to understand the physical brain and its functions, which is the control center for the psychological make-up of a person. We open the doors to mental and personal awareness and personal well-being, and to do that we use 10 steps in cognitive behavior identification and modification.

We also deal with the evaluations of stress, assessments of the stresses and analysis that measures the stress. When a person deals with these methods they should not deal with any problem without realizing, if they open old wounds, there is a need to finish the healing process. In some instances people second guess their thinking it is better to leave those old feelings alone until a person is ready to face the problem.

We open three doors mental, personal, and psychical

I have been in counseling and group sessions for over twenty years. We will show you how they work as we deal with what's under neath the paint and glitter.

During counseling or group sessions we teach people how Life Enhancement works. Some become core group facilitators and they learn how to mentor people. This understanding helps people who are struggling with relationships and addictions. There was a time when I felt like a victim, but my life was changed. I have seen other lives changed and I have seen marriages restored and people recover from addictions through our methods.

In this book I will help you to be able to live a better life. If you do not understand how to do this it is like the blind leading the blind. Many of our problems come from our childhood disorders and problems.

Life Enhancement Skills

Our methods have helped people find their way. In family counseling we have over 75% success, and in addiction counseling it is more like 20% success. At the boys' ranch we have around 75% success, because they are in a controlled environment for at least a year. We are not able to do this in our counseling, but we do have people in our group sessions for over a year and that is why we have had such a high success rate when they stay.

In this book we will study methods of cognitive behavior identification and modification, and our reinforcement axioms. I have dealt with sexual abuse and sodomy cases over the years and do relationship and marriage counseling.

A young lady, in her early 20's, came to my office and asked if I thought I could help her? I ask her to tell me why she felt she needed counseling? She told me she was molested as a four year old child and had suffered from a host of emotional reactions and problems over the years. She brought her grandmother to the session to confirm what had happened, I asked the grandmother if she felt she needed help.

There were definite signs of psychological problems that were affecting her mental-well-being. She had been deliberately violated. We discussed sexual crimes, but I told her, generally speaking, that there are none more severe than sexual abuse, and they cause psychological reactions and are more violent than other crimes or property crimes. There are also two types of hidden sexual assaults: The victim acknowledges to herself and perhaps also to others as to what happened. In this case she had been molested, maybe more. The situation matched the legal definition of rape, but the victim, for different reasons did not see it as such and felt it was her fault. I asked her to think about it before committing to counseling. The counseling would not help unless she saw it through.

During the second session she agreed to see it through. I ask her to tell me what had happened. She told me of suffering intense emotional reactions over the years and wanted to get past those feelings. The visions started when she was a teen. She said, "I would wake up with this man coming on top of me and I couldn't go back to sleep. I can't sleep at my mother's house because it happened there. I explained the reason they started in her teens. The Prefrontal Cortex starts developing which has to do with her memory as a child. I said,

"You were told not to talk about it and it would go away and she suffered rejection from her mother." I described the events as personal crises and the person usually experiences of fear, agony and anxiety, mixed with emotional numbness at times. Her childhood was filled with those emotions. It is common to have severe reactions for months and they can come back after a few years. I asked her if she had disturbing emotions combined with low self-respect and sexual dysfunctions and she said, "Yes."

I took some time to go over some defense mechanisms such as denial, the function of suppression that could block-out the strong emotions and thereby she had tried to escape the painful feelings over time which can be psychologically helpful and exhausting. She tried putting the worst parts of the assaults out of her memory and she tried to put them out of her mind, and did at times. Victims often try to avoid the immediate distress and try to shut it out of their mind.

I told her that disassociations are a part of the problem, another defense mechanism which can be employed during painful physical attacks and abuse, and was the reason she was unable to escape the memory. There was survival techniques taught as we talked in these sessions. I would ask her to remember as much of the details as she could as we went through each session. Each session we would go over the same situations. I told her the more we talked about it the easier it would be to deal with. It is called cognitive reinforcement.

Because we will have to break down these defensive mechanisms that affect the victim's ability and motivation and to talk about the abuse they suffered. I told her it was important to continue with the sessions, because, if not she would suffer deeper depression and anxiety. I describe them as long-lasting traumatic reactions, avoidance of certain thoughts, feelings and situations that remind the victim of the abuse. In her case the mental images of this person over her body two to three nights a week. Avoidance behaviors are psychological defense mechanisms against severe anxiety and tend to be long-lasting.

One of the most common affects is depression and withdrawal, which can last for years. She attempted three different suicides, and had sleep disturbances starting in her teens, especially when the victim is assaulted. In this case it happened in her home. This would happen when her mother was at work. She started staying with her grandmother to get away from him. Consequently her grandmother has raised her. She visits her mother from time to time.

She was unable to use rationalization as a defense to cope with the attacks. She seemed to feel a greater sense of betrayal and was more confused about the meaning of the acts.

In the third counseling session she told me what had happened. Her grandmother said she complained of irritation and tenderness in the vaginal area at the age of four. The grandmother saw it for herself, but her mother didn't believe her and still is in denial. To some degree her mother wanted her to get help hoping to prove she was wrong.

Ongoing violence and rape sometimes happens within a close friends, family, and may result in affect that is com- parable to those of torture and war (PTSD). This is due to the repeated violence, such as physical harm, threats, and often is intensified as trauma.

I explained that the perpetrator's first objective is to gain control of the victim. In her case he was setting her up for the violation of her body. She knew it was wrong at her age, and his intent was to complete the action. I have a sister that was molested by a neighbor when she was four. They want to control a person. Some use physical violence, and threatening violence. In her case it was scare-tactics. In this case his strategy was to gain her trust and create a situation she could not get out of. He was dealing with a child. He wanted to take control of the victim in some way.

In her case she tried to avoid the attempts by staying with her grandmother. It has been my observation in these cases of abuse. There needs to be a resistance and find some way to defend themselves. There should be an attempt by the person to defend themselves against the aggressor. Her own home was not safe. However, there are two obvious problems with this viewpoint of defending themselves. First, the non-resistance may be used against them, because they are going to hurt or kill them, some feel they are to blame or it will be used against them in court.

The recovery process largely depends on the person and reactions by the family, friends and professionals. It is important for the victim to be able to talk about the assault without being interrupted, questioned as a person, and the trauma is not minimized or explain away. Therapy and counseling may be necessary to help the victim work through the traumatic experience. It is important that the person is not made to feel guilt or any responsibility after the assault, which harms instead of helps, and to help her understand the real reasons why she needs to deal with the abuse.

At this point in counseling a person needs to understand the psychological defense of the mind-set. It has to be changed partly as a result of an unconscious conviction that those who behave appropriately will escape trouble; which also strengthens their own sense of security and control. Another reason is placing the blame on the perpetrator who caused the abuse. It relieves oneself of the responsibility of feeling they are to blame. There is a need for action under the guidance of a counselor. In this case it helped her take action and helped her.

In counseling session four we got a real break. She said, "I saw him at a gas station last week. I don't think he saw me. I was trembling and cried for a while before I could drive my car. I was so unsettled that I couldn't go to work that day." She asked me, "What do you think I should do? I said, "What do you want to do?"
She replied, "I want them to put him jail." I said, "I think that is a good idea. I think you need to go the police and report it to them."

The next two sessions we continued with reconstructing the values of her self-image and putting the blame on the other person because he had caused the problem. Each time we talked about how she felt that week and is it getting better. By this time we were meeting every two weeks. She went to the police and her grand- mother went with her. They said it had been too long ago and they couldn't do anything about it. They said that they would check his record and try to link you with someone else and see if they had made any charges. All they could find was a speeding ticket. That does not mean there weren't others they may not have reported it.

This can intensify their feelings of alienation and feeling

powerlessness. One of the tasks of the counselor is to build a family and social network for the victim. Others are judgmental, particularly when they do not approve of the victim's behavior. They may exacerbate existing conflicts over this. Some families respond with anger. The thing that helped her was her taking action and doing something about it. If she had not faced that incident, and let it pass, and had done nothing, she would have let him control her even when she had nothing to do with him. I asked her if she felt better and she said, "Yes!" She was glad she went to the police.

Let me explain how these faith-based methods work. There is a new method of counseling called, "Competent Nouthetic Counseling." This method is based on letting the person make their own decisions, with the guidance of a counselor or therapist. For years counselors and therapists controlled the person, and the person was dependent on the counselor or therapist. This is a new approach to counseling a person. People who go through these sessions should be expected to go through life with a successful ending, and find solutions to their problems and experience healing at the same time. That is what this study is about; creating a non-dependence on the counselor. If you believe in these methods you will learn how to deal with your own problems as well the problems of others you know, and this will enhance your life and theirs.

Chapter 1-The Function of the Brain, has to do with getting acquainted with you: let's start with who you are, and how do you feel about Life Enhancement? We will be able to answer that question better as we develop this study, and then we will ask the question, "Does the brain have any authority over what a person does or thinks? The importance of this study deals with how people feel about themselves and others, and what drives their emotions. What does motivation have to do with your thoughts and thinking? The question comes down to how do you "Control the Brain Functions?" In this study the brain influences have a lot to do with human behavior. I will answer that question and other questions in these Life Enhancement studies, you will find out what problems you are dealing with and how the brain works in Chapter 1 and what it does.

Chapters 2-7-Behavior Identification: We will deal with "Mental-Awareness." It is about how a person thinks, but more than that, meeting the many needs of the individual. People do fall short in dealing with their "mental-well-being;" I want to present how to have a balance in life

Chapters 8-10 Personal Behavior Modification: The challenge comes in different methods of changing human behaviors. There will be the challenges to do right, and accomplish things. There is also a conflict of what to do. The way to do this is by being able to relate to your personal-well-being life experiences, relationships, at work, and play.

There have been advances in mental-health, and personal-well-being, but there have been greater advances in self-help books. Over $11 billion a year alone is spent on self-help books.

This has revolutionized the way we deal with the mental and the physical well-being of a person. There is a need for such information in today's society, because there is more stress, anxiety, depression, and many phobias.

Why should you take up my studies on SOS Life Enhancement? I believe people want more out of life, not just getting by while dealing with a situation, but living a meaningful and fulfilled life. I believe some of this information in this study on Life Enhancement Skills will benefit a person by using counseling techniques, which comes in the form of behavior modification and identification; it involves dealing with patterns of all kinds.

Support Outreach Services is a neutral party, but my objective is to unlock some of those doors to life.

Support Outreach Services are available through our website. http://www.sosselfhelpbooks.info. You will find a list of (SOS self-help books) (Training Booklet Mentoring & Coaching) (Training Manual on Leader Ship Training Manual / Counseling in Group Sessions).

Book:How I got answers to my Prayer & Spiritual Warfare in Prayer!
1. Standing in the GAP for others, (God Answers Prayer).
2. Co support & Co-prayer-support for others.

DISCOVERING THE REAL YOU?

Booklet: (Free) (Rehabilitation & Forgiveness) My Testimony: Life can cast a "Shadow of doubt in a person's life?" & falling by the way (backsliding as a Christian)! We discuss my testimony and what happens and the changes in my life.

Questions I had to answer, Christian Methods, Values, & Biblical Principles.

(Booklets)

What are some Secrets for a Happy Christian Life? Secrets to Happiness.

Common Enemies of Man-kind / Christians.

How Can Christian's "Develop Control & Balance while Maintaining a Disciplined Life.

Understanding & Creating a New Life in You!

Comparing the modern age of psychology and the

Self-image has to do with the character of a man or women.

Scriptural view of Self-image.

The modern age of methodology in terms of the Scriptural view of the person

A. A down-hill-spiral exposes the weaknesses in man-kind/Christian.

Burnout - Depression - Anxiety in Christian's,

Why is the New Reformation Wrong?

Biblical out looks on divorce. Or (Booklets & Video)

Chapter 1

STEP 1:
IDENTIFYING YOU

Door 1: Mental-Awareness
Who is that person in your mirror?

I have often used the phrase, "What is ticking and clicking?" Are you a time bomb on the inside? Are you ready to explode some days? I know how that can feel as I look back at my personal experiences. All it takes is the right set of circumstances. I have been there and have gone through some pretty serious situations because of a divorce. My life was threatened, and my house was broken into. I had to get a firearm for protection, all under the guidelines of self-defense.

Then next were serious bouts of arthritis and another divorce. The hardest blow was the last divorce and the last arthritis attack that just about crippled me for life. In the midst of this there were three heart setbacks and high blood pressure each time. All of this has left me with physical limitations and a disability that I have had to deal with. With God's help I haven't let the circumstances get me down.

Each situation adds to the stress and pressure, and that will have a definite impacted on the next situation. Now let's see how multiple forces are happening at the same time that is what I had to deal with. I thought I could beat the odds because I don't drink or smoke, and I live a clean life, and I consider myself a good Christian.

There is an internal compass in everyone that points to what direction to take, but people don't always go in the right direction.

Why? I thought I was a well-adjusted person, but it wasn't as easy as it sounds to be able to understand my emotions, feelings, desires, and motives. I wanted to do well in my life, and that was a force because I wanted to be successful. I thought I was able to relate to the meaning of such actions and reactions taking place in my life.

I felt I had come a long way in a relatively short time, how I did it is a relevant question at this point. We must be able understand the whys, if possible, and what makes us "tick." I look back on those situations and wonder how in the world I kept from exploding or falling into the depths of despair, but I didn't, and I thank God for that.

I am going to look at what makes us tick or what is clicking in this study; I will refer to the Emotional Balance, Control or Out of Control, relating to Stress, Anger, Anxiety, Depression, Guilt, and Criticism, in relation to a situation or problems in this study-guide. "How did I climb the highest mountain" in my life? I believe in respect for others and getting my life under control.

In our first chapter I am going to introduce you to some exciting new information, and I want to show you how SOS Life Enhancement will help. This is going to help guide you so you will know what to expect in life.

That is the reason I use terms that are relevant, and in a way a person can understand what is happening in their life. I have been at the bottom in my life, and that is why I feel you will learn from these studies, because I use methods that worked in my life. Some of the information may take more time to get through what needs to get done as we deal with issues in a person's life. Another problem is discouragement; I use basic psychological methods in meeting the needs in different areas.

I will use other authorities, references, and profile the different subjects that relate to the different problem areas in a person's life.

FORGIVENESS, Your FLAWS ARE SMALLER THAN YOU
THINK. LOOK PAST
YOUR MISTAKES ARE JUST STEP PING STONES TO SUCCESS,
and LEARN TO DEAL WITH YOUR STRESS. WHY LET
ANYTHING STOP YOU FROM LIVING LIFE TO THE FULLEST?

One: does the brain function independently? To some degree the brain does, that is why a person needs to control what goes through the brain.

Two: you need to know how the brain works so that you can understand the psychological make-up of your decisions and analyze the problem and work on problem solving, and how it affects your well-being. A person is not only limited to their mental health; the results may influence a person's physical health.

One of the biggest problems has to do with the battlefield of the mind. I know some will say the physical battles are the toughest, but these mental conflicts are a product of how a person deals with them.

Once-in-a-while a person just needs someone to talk to, but it should be someone who cares and understands. They may be able to say the right thing at the time and that can do wonders, and help a person get back on track. Three goals for self-discipline:

Challenge yourself!
Believe in yourself!
Focus on your life and your goals!

People should take advantage of wise counseling, but most don't look for the right kind of help. Most people seek advice from someone who will agree with their ideas of what is right and wrong in their life. People have a tendency to believe they are right and they think they know what is best for themselves and others. Others get advice from a spouse or friend, rather than seeking wise counseling from a counselor in the field in which they need help.

My dad said this about seeking wise counsel, "Go to a person you respect and that has knowledge in the specific field you need help. If you have a plumbing problem, go to a plumber, if you have a problem in finance, go to a banker or stock broker for advice, and if you need personal counseling, go to a respected counselor."

Let's look at a person's life, and see if we can look at it like a rock or stone, before the sculptor takes the chisel in his or her hands and starts to work on the stone. There is a reason he or she has to use a chisel, because the rock or stone is hard.

A person's life can get hard to deal with over time, and some- times it takes a chisel to reform their life. The rock comes from hardened clay that takes years to form. That is very much like what happens to a person.

When looking at a person's life, it is like clay in the hand of a master potter. It may stay soft and pliable for some time. The potter can make things out of it when it is soft. That relates to childhood where a life can be molded, but when a person gets older they may get hardened over time and it is like the clay that gets hardened into a rock, and the rock needs a chisel instead of gentle hands. At one time just the gentle use of the hands was all it took to form a child's life. No person knows what is going to happen until it starts to take shape.

A person may have an idea where they are going, but if the sculptor or artist makes a mistake they can ruin the work of art. They might even have to start all over again and again, or they might be able to work around a mistake or mistakes. It may even make it a better work of art, and sometimes it becomes a priceless work of art. He or she will have a vision as to what they want the sculpture to look like. They may have to work on it over and over again until they are satisfied with the completed piece. My life story fits into a work of art. There had to be a lot of chiseling done in my life before it started to take shape.

My mission as an author is to help a person get their life together. The ideal in this study is for a person to feel free to stop at any time and then restart. I know there will be a lot of information to take in at one time, and that is why I have different places to stop and different subjects relating to each person's needs. This is my burden for others; Gal. 6:1-3, "Bearing one another's burdens".... I do not claim to know all the answers to every person's problems and needs. I use excellent references and personal profiles in every avenue of our studies.

What speaks volumes without saying a word is how you live your life, and what speaks louder, but it shows up in your actions and reactions in a situation.

A person's mind-set declares their intentions!

The Big question is who are you? That is what we are going to find out; where are you going in life?

For the most part, people are looking for the easy-way-out, or quick-fixes for their problems and situations. Life is usually much more complicated when you are dealing with problems and situations and how those problems and situations relate to your life. It all comes down to how and what a person thinks. What a phenomenon, knowing how the brain works!

The brain is a receiver, much like a television set, which picks up a signal from the network station. Your spirit works in the same manor. The information comes from a person's spirit, some call it the soul, the conscience and it sends and receives a signal like the television station. The brain is like a computer that stores information. Does the brain actually think?

No! In the same sense the spirit of a person functions quite independently and it communicates the feeling to the brain. The information is stored and then a person makes a decision to recall the information. I think of the soul and spirit as the inner being, not the brain. The conscience and sub-conscience make judgments according to a person's feelings. If they are upset, it's probably going to be a bad decision.

This is never more evident than when a person recognizes the hindrances, or things that upset the harmony in their life. There could be many reasons why things happen. Something needs to be done in those kinds of situations! There is a saying, "When things get tough, the tough get going." Some people fall apart when things happen or something doesn't go their way. Sometimes they shut down and can't function. How can I help you climb your Mountain? What are the next steps that unlock the doors to life and happiness?

Getting down to the task of "why you do and say things?" It helps to start with one's self!

Climbing your mountain is about making the right choices!
- I believe there are certain principles involved in determining these factors!
- I believe there are some basics in determining "who you are!"
- I define them in two ways; Primary & Secondary Influences, second is personal wants, needs, and despairs!

In this book we will try to find simple solutions to complex problems, in relation to the circumstances within the situation! Then, we will define the mental, emotional, & physical actions and reactions from within and from without!
- It is paying attention to the realities in a person's life!

- Not hiding or covering up the struggles or conflicts, and the hurt, anger, hostility, and bitterness inside!
- What people often see is the outside, but they may not be aware of what's going on inside!
- Some of the time a person is overwhelmed by what's going on inside and out!
- Making choices - dealing with reactions.
- Normal reactions - impulse emotions.
- Abnormal reactions – impulse emotions.
- Out of control, dominated, co-dependency - an improper balance.
- Stressed-out, stress, stress level, burn-out, - even depression.

You should be looking for a solid foundation to build on.

There is power in knowledge and understanding of one's self.

Living up to the inner-power from within, not living it down; but living up to *your* expectations makes the difference.

Certain events cause a person to STOP living a successful fulfilled life as such while a person's heart keeps on beating and breathing, in some cases they can't face what has happened.

When the QUALITY of life has been ALTERED, even slightly, or in some cases the past problems has destroyed them mentally, emotionally, and their physical ability to cope.

There is a problem when a person keeps looking back and sometimes the old problems are a part of everyday life!

All of us have / or had to deal with those feelings of the past, and how those emotions affects our present feelings.

You say some of these those feelings sound a little familiar; I want you to find out what is going on in your life.

When there is a trauma mentally, emotionally taking over your life, and there is a breakdown!

√ SOS Support-Groups are one of the more popular self-helps in today's society.

√ SOS Study-Guide, for the person looking for Self-Help information

√ If these self-helps do not work, then the next step is professional counseling.

√ At this point see who you are as a person?

√ To see if your back could be against the wall.

I want you to find out who you are and find the real you, and the person you really want to be. I want you to keep an open mind as we go through this book on life skills, and my hope is you will see how these \how these Life Enhancement studies can help a person. This is a partial picture of the total program and work. I hope we will hit the target I think of this as just one part of the total SOS Life Enhancement program, the heart and soul of a person lies in these life enhancement skills and studies.

This is where it all began in my life, how it progressed over the years, and how I dealt with the different situations in life. Through all the trials, I learned how to solve problems. My hope is you will want the entire study to give you the total picture, depending on what has happened in your personal life.

Most of us have an interest in our own well-being, and the need to fulfill those personal needs. My hope is that you will identify with those feelings. Each of us can identify and bond with each other in some way. There is a great feeling when that happens, and I want you to know that there is someone out there who cares for you. To find your way is so important, and then to get on track can be exciting. I have spent a great deal of time in these studies and research, also searching within myself to find a way that makes sense of what happened in my life and to be able to pass it on is my goal. I would like to tell you what happened in my life, and my hope is you will enjoy my experiences as I try to help you.

I have spent several years trying to understand why things happened, and the purpose behind them. Because of the victories I have experienced, I find that I'm more at peace with myself   than I have ever been in the past. What was it that brought about this change in my life? I am a Christian, but that was not all of the answer. So what happened to bring about this peace that I have, and how do I pass this on? I must have done something right, or was it just luck, or do we have some control over our lives, and are we able to change things?

I have dedicated my life to life skills studies because I want to see it work in others, if for no other reason than to know that they can do it. You are welcome to come along and see what happens. The best part is learning how to use these life enhancement skills will be for me to help someone along the way and if I don't, I have had a good time doing what is in my heart. This journey has been fun, to say the least. Maybe I'll inspire you to do something you have always wanted to do. The main thing I want is for you to be able to find yourself and a joy and peace in your life.

This was my very first thought when I started writing my life story. I remember back when I was in the first grade. The very first book we learned to read was "Run Dick Run" and Dick said, "Run Jane run," we read it over and over again. The subtitle of my life story, Run John Run, has nothing to do with that book, but it fits the basic principles involved in changing my life.

Let me take a step back in setting up the title of my life story. It goes back to my high school days. The coach of our football team said, "If you want to play football you will have to go out for track in the spring." So I did. I practiced running for a couple of weeks, and he set up time trials to see what event we were best at. Mine turned out to be the 220 long distance dash. It took stamina and strength to run that kind of a race, and that fit my physical ability to a tee. I was the best runner in that race. So the coach put me in a track meet with some other schools. I was always good enough to make the team, I never had the special abilities to be a star, but I had a great desire to compete and be a part of the team.

The night of the track meet was early in the spring, and it was very cool that night, I still remember how cold it was. A buddy and I did everything we could to keep warm, my feet were very cold, we had sweats on and we were still cold. My race was one of the last races that night, I ran as fast as I could, and every time my feet hit the ground I could feel the thump all through my body. It felt like I was running in slow motion like you see on TV. I did not win the race nor do I remember where I finished, I was just glad it was over.

That was the way my life felt for years, every step seemed like a thump for a long time, and I think my life was running in slow motion as I tried to handle my problems. Now you know one of the reasons I chose the subtitle Run John Run, but there is even a more compelling story, and that was being able to understand the person inside of me. That was a challenge I was not expecting, so when these thumps happened, I thought everything would turn out better as life went on.

Back in 1987 began a dark time in my life, because of the pressures of life were caving in on me I thought I was going to have a heart attack any time. I had no idea where I was going, I was living day to day expecting a heart attack or I was faced with a divorce. Ten years went by, and no heart attack. In May of 1996 I knew I was going do something, but I didn't know how I was going to do it? So I got down to the serious business of dealing with my health and I started writing about how I had gotten better over the years.

I think I have some idea of how a woman feels when she carries a baby. The agony and travail of writing about my health has given me some of the basics on how to deal with mental health and well-being. I am human, because it has taken me years to get to this point, and that has taught me how to prevail over certain situations. I will share this in more detail in as we go through each book.

Then the study and writing of the different books has been a major undertaking. Now maybe you can understand why I think of it as a birth, and it really is. Bringing it to this stage has been a wonderful experience; this is a conception from within me. I hope you will stay with me as we go on.

Who is that person is in your mirror?

I want to take you through step one: The key that unlocks the door to Life Enhancement, opens into what I think is the most important part of our Life Enhancement skills. This will set the stage for my biography "Facing the real me Run John Run. The hurt and pain, and the real cry for help, and the real changes in my life" it is actually an introduction and conclusion to my life's studies and how dealing with my health saved me from living a life of disappointments.

This part of our study guide will help you understand how human behavior modifications and identification works for and against you.

These methods and principles are helpful as we go through how to deal with your life. I would like to give a little bit of a profile of how I am going to approach these evaluations, assessments and analysis. I have shown you a picture of the mountains and a stream going down a mountain. I have provided a picture, but now I want you to get a mental picture as we look how the process works for your good.

There is a lake at the bottom of this mountain. The theme is "still waters run deep." I want you to carry out this thought as I introduce how to understand behavior identification.

When a person approaches a problem or situation, it is easy to compare it to a mountain. The climbing of that mountain can be slow and very tough getting to the top? Then going down the mountain can be very fast and dangerous because a person is likely to be running down the mountain or walking very fast. I would like for you to picture a stream flowing down the mountain at the same time. The farther it flows down that mountain the faster the water is going, and also there are rocks and boulders as the water goes around and over the top, and then down the mountain.

Then we see a beautiful lake at the bottom of the mountain, and it looks so calm and peaceful. A person usually doesn't relate to the fact that all of that turmoil had to happen before that water could become a beautiful lake. This can be true in your life after all of the turmoil in your life. The fact is there can be peace when you understand your life and depth of how to make good decisions at the same time.

Remember, it can be hard to climb the mountain, and yet it may be the best part of the experience. It can be exciting as a person is going down that mountain and dangerous at the same time. I want you to be aware of that fact, but I want you to enjoy the climb because it will be the toughest time, and it will be worth it when you get to the top and down to the peace in your life. I think my life reflects some of all those facets as I look at it. I love the still waters now, and I want to pass all of that on to you as we go on.

Also, I want you to know that these studies reflect that kind of character. So, keep this in mind, I want to be helpful at the same time.

I think one of the first things I have to do is help you get your priorities straight. What is it that you want to do, or what are you wanting accomplish in your life? What is the purpose for your life? Everybody will likely have different answers to those questions because of their age, and their sex will determine some of their priorities.

My hope is to give you a hint in the direction you may want to go. Sometimes a person needs to stop and get their bearings and see where they are, and what needs to be done! That means you are going to have to stop, look and listen! People get so busy living their life and don't realize what is or has happened, and why their life is in a mess. That is what happened to me. I got blinded by what had happened, or in some cases I tried to ignore what was happening, somewhere along the way I got lost in living my life. Does that sound familiar to you?

What makes our Life Enhancement unique? I present it from a laymen's point of view. Each book in the series has its own character, and the way I see life and what happens.

There are many ways of dealing with your life! There is a common denominator in each of our lives, and the fact we all have to deal with problems in some way.

The question is, "Are you doing the right things, and are you really solving the problems?" Let me set it up like this, and see if I'm on track. A person may take shortcuts to solving a problem, and they say, "I will take care of this later." Does that sound familiar? To those hard problems and crises there are no easy answers!

The advice you get is not always the best. Because your family, friends, are not counselors, but they should be a part of your support team. There are books a person can read and some are not always helpful. You may say if that is the case what should I do now, and that is a good reason for wanting the right kind of help. I know, I have been there, and when I listened to others and society influenced some of my decisions I made and again I made my own mistakes. I had to learn the hard way; I don't want you to do that. When I made a mistake, did I ever hear about what I had done wrong? It seemed like I always made the wrong decision in who I married! I have learned to live with my past, and not judge myself in the way others see me. But, I began to understand that I'm only human. I learned why I made the mistakes in those relationships, and my quest is not to make the same one over again.

That is where I can help you. Learn your weaknesses and strengths, and when over reactions take place and when it happens over and over again it has a pyramid affect. My problem was I thought it won't happen again, and I was determined not to make that mistake again. The internal grief comes from inside feelings, and they can be devastating to deal with. Here is where the over and under reactions are taking place.

To get a clear-cut picture of a situation is hard to do because there are so many variables to deal with and that is why it is important to deal with the last four steps in behavior modification. A person's past has an influence on the rest of their life effecting every situation, and the way you know this is by the walls and blocks in your mind. The brain has a protective mechanism built in to protect you from pain.

I have tried to look at my life with an open mind because I'm not going to live up to some and their expectations of me. There are some who will see you as a failure regardless of what you do. People tend to think of a failure as weakness, but failure can become a strong point if you know how to deal with it. I try to look at the good in the bad and try to see the bad in the good. If a person looks close enough they will be able to see their strong points and their weaknesses, and how to deal with them is where we are going start.

It is also difficult to understand what is happening to a person because of their excess baggage that can come into their lives. This can be particularly true in adults and teenager's lives, but children face their own set of problems too. How can a person keep their PERSPECTIVE on life?

We are kind of like a person that walks a tightrope; we have to keep our balance and focus. I have seen tightrope acts, they usually have a safety net to catch them when they fall, and they always go back up and do it over again.

We had a rail fence around our barnyard as a boy, and I always had the challenge of trying to walk that rail fence without falling off, and if I fell off I would get up and continue walking on the fence. Sometimes my friend and I made a game of it. The object of the games was to see who would not fall off and reach the end, if one did he would have to start all over again, and sometimes we would see how fast we could go and how far without falling off, and they were the winner. There were posts every so often where we could get our balance and go on.

Have you ever had one of those days when everything seems to go wrong! And wondered "why me?" The stress point peaks and you say, "I'll be glad when this day is over." Sure you have. Have you ever had situations or problems that you thought were impossible to deal with and you questioned why they happened to you or will you ever get through them.

Every time I thought everything was going to be all right, something else went wrong. This is a good example of how things can happen. It could be a health problem or a physical problem, and yes, it could even be a personal problem that is making your life so hard to deal with.

We should not judge a book by its cover. In other words, we should not judge another person until we have "walked a mile in their footsteps."

Then there is the personal side, like what are the contributing factors of what a person has done. How do you fit into the equation of what is happening in your life? When you make a decision or a promise in your heart and mind, you may do one of two things. You may pray about it, or you may think you know what is best for your life. Then again, some choices you make always seem to be wrong. My hope is things will work out better if you make an effort to change things and find a solution.

Sometimes a person thinks everything will be all right when they know better, and they think that is all it takes and they won't have any problems because nothing will go wrong. I found that to be true in my relationships, that thinking caused me major problems, not so much what I was doing, but rather the way I was handling them. This is a major case in point. There are always choices; one of them has to be wrong for you and one has to be right.

Now let us look at the reality of the situation that is good for you? It takes determination and perseverance to change things and then see those things through. That can be good if you do what is right for you. What if the other person doesn't agree with you? Let's look at this way. Let's say you are going down a one-way street in the wrong direction, now you are in real trouble. Remember one thing at this point, you are likely to rationalize or even make excuses for what you do and what was the turning point.

Now let's look at it from this point of view. You may be going down a one-way street in the right direction; and the same can be true in life, you are going in the wrong direction in either case, again you're in real trouble.

I don't have all the answers! It is not easy to understand what is happening when a person is drowning, so to speak. You may be fighting as hard as you can, but you are going down for the count, and that is why you need help.

There can be true peace in the midst of all the turmoil if you are dealing with the situation. There can be a depth at the same time because you are trying. This happens in everyday situations too.

I think one of the first things you need to see is how to get your priorities straight. What is it that you want to do and want to change in your life?

There needs to be a purpose and plan in your life, probably up to now you don't have a plan, knowing what to do, and what you want to accomplish in the future? I hope this gives you a hint in the direction you may want to go. At this point I recommend that a person needs to STOP and think! STOP and get their bearing and see where they are going, and how their situations are going affect the rest of their life! Is it worth the pain?

That means you are going to have to stop, look and listen to what is happening and are you willing to except the changes needed! A person can get so busy in living their life that they probably don't realize what is or has happened to them along the way. You may be living with the status quo and thinking nothing needs to be done to change things. If you accept the status quo, that means you are willing to live with the past and not challenge yourself for a better life in the future.

That is what happened to me. I was blinded by what had happened. Somewhere along the way I lost my direction in life, and where I was going.

There are many ways of dealing with your life! There is a common denominator in each of our lives, and the fact that we all have to deal with life in some way. I want you to ask these three questions:

are you doing the right things and for the right reasons?
Are you really solving your problems?
Are you happy with the results?

Did you listen and learn from your mistakes, and if not, why? When I didn't listen to what I believed to be right it was an entirely different matter. As I look back on what happened in my past, it seemed like I always made the wrong decision and choices in my relationships and even some of my business decisions!
The hardest thing was to admit I had made a mistake. When I learned to understand why things went wrong, then they became stepping stones, and I was determined not to make the same mistakes again.

Whatever weaknesses you have they are likely going to happen over and over again. Even when I was determined not to make the mistake again, I did it anyway. The internal grief I experienced was painful. It was hard at the time to live up to my expectations, let alone what my family expected of me and all of that became like the proverbial noose around my neck. It tormented me on the   inside and that part was the most devastating thing to deal with. Here is where some over and under reactions were taking place, the way I felt about myself affected my attitude. I felt I was a bad person because I had let God down.

We have a tendency to look at another person and see how they should have handled a situation. I want you to look at the contributing factors in your life. A person may not be so critical if it is happening to them; do you get my point?

What happens when a person's life is wrecked and has no place to turn? At this point a person may feel like they are fighting as hard as they can just to keep their sanity, but they are going down for the count. I want to stop it before you go down and lose control, and feel you have no place to go.

The Physical Function of the brain

The human behavior that pertains to a person's thinking and what resides in them are stored in the brain. The brain can control their thinking. Prior information that is stored in the brain is separated into the different functions of the brain. Another factor is the genetics passed on from one generation to another. The next influence is your environmental cogitation which is developed from the family history. This allows you to understand the current physical structure of the human neurological system. We will study the cognitive aspects of human behavior within the person.

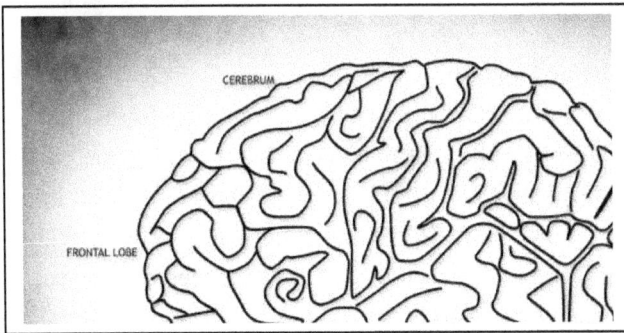

The overall goal of SOS Life Enhancement is to help you understand the brain and why you do certain things, and why things don't change easily. The brain does not stand alone because the brain is an important part of our study guide. I will use developmental charts, axioms and profiles in human behavior identification that are based on the nature of a person, and for the use in developing a life of happiness. To do this we must use the educational, psychological, sociological tools necessary for the formation and maintenance of the individual's behavior identity as a person.

There are basic reasons for using these studies in the areas of the brain, and they're not erroneous theories, nor are the development of these studies pure conjecture or imagination.

The following study of the brain is confined to those features of the brain which determine or contribute to human behavior.

Defining the function of the brain

The brain gives out several signals in Milliseconds and there are things happening at the same time in milliseconds, faster than you can blink your eye this will reflect in a person's actions or reaction.

A response can be different than a reaction; however, both are being triggered by a person's response. A response may not be a reaction, but a reaction always takes place when a person takes action. The response is also the result of an evaluation , or command given by another person or by the person's inner feelings, and the brain takes on some form of action, but a person has brought it a about by some kind of feelings.

The Geography of Thought

Each cerebral hemisphere can be divided into sections, or lobes, each of which specializes in different functions. To understand each lobe and its specialty we will take a tour of the cerebral hemispheres, starting with the two frontal lobes, which lie directly behind the forehead. When you plan a schedule, imagine the future, or use reasoned arguments, these two lobes do much of the work.

One of the ways the frontal lobes seem to do these things is by acting as short-term storage sites, allowing one idea to be kept in mind while other ideas are considered. In the rearmost portion of each frontal lobe is a motor area, which helps control voluntary movement. A nearby place on the left frontal lobe called Boca's area allows thoughts to be transformed into words.

When you enjoy a good meal—the taste, aroma, and texture of the food—two sections behind the frontal lobes called the parietal lobes are at work.

The forward parts of these lobes, just behind the motor *areas, are the primary sensory areas. These areas receive* information about temperature, taste, touch, and movement from the rest of the body. Reading and arithmetic are also functions in the repertoire of each parietal lobe.

As you look at the words and pictures on this page, two areas at the back of the brain are at work. The frontal lobes are called the occipital lobes, process images from the eyes and link that information with images stored in memory. Damage to the occipital lobes can cause blindness.

The last lobes on our tour are the temporal lobes, which lie in front of the visual areas and nest under the parietal and frontal lobes. Whether you appreciate symphonies or rock music, your brain responds through the activity of these lobes. At the top of each temporal lobe is an area responsible for receiving information from the ears. The underside of each temporal lobe plays a crucial role in forming and retrieving memories, including those associated with music. Other parts of this lobe seem to integrate memories and sensations of taste, sound, sight, and touch.

The Inner Brain

Deep within the brain, hidden from view, lay structures that are the gatekeepers between the spinal cord and the cerebral hemispheres. These structures not only determine our emotional state, they also modify our perceptions and responses depending on that state, and allow us to initiate movements that you make without thinking about them. Like the lobes in the cerebral hemispheres, the structures described below come in pairs: each is duplicated in the opposite half of the brain.

The hypothalamus, about the size of a pearl, directs a multitude of important functions. It wakes you up in the morning, and gets the adrenaline flowing during a test or job interview. The hypothalamus is also an important emotional center, controlling the molecules that make you feel exhilarated, angry, or unhappy. Near the hypothalamus lies the thalamus, a major clearinghouse for in- formation going to and from the spinal cord and the cerebrum.

An arching tract of nerve cells leads from the hypothalamus and the thalamus to the hippocampus. This tiny nub acts as a memory indexer—sending memories out to the appropriate part of the cerebral hemisphere for long-term storage and retrieving them when necessary. The basal ganglia (not shown) are clusters of nerves cells surrounding the thalamus. They are responsible for initiating and integrating movements. Parkinson's disease, which results in tremors, rigidity, and a stiff, shuffling walk, is a disease of nerve cells lead into the basal ganglia.

Making Connections

The brain and the rest of the nervous system are composed of many different types of cells, but the primary functional unit is a cell called the neuron. All sensations, movements, thoughts, memories, and feelings are the result of signals that pass through neurons. Neurons consist of three parts. The cell body contains the nucleus, where most of the molecules that the neuron needs to survive and function are manufactured. Dendrites extend out from the cell body like the branches of a tree and receive messages from other nerve cells. Signals then pass from the dendrites through the cell body and may travel away from the cell body down an axon to another neuron, a muscle cell, or cells in some other organ. The neuron is usually surrounded by many support cells. Some types of cells wrap around the axon to form an insulating sheath. This sheath can include a fatty molecule called myelin, which provides insulation for the axon and helps nerve signals travel faster and farther. Axons may be very short, such as those that carry signals from one cell in the cortex to another cell less than a hair's width away. Or axons may be very long, such as those that carry messages from the brain all the way down the spinal cord.

Scientists have learned a great deal about neurons by studying the synapse—the place where a signal passes from the neuron to another cell. When the signal reaches the end of the axon it stimulates tiny sacs. These sacs release chemicals known as neurotransmitters into the synapse. The neurotransmitters cross the synapse and attach to receptors on the neighboring cell. These receptors can change the properties of the receiving cell. If the receiving cell is also a neuron, the signal can continue the transmission to the next cell.

Some Key Neurotransmitters at Work

GABA (gamma-amino butyric acid) is called an inhibitory neurotransmitter because it tends to make cells less excitable. It helps control muscle activity and is an important part of the visual system.

Drugs that increase GABA levels in the brain are used to treat epileptic seizures and tremors in patients with Huntington's disease.

Serotonin is an inhibitory neurotransmitter that constricts blood vessels and brings on sleep. It is also involved in temperature regulation. Dopamine is an inhibitory neurotransmitter involved in mood and the control of complex movements. The loss of dopamine activity in some portions of the brain leads to the muscular rigidity of Parkinson's disease. Many medications used to treat behavioral disorders work by modifying the action of dopamine in the brain.

Neurological Disorders

When the brain is healthy it functions quickly and automatically. But when problems occur, the results can be devastating. Some 50 million people in this country—one in five—suffer from damage to the nervous system. The NINDS supports research on more than 600 neurological diseases. Some of the major types of disorders include: neurogenesis diseases (such as Huntington's disease and muscular dystrophy), developmental disorders (such as cerebral palsy), degenerative diseases of adult life (such as Parkinson's disease and Alzheimer's disease), metabolic diseases (such as Gaucher's disease), cerebrovascular diseases (such as stroke and vascular dementia), trauma (such as spinal cord and head injury), convulsive disorders (such as epilepsy), infectious diseases (such as AIDS dementia), and brain tumors.

Neurons

"Your brain is full of billions of microscopic cells.
Many of these cells are special messengers called neurons. Neuron means "nerve cell." We have about 100 billion neurons in our body. To picture the size of a neuron, think about the fact that 30,000 neurons can fit on the head of a pin! Neurons carry special signals back and forth throughout your body. Billions of neurons are chained together in a network of nerves. Nerves are a large amounts of neurons linked together in a small place. Your nerves send tiny electronic signals through your body to the brain stem and to the main brain.

The neurons inside your brain have three basic parts. Every tiny neuron consists of a cell body, an axon, and a dendrite. Neurons "talk" to each other by sending chemicals to each other across a very tiny space called a synapse which is the firing within the brain. Learning what happens when two neurons "talk" to each other. As the brain makes connections, it actually grows dendrites and makes stronger synapses. That means that the more you learn, the heavier your brain gets! So that means you really can "grow" a better brain. Your brain is full of billions of microscopic cells. Many of these cells are special messengers called neurons. Neuron means "nerve cell." We have about 100 billion neurons in our body.

To picture the size of a neuron, think about the fact that 30,000 neurons can fit on the head of a pin! Neurons carry special signals back and forth throughout your body. Billions of neurons are chained together in a network of nerves. Nerves are a large amounts of neurons linked together in a small place. Your nerves send tiny electronic signals through your body to the brain stem and to the main brain. The neurons inside your brain have three basic parts. Every tiny neuron consists of a cell body, an axon, and a dendrite. Neurons "talk" to each other by sending chemicals to each other across a very tiny space called a synapse. Learning happens when two neurons "talk' to each other. As the brain makes connections, it actually grows dendrites and makes stronger synapses. That means that the more you learn, the heavier your brain gets! So that means you really can "grow" a better brain.

Do people loose brain cells as they get older? Yes, you lose brain cells every day because of decay and disuse. Scientists aren't sure how many you lose each day but you don't need to worry. You have enough to last for your whole lifetime.

Some people think that your brain can never grow new neurons. That isn't true. Scientists have found that one area of the brain called the hippocampus can grow new neurons. They are doing more research to see if there are other areas of the brain that regrow neurons.

Principle 1: Personal-attention & care: Who am I?
Profiling patterns in the mind-set

Let's look at patterns in a person's mind-set and how the brain aids the process, and how they relate to a person's mental-well-being. Believe it or not, what you do every day becomes a way of life and sets a pattern of behavior. I am going to remind you, old habits and patterns are hard to break, and to develop new habits and set new patterns is even harder to do.

Let me illustrate what I'm talking about. The city had scheduled some road construction on the route I took to work. I had to change my route to work that was part of my daily routine. The first day wasn't so bad. I made a conscious effort and watched where I was going. The next day I watched real close and I made it just fine. The third day I must have had something else on my mind and I went back to the old route without thinking. I knew I had made the wrong turn, because I had gone back to the old route and the road was blocked. Now you see a good example of what I'm talking about. The subconscious took over and I fell into an old pattern in my life. I have been there and gone through these kinds of situations in my life, but you may be saying, "I like things just as they are, I don't want to change, I'm okay; I don't want to do that Dr. Barrett."

May I remind you again you may be going down the road in the wrong direction, and to change things is going to be an uphill battle all the way even if you want to change? Let me take you a step farther! Have you ever said something before you really thought about it, and thought, "Why did I say that?" I have done this many times in my life, and it becomes a pattern of behavior. The question is how do you change that way of thinking? I have done some things without thinking, and even when I thought it over I still thought I was doing the right thing. Consequently, it didn't work out like I thought it would.

I have gone through that whole routine and that resulted in bad things happening in my life and life went on, but I was not the same person afterwards. I had to live with the consequences, even when they were innocent mistakes. A person means to do right and make the right choices, but things don't always turn out right.

There is a motto, "Don't ever say I won't do anything" because that may be the very thing a person ends up doing. Another problem is not looking at all of the consequences! I have even worn that old T-shirt a few times, in a manner of speaking. I hope you are beginning to see where I am coming from.

What is your destiny, more than that, what is your life all about? To accomplish things and succeed is a goal, but experiencing life can be the greatest feeling, especially if you are going in the right direction.

Sometimes, with all of the confusion, battling, and fighting, it is so hard to raise a family because they are affected by these influences. A person's job and family finances are one of the things people worry about, and if that is not enough, a person can get so busy with their job and family they don't see the real problems.

I want you to stop and find out what is causing the problems and confusion. I hope you will be able to find out what the real problems are in your life and how to deal with them, and then how to solve them to some degree. As we go on with our studies, we have more clues and answers to these questions. We will be looking at a man or woman, and how they are dealing with their reactions, feelings and dealing with their emotions in their relationships in the next chapter. Now let's look at mental-awareness, as it relates to who are you?

Now we're going to dig a little deeper into, who you are? We are going to look at some the same issues from a different viewpoint. We have only scratched the surface as to who you are? We are going to look at ways you can help yourselves & understand where you are going. The second aspect of our studies deals with behavior modification we will deal with in steps 8 - 10 based on practical applications, evaluations, assessments, and analysis, based on profiles and charts and axioms.

Part One: Defining the Problem

When a person has problems in these areas of living there is probably an under lying issue in personal fulfillment at home and at the work place. The defining process may involve plans in evaluations and using good value principles and common sense. This is one means in how a person can puts them into practice on a daily basis.

Another is establishing and facilitating communication skills in changing behavioral patterns, and we as a (group leaders and care persons) must provide supervision allowing for growth in different areas of a person's life. Without providing a consistent framework for insight into the symptoms of behavioral patterns, phobias, anxiety, panic, and depression disorders this cannot be done without personal discipline on the behalf of the person involved in changes. This also cannot be done without making an emotional investment in their relationship or relationships, and without creating help in the social adjustments and cultural dynamics in the relationship.

The importance of listening without preconceived ideology's as to what the person is saying, and a person should never base an evaluation on a single piece of data. In any case additional data must be used and wise assessments based on the interview in the "group session" is essential. The knowledge and experience work hand-and-hand and can provide a wise foundation for help as a person tries to live a better life.

Objective observations are better than subjective judgments. Similar to the principles above, but this principle challenges their reference point and it is important for them to create a criteria for change and help them create an objective view of the situation. Bring in objective information rather than relying exclusively on intuitive hunches and impressions, no matter how good one may feel about their situation.

These five basic rules:

Cognitive-disorder rule trumps all other decisions in the session. This is due to the sometimes life-or-death reality of certain cognitive disorders or trauma.

Parsimony rule dictates the simplest path for the best results. A close corollary rule is that fewer details are better than many.

DISCOVERING THE REAL YOU?

Chronology rule places priority on the problem that has been presented. The logic of this rule is that the longer the discussion, it is more likely to find their primary area contention (and not a secondary issue- not related to the problem or functional disorders.

Crisis rule gives priority to resolving crisis problems first. The nature of the crisis is such that it consumes nearly all the time, attention, and energy of the person embroiled in it.

Some cases are life-treating and demand attention... helping to resolve the crisis may stabilize a person's life and priority.

Safety or outcomes rule all the physical and mental disorders can be placed within a rough safety zone or outcomes...the rule suggest that treating the safest issue problem come in order-the one with the best prognoses or outcome – may be the wisest choice.

But there is order in solving small problems first to give confidence as they take on bigger problems.

Chapter 2

Step 2:
AWARENESS OF YOUR FEELINGS

In this chapter we will be dealing with psychology in conjunction with the working of the brain, I will give you tools to help you understand what you are doing, saying, and feelings.

Step 2 unlocks the door to mental awareness and behavior identification.

How to deal with your feelings

The body, soul and mind may be crying in some way. The mental and physical aspects will be so important in a good healthy mind, and attitude, but there is a negative side. The soul of a person and the heart of a person are that driving force inside, but the brain's analyzes a person's mind-set is the difference between what a person does. Let me say the mind is a terrible thing to waste and that also applies to a person's life.

There is another twist in how the brain works. A person can be misled by their conscience, which is governed largely by their self-esteem/ego, and by not fulfilling their wants, needs, and drives. The emotions can be driven by anxieties, and a person's imagination can run away with them because of fear. They can be influenced by negative forces of the mind, and it can get pretty confusing when a person is in that state of mind.

There are so many ways that a person can look at a situation and justify themselves. It all boils down to what a person thinks is best for them or not. There is always a time of anxiety, when a person doesn't know for sure what to do.

A good illustration of this can be seen when a person is thinking about getting married. There is always some doubt; "Is this the right person, or is this the person I pictured before marriage?" Sometimes they seem like two different people after marriage. The person they dated and the person they married!

Another thing that happens, life does not always turn out like they planned, like the number of children, and how many boys and girls they want. There is a conflict when two people want different things in life. This may bring about a cry for help before and after the decision to get married. The cry from inside will let them know something is wrong, but couples don't always listen. At this point they need to slow down and find some common ground before they get married, if not, what is likely to happen after they are married? The anxiety is not always a bad sign and a couple should always do the "right thing" for both to be happy, if not one or both are going to be unhappy. Now think with me and follow my line of thought.

Some clues:
1. When the mind cry's out in confusion.
2. When the soul cry's out in anguish.
3. When the conscience cry's out in pain.

This is where the mind-set comes into play and how a person deals with self-esteem, self-will and selfishness will dictate the way a person feels about themselves and what they do. There is a twofold part in how a person deals with others. "You're going to say what does that mean?" That is a very good question, because that is where I am going next.

This is where low self-esteem comes into play; anxiety has a negative influence and may well cause a person to feel people don't like them. It will cause over and under reaction when someone is angry and upset for no reason. There is always a time of anxiety, when a person doesn't know for sure what to do.

While others take advantage of others that is not a good sign and when they look down on themselves, and degrade their self-worth.

On the other hand, self-esteem and self-will can also take on positive characteristics. A person may want something so bad they are willing to do anything to get it, figuratively speaking, even if it kills them. Sometimes it's hard to know love how fits into that analogy when it takes on the form of self-denial; this kind of love can lead to self-destructive attitudes and brings about a bad relationship.

When bad things happen in a relationship, it may bring on depression and low self-esteem to deal with. In that case how can that relationship work? Sometimes it's hard to know how love fits into a bad relationship. It is hard to know the difference between love and desire. They may feel they can't live without a person because they feel needed. The conflict of love and desire is not always easy to distinguish between love and a need for love. This kind of relationship can affect their good judgment and there are other reasons are not good for the person.

This is another good example of an improper balance. A person can feel alone in this kind of relationship and live with a great deal of anxiety and depression. This brings up the question, "Are your problems worth the anguish?"

Over critical obstacles in a person's life and love

Another thing to consider is this, has either person's love been violated and to what degree, and how much damage has been done? A person needs to consider themselves in light of the situation and make it a priority as to how important the relationship is to them. Commitment to a relationship, marriage, or dating should be of the up most importance. A failure here is damaging and will affect the situation a person is dealing with in the relationship, and as they take the next step in their life.

The one big question comes into play when dating the right person? It is very important in dating or marriage has a person violated your love and trust? The point here is evident, when they are dealing with problems and where did they come from.

What is love? Love is a natural feeling, especially in any relationship, and at the same time conflicts are a natural part of life. How does a person know the difference between conflict and abuse? One way is how you relate to "God is love" and what does that mean. God forgives when a person asks for forgiveness. That should be your guide. If a person doesn't want your forgiveness, can you forgive them and go on with your life. I hope these examples will help you in how to deal with your relationships. It doesn't mean you don't love them, but you can't live with their bad treatment or abuse.

How can a person say I love someone, and at the same time they are having problems dealing with each other? Love is not at all inclusive in how to deal with a relationship. A person can love someone and live in constant conflict; that is not the true test when it comes to love? The need for love is one of the strongest feelings, but why they live with conflict is a telltale sign as to how much they can love the other person. Saying, "I love you" is not enough. Proving it is in doing it.

If a person can't forgive and can't respect the other person, their love does not mean as much. To sum up the question of love, it is more than just saying, "I love you," it is putting love into action, and actually proving your love. Love should be the ingredient that makes the relationship better, if not it is not the right kind of love for each other and the love will not grow, but emotions of love can be over stated. It is putting your love into action that counts.

I've wanted to give up over the years, because I felt my love was violated in my own mind, and thought I would not be able to overcome the divorces and health problems. At one time I didn't think there were any answers to my problems.

May I say something, there are reasons for everything that happens, and I don't have to know all the answers. In my own life I made my choices and things certainly did not turn out the way I wished. I believe that some good came out of all the bad things, and some bad came out of the good. I know that I may be overly simplifying my life, but these are some real good principals that came out of all that happened.

People do change and yet I know people who have gotten back together, in every case the person who was in the wrong had a change of heart and mind. It worked when the other person was willing to forgive.

How emotional feelings relate to how a person reacts?

Emotions might be the most complex characteristic in a person's interactions, because they are a person's feelings. These feelings are very difficult to comprehend when a person is dealing with a situation or personal problem.

This hypothesis states they are dealing with their emotional experiences relating to their feelings and how are they relevant to a person's conscience and subconscious feelings. Is it possible for the brain to control the conscious emotions if they are out-of-control, or is the person unable to control them at the time? The brain allows for awareness, but because of previous experiences the brain has stored it can only act on what it perceives is happening. If there are no variations when it comes to perceived thoughts this is brought about by what the mind perceives, the emotions are unconsciously perceived. The brain takes action based on a person's feelings from the past.

Consciousness is a state of the heart and mind at the time, which can be occupied by a person's mundane thoughts, consisting of emotional highs or lows at the time. If this hypothesis is true, there may be some contradictions in the previous theories of self- worth. What happens if a person's emotions cannot be controlled in a situation? Perhaps if emotions are perceived as a state of conscious feelings, a person could begin to attempt controlling their emotional highs and lows a person does this through their thoughts and feelings. What happens when a person is having a bad day, they may react differently because they are upset?

However, sometimes I find myself not so sure of myself   and question whether I can even control all of my thoughts and feelings. Sometimes I can't control my emotions. That is why you need to learn how to control the inner person, and I will give you some methods I used in helping me to enhance my life.

Self-help books can help a person be responsible for their emotional out breaks and uncontrolled emotions, but what happens when a person feels they can't control their emotional feelings. Do they feel responsible for their actions? There has to be a reason to override certain emotions because of past feelings, for instance if both fail. This may lead to people committing a crime and then a legal penalty comes into play or punishment may be in order. The legal punishments are brought about by laws, but in such cases of emotions, emotions are not laws, only the heart and mind governs a person's deeds. It is more common when human reactions create a cause and effect in a situation. Thus some people have a milder form of accountability. A person may not want to live with someone who has hurt them.

There is an indirect sense, if a person does not feel responsible for a particular emotion or up-set; they feel they are not responsible, which makes it a negative assessment to how they have responded. In this case their analysis may be they don't feel responsible for their emotional out breaks, they feel they are justified because they have always acted that way. They may feel the other person is responsibility for their emotional out breaks. The important thing is how they feel about why they did it. In their mind they may think there is no legal penalty for hurting someone so it is not wrong to hurt them, but there is a moral responsibility involved in making things right with others.

A major reason for the more direct mental control over your emotions brings about a person's responsibility for controlling their emotions. This may be expressed in a particular act from the other person's emotional response. Now you have two people out of control, but in being able to control the emotional mechanism there is an underlying problem in the way a person responds, by letting a person become out-of-control in the first place. But, a person is responsible for their emotional response.

I do not defend this view which implies that a certain type and degree of emotional responses are justified. There may be a mental problem if a person's feels justified. I believe this avoids two extreme positions held by some: emotions are manifestations of a person's freedom of expression, and compared by those who believe people can never be responsible for their emotions. Of course a person is responsible for their emotions, but there are some who may need professional help when they are out-of-control of their emotions and when it happens over everything or even little things that annoy them.

The brain really kicks into gear

A person is preprogrammed to a certain degree to react because of their past personal experiences, interwoven or fabricated by the makeup of their genetics' ties to parents. Their personal feelings are involved because of their wants, needs, and desires. Now I want to look at these four aspects of a person's inner feelings. If there is hurt, anger, hostility, and bitterness involved they become a part of a person's personal make-up. This make-up has to do with what has happened to them. When the personal influences get out-of- control they become controlling factors. A person is going be under minded to a degree by their prejudices, their biases set forth in their life, and certain influences that govern their lives. They also show up in almost every person's reactions.

The personal thought process is clouded by influences and a person's mental-well-being. While the past influences weigh heavily on the present circumstance in the situation, in the process a person can hide things. Yet, all of these actions or reactions take microseconds to be discerned by the brain, but they may have been influenced from a person's childhood up to the very second.

• Real feelings are revealed by their happiness or by the baggage in a person's life.
• Personal feelings can be affected by their emotions, body's metabolism, and personal balance.
• Emotional Feelings can affect a person's mental-state of mind: conscious feelings in respect to the situation.
• There is always going to be actions and reactions taking place in any experience, "good / bad or in between."
• Personal actions and reactions can start with a mere thought, or in the thinking process.

Real and Superficial Feelings?
We will now look at a guide to help you understand what kind of feelings you are experiencing.

Let's try in our own way to get past:
• The old adage, "Everything is all right" when it isn't?
• Those excuses & underlying liabilities.
• Those misnomers and misunderstandings.
• We try our best to get to the bottom of things and work our way up.
• To get to the heart of the matter is more like it.
Different emotional feelings
• The body may respond according to its physical chemistry (like or dislike in foods).
• It could depend on how a person feels that day (good mood or bad mood).
• The mind or mental-state – conscious responses are they negative or

positive.

- The heart beats faster because the person is scared or frightened.
- You may respond with happiness or joy, or utter dismay or depression.

I believe a person has to be honest with their feelings, it is normal for the mind and heart to react to a person's feelings, and feelings show up in a person's ego, and emotional reactions! It is how a person deals with their feelings that make it so critical!

- Trying to get to the root of the problem!
- In most cases a person tends to deal with the symptoms, rather than their real feelings?

A person may try to sort out those feelings before they find out the real truth about their feelings. Sometimes they don't express their true feelings because they don't want to hurt someone or it hurts for them to talk about it.

Sometimes people get the idea that they are the only person on earth, nobody cares, or everybody is out to get them. Now they have created a self-complex! The trouble is they only think of them- selves. But, they need to ask how the other person feels or thinks about them? That is a different question.

When it comes to real feelings, a person could be dealing with major or minor issues, not the significance of the issues, and not prioritizing their real feelings. But, what is a person doing in reality? They may be defending their on their feelings in the wrong way, and feelings can make a person feel good or bad in a false sense.

When something makes a person feel good they may think things are all right, and they are making progress when in reality they are not. Feelings are good, but they can be deceptive at times. Feelings can be misleading when they are not based on true principles and facts. Just because something makes a person feel good may not be the best for a person, and knowing what a person has done may prejudice their feelings in the right or wrong way. Feeling things for the right reason; the right kind of feelings is what a person is looking for.

A person may have a tendency to hide their inner feelings and thoughts, and there may be a reason why they don't talk about their real feelings. The real truth is its hurts to talk about them, and it's hard for people to talk about their bad feelings. Others are very sensitive and get their feelings hurt very easily and they dwell on their own problems. They can talk about someone else and their feelings, what they should say and do, but the real truth is that it is usually not easy to talk about someone who has hurt them and ignore their own personal feelings.

This may sound odd, but a person hides things from them- selves, and even covers up why they are not dealing with those hurt feelings. In some cases they are hidden so deep in their subconscious they can't accept or recognize those feelings for what they are doing to them.

A person can pretend and even think everything is all right when it is not or they can think everything is wrong. They think no one cares and knows what is going on inside. Be honest with yourself first, and then others. I know it is human to blame it on the other person and see what they have done wrong, and blame them for your own misgivings. But, as long as you're looking at the other person and blaming them, you're likely not looking at yourself. Most people don't know their real feelings because you say everything is all right and pretend everything is all right.

Take off your mask and see what others think of you. When you take off the mask, others may see you in a different light. All things being equal a person may need to do it for their own sake; it will help you to be honest with yourself.

I think a person will be able to use some of these miss conceptions and apply them to other parts of their life. This is setting the tone as we continue dealing with these self-help studies.

Personal feelings

I wanted the pain to go away and the hurting to STOP! The hurting had built up over the years and I was angry because of what had happened in my life. Each situation was building and had left its mark on me. Each divorce and health problem created a crisis that I had to deal with. I would say to myself, I won't make that mistake again, but I did. I said after each marriage, I won't marry again. Instead I even tried harder to get it right, thinking the next marriage would be the right person! That is the best way to describe my feelings. I did not realize I had not dealt with my previous feelings about why it happened.

As I look back, they all had something in common. They had just gone through a death of a husband less than three years we were married and they were very emotional times for them. They had gone through a traumatic experience, and they had not gotten over the death. I could never live up to their image of that death. I don't know why I was attracted to them or why they were attracted to me.

I was a Christian and youth minister. I felt I could understand how she felt, her first husband had died in a car wreck, but she didn't tell me of a divorce until later because she didn't think I would understand and she was right. She didn't lie, but she did not tell one detail that would have changed my mind. I knew people would not expect a minister to marry a divorced person. She had an afar, I felt betrayed and hurt.

The one thing they had common they had not gotten over the death of their husband. That puts a strain on the other person and marriage. Each one of them had multiple marriages afterwards and so did I. I know now it was too soon for them to remarry. There was anger in each of them and they seem to take out their frustration on me and on the children, in reality blaming me and others for what had happened, and I could never live up their expectations. Now I know from studies they should have waited at least six years before remarrying.

At the time, the divorces had become a down-hill spiral in my life. I was not happy because I didn't feel I deserved all of those problems that had happened during the relationship and marriage. I didn't feel I was to blame either, for all of the things that had happened to them and I know it takes two to have problems. At the same time I felt out-of-control because I was unable to change the situations in our relationships. I felt I was a good husband in each case and they left me with some bitter feeling because of their problems.

I didn't want to go on with my life like this and have all of that bitterness and pain. The mental anguish and grief was an overload on my mind, body and in my soul there was the burden of guilt. I cried within myself because of the pain I felt I was to blame for what had happened.

There has to be a better way of dealing with my pain and they have to find a way to deal with their problems. I had to do something to get my life strengthened out and get the pressure off of me and get my life back on track. I stopped and took a look at myself.

I felt I was running for my life and other times I was running away from my life, "dodging the bullets" so to speak. Another way to look at life it is like a thread. You know how a thread can get unraveled in clothing and the more you pull at it the longer the string gets. You have to cut it off at some point. You know if you keep on you are going to run out of thread. You are going to have to stop, but knowing when to stop is the hardest thing we deal with. The same is true in divorce.

I'm the normal every day guy you meet, except for the fact that I have had four divorces and numerous health problems. I have lived through them and lived to talk about them. There is nothing special about my life. I have never amassed a great fortune, or been a great athlete, or a great Spiritual leader, or a great author either.

I have a ministry and business background and a full time professional occupation up to this time. I have worked hard and had some real successes and disappointments, failures and some life threatening health problems to deal with. Each sequence of events has led to another then another.

As I continue on with my life I have determined to look at my problems in a different way. Problems will continue to build-up like a ball of yarn until I do something to change the cycle. I hope you can understand the series of events that had built-up and threatened my well-being, until I took steps to change them.

So hang on as we go on our journey. I have lived a very healthy life as a whole, but abnormal at the same time. I am a good example of a person who overcame the bad. The reason for telling you this is that I would not be the person I am today without what has happened. I will show you by example how not to do things in your life. There were some lessons to be learned as I reveal those feelings of despair and guilt.

May I emphasize again that my life is the key that unlocks the doors as we go on. Everybody has their own keys. It is important how you view your life. That is what makes your life and mine special.

A person needs to know how to deal with their personal feelings, but this can be a little bit more confusing because personal feelings are linked to the hurt, anger, hostility, and bitterness. A person needs to see that they are not getting to the root of the problem. They may be showing up in how they are covering up things while they are exposing their personal feelings, the real truth is in how they see the situation.

There is one way a person tries to cover up their feelings; if you don't feel it, then nothing is wrong. Think of a cat using a litter box, the smell is still there, but you don't smell it. A person can say everything is all right and cover up their feelings. They are just covering up their true feelings, but the feelings are still there even if they don't leave a hint of anything. How does a person find a better way to deal with their personal feelings?

The answers are hidden deep in a person's feelings, but if they don't know their true feelings, how are they going to deal with those feelings? The next question is how are they going to relate to those feelings in a better way?

First, face the reality of who you are, and then face your true feelings. This is not an easy task! The different circumstances and influences that control a person can affect their feelings.

Let me make a statement, and try and prove my point. Let's look at a supposition. Does time heal all wounds and feelings? My contention is in some cases it never gets resolved completely, but hidden or put in the back of the mind. Therefore, time does not heal all wounds and bad feelings never go away; it only puts a distance between those feelings for the person or persons. Those feelings can harden over time, but the remorse sets in because those feelings get harder and deep rooted, but usually nothing has been done to solve the hurt, anger, hostility, and bitterness that brought about those feelings.

So, the saying, "Time heals all wounds" is not always true or an accurate statement, but it does put distance between the next event that reminds them of what had happened, but the under lying problem is in the memory which never forgets those feelings and they affect the present situation. It may not have the same significance or impact it once had or yet it could get worse because it builds up and adds to the existing circumstances. They will show up in other situations as life goes on.

Let's bring up another situation when someone wants to hurt a person at their expense, and make them pay for something they have done wrong. This is usually at the expense of a person harboring bad feelings, because of what someone has done to them. In other words, dwelling on the hurt doesn't help the present situations, but a person thinks they feel better punishing the other person who has hurt them in the past, and a person can even plan revenge, and that usually beings about a spiteful attitude.

This is the worst thing in this case, because they are also hurting themselves in the process. This only damages their own ability to feel good, and they become a victim of their own devices, thoughts, and feelings. They have created a monster from within.

I think I have reached the point where I can express my feelings, and I hope I can put my hurt feelings aside. I am not here to cast a shadow on anyone, including myself. I will not bore you with the trivial stuff about my life, and yet that might be more interesting and fun to talk about. I am beginning to express how I felt about things as they happened in my life without going into things that won't hurt someone.

I'm going to pass on some of these deep feelings, but on the other hand it is hard to do because it brings back the old feelings. There was a time when I would get upset and mad just thinking about those old feelings. When I think about those events it is still just like they happened yesterday. Yet some of them are very special feelings because now I have gotten control of my thoughts and feelings, and I look at the situations differently now. I even feel good about them now.

I believe a person has to answer to themselves, but not at the expense of others in regard to hurt feelings, first-and-foremost. I hope by using my life as an example that might help someone else. I do not want to cause any personal harm in regard to their personal feeling. I may not be able to carry on a conversation with the person who hurt me, or even want to be personally involved with them. My goal is to live and let live as much as possible, and to get along with others when if possible.

Nor do I expect them to feel any different about me and that it is okay, but I do respect their feelings. I do not wish them any personal harm. They don't even have to like me, or forgive me, but I would feel bad if, after all these years, they still wanted to cause me harm.

Consequently, I'm a happier person because I can go on with my life. Although, I've tried to understand the whys and why fore's, I usually come up with some dead ends. The most important thing I've learned is to take life one day at a time. Looking back at those choices, they seemed right at the time. It doesn't seem so bad now, but in some cases it seemed like a nightmare at the time.

It is much different now, because I like where I am going, although it was a terrible experience at the time. That is the best way to describe it now, it seems like a bad dream, but I do feel like I'm a better person because of those bad experiences. I know who I am, and it has humbled me it's important how a person deals with those bad feelings. I am better off today because that is who I am. I don't wish those bad feelings on any one; things could have been different. I did what I believed to be right at the time, and maybe it wasn't all wrong.

I had an opportunity to know them and love them. I can say my life has been enriched because of the experiences. I would not be who I am today without living through some of those emotional upheavals, because the experiences of going through those divorces did not change me, maybe that's what it took to make me a better person, never-the-less I am who I am by the Grace of God.

I felt like I had lost the battle, but I kept on going. I never gave up on myself. In my life story, I will take time to express my real feelings. Now let's deal with difficult feelings in a situation.

I want you to evaluate those superficial feelings in your life, as I did. My hope is to save a person from some of the heartaches I went through. These evaluations are private and confidential, only the person you are sharing it with will know what is in a person's profile. One the most important steps in the healing process is being able to talk and share your experiences. At Support Outreach Services we offer that opportunity for you to share your life story.

When a person has been hurt so badly, they may have buried their problems or covered up their real feelings. Support Outreach Services wants you to bring out these hidden feelings, and talk about them with some who cares. This is where a neutral party is so important in helping a person find a way to deal with their feelings. Feelings can dominate and control a person's way of life and even take control of their thinking. Life goes on, but it is important to take control of those feelings.

Emotional feelings

Emotional feelings, like everything else, go through the thought process first, and physical emotional responses show up in a person's body language.

Their emotional feelings are a part of their personal makeup. Say, for instance, a person has a bad temper they can't control; they will have to deal with those emotions. These kinds of emotional feelings can dominate/control the person in any given situation. The conflict is evident by the amount of emotion.

I have set up some guidelines to help a person decide what areas will help them. I think it would be good to look at all areas of your life.

Profiling the stress in a person's emotions and feelings

At my age I have finally gotten some peace and control of the storms in my life, but that was not always true. I started off on the right foot. What happened to change my life, and how did all of this affect me? I made a series of bad decisions and lived through some bad circumstance. The best way to explain it is that I had gotten off track in what I believed. It seemed like a roller coaster ride for a while. How did I get off-track is a question I asked myself many times, and I came up with the same answer? My process for recovery started by identifying with this fact, I was dealing with the same problems over and over again. I learned how these axioms worked and profiled these behaviors.

Now, let's look a little closer at the emotional experience in relation to the number of conflicts. Also, when you look at the emotions inside of a person, there will be stress. I want a person to be able to measure the stress level, and understand what stress means to their well-being. The stress demands are responses to the actions or reactions taking place because of someone or something. A good example is when someone expects them to do something, or when someone makes demands. The next word is crisis, and a person will probably deal with some kind of crises at different times. The amount of stress is the key factor involved in any emotional experience.

Stress

I was living in the fast lane and I was king of the mountain for 15 years or so. I had geared my life to the point that I didn't need much sleep. I lived off of my own energy and adrenalin and that was the highs for me. There are some good things about this kind of life and some that weren't so good. The fact that I was in good physical shape was one of the reasons I could do all of this and do what I did for so long.

I was shocked when I had my first arthritis attack and I didn't know what was going to happen to me let me explain.

I had a great job working at a local power plant. Every five years they had to do what is called a turbine over-haul. The plant would have to shut down to check all of the parts for wear. The stress factor on the parts could be compared to the wear on the body. I was a maintenance foreman and I really liked the job and they treated me very good at the same time.

The turbine had three different steam chests and the intermediate steam chest had gotten too hot. The bolts had seized up. Somebody had gotten the steam chest to hot at some time before the over-haul and there was no way of knowing who did it or when. We used pneumatic air hammers and they wouldn't loosen the bolts. We finally had to use 18 pound sledge hammers and pound on those bolts 16 hours, two shifts a day for about a week. There were three men to a hit on each bolt. Each one hit as hard as he could for as long as he could, and then the next man would take over.

This was too much for my hands and they couldn't take the pounding. We were just about to finish with the over-haul when my hands and fingers swelled up like balloons. I couldn't move my fingers at the time and the pain was very severe. I had to take some high powered medicine to alleviate the pain because it was so bad. I was no longer able to work. I was unable to get my retirement and social security because I was 42 years old. I didn't know what I was going to do at the time.

There were a lot of factors to deal with. All of the doctors and all of the tests I had to go through turn up negative. The most painful were the Prednisone shots into the founts of my fingers and I also took steroids at the time. Every doctor seemed to have different diagnoses as to what kind of arthritis I had. The test did not show any indications of Rheumatoid Arthritis. We finally got a break through when I got another doctor's opinion. He said that he had a friend who had a doctor with the same kind of arthritis. He said you have a very rare kind of arthritis and in the acute stages it re- acted the same as Rheumatoid Arthritis. The term is called Psoriatic Arthritis and it cripples and mangles the joints. I always say at this point, "I would like to stay out of those joints."

What was it that brought all this on there was too much physical stress and I had also created too much stress in my lifestyle that was a contributing factor and it left a big question mark at the time.

I have tried to see if anyone has had this kind of arthritis in any of our families, but I haven't as of yet. One doctor gave me ten years to live and I thought he didn't know what he was talking about, but I learn over the next 10 years he was almost right. Believe me this is going to be one of the toughest battles of my life. The three divorces were a mere challenge compared to what I am going to face in the next fifteen years of my life. Everything that has happened up this point may have had a contributing factor to all that has happened. I did get my Social Security two years later. The psychical therapist said this was the worst case he had ever seen.

Stress is in all three elements: mental, emotional, and physical. There are always causes to behavioral responses from a wide variety of different aspects of the personal experience. Contrary to popular belief, stress is not necessarily caused by an actual upsetting event; it is a common denominator in every situation.

The term can refer to demands placed on the everyday experiences that result in the body and mind being aroused by mental, emotional, physical responses. The physiological aspect of a response in meeting those demands is what causes stress. Stress in these areas could mean more strain or pressure placed on the mind and body system. With some stresses the body system adapts quickly, and changes without identifying the behavior. Sometimes a person becomes stronger without doing anything about a behavior. Let me explain, behavior modification does not come automatically. With too much stress, the body-system can reach a point where it will reach the breaking point.

Stress is an unavoidable part of living. To be alive is to experience the joys and frustrations of life. Some stress is good for a person, and there are other things that help "spice up life." Other stresses can be harmful, if interpreted in a negative way, while other stresses are useful. If it serves as an incentive or motivation for a person to develop better ways to deal with a situation, that is a good kind of stress. Since stress is inevitable, it's important to learn how to live with it, and make it work for a person.

Some have the mistaken idea or belief that stress is a sign of weakness or failure when they have experienced a stressful situation. Problems develop when people don't recognize what kind of stress is causing some of their difficulties, or if it is not successfully managed. How does an individual respond to stress? Some people seem to thrive on deadlines and others get anxious. It may cause someone else to become upset, procrastinate, and lose sleep, worry, and finally some stay up all night trying to finish the project or test.

How the body and mind reacts to any given stressor is different in each individual person. When too much stress is observed, eventual dysfunction will occur.

Stress is more than an isolated incident in a situation; it is the provocation that moves the person to act. It is also the product of many aspects of a person's lifestyle and environment. To reduce and manage stress, and its potential affects, can change many aspects of a person's lifestyle and environment. In some situations it will cause the stress level to change. In that case a person can do this by learning techniques to reduce external stress or to manage some causes of internal stress, and to handle acute stress.

What are the dangers of not controlling stress?

1. Alarm: as the body and mind is aroused by stress
2. Resistance: as the body and mind tries to adapt to stress
3. Exhaustion: as, with continuing stress, the body and mind reaches the end of its abilities to handle the stress
4. Muscles: chronic contraction and tightening the muscles,
5. Digestive system: difficulty with digestion, ineffective spastic contractions of intestines leading to diarrhea or constipation; excessive acid in stomach.
Cardiovascular: increase in heart rate; increase in blood pressure, constriction in the blood vessels; increased and it overloaded the heart.
6. Skin: decrease in temperature; increase in skin sensitivity, eczema (itchy skin eruption), acne, hair loss.
7. Endocrine (hormonal) system: increase in glucose, salt, and water retention; decrease in protein formation; decrease in immune resistance; muscle wasting.
8. Brain: increased arousal, mood changes, irritability, fear, anger, and confusion; difficulty concentrating; difficulty sleeping.

How can I tell if a person is under too much stress?

1. You are always rushed and cannot take enough time to do things well, or get in a hurry to get everything done.
2. You can't slow down and relax, even during weekends or vacations.
3. You're irritable or moody, get angry, or cry for no obvious reason.
4. You find it hard to concentrate or to pay attention.
5. You don't follow through on deadlines or you forget to send a birthday card to your best friend or family member.
6. You cannot seem to find time to do something you enjoy or just being able to relax.
7. Your mind is usually racing or confusion itself. You are up to your neck in details and you are constantly thinking of more things to do, which makes it hard to focus attention on the problems in front of you. You're not fully "there" when people talk to you.
8. You have difficulty sleeping even when you're exhausted. Your

mind is racing when you should be resting.

9. You feel pressure and an urgency to be active and accomplish something almost all the time.

10. You become irritated at the minor inconveniences of life, such as standing in line at the cafeteria, waiting for an elevator, or getting caught in traffic.

Much of the stress a person experiences is brought on by the mental or physical pressures affecting a person's energy. This causes a misconception of one's self and what they want to accomplish, which interprets and should give meaning to the events. The way in which an individual thinks; more importantly is their motivation and self-perception can increase or decrease their reactions to stress and the stress factors. How a person interprets the events or situations is important too, and therefore how they see the experience is often determined by their personality traits. If you become aware of these thought patterns, you can work to reduce negative thought patterns and stress responses.

Some of the other aspects relate to emotion, such as love, anger, crying or being angry are an emotional expression of what has just taken place.

At SOS we will look at several kinds of normal reactions and how a person reacts to stress. You will see how the ups and downs work in a person's life, and how a person reacts normally or abnormally, the important aspect is how quickly, or in a short period of time life goes back to normal. The mind and conscience sort out things rather quickly, and the decision is made even if a person is not happy with the decision.

Patterns

A person also has to watch for the patterns in their life. There are patterns in how a person lives or deals with their stress, because it is important to be able to measure the stress level in a situation. As a person develops stress patterns, demand patterns, and crisis patterns, they can watch how those patterns change when there is too much stress. These patterns have been developing since childhood, and now a person becomes set in those patterns, which relate to how a person feels, it best described by the good or bad feelings. The worst thing about patterns, a person becomes unaware of how they are controlling them, and they don't realize what is happening.

There are other aspects in patterns such as selfish motives. When they know it is the right thing to do, but also know something is wrong and don't know why, and they still end up doing it any way.

Demands

1. How can I refuse other people's demands without making enemies?

2. A basic premise of assertiveness training, gives a person the right to say no to certain demands, and not feel guilty. You do not have to meet everybody's needs, or agree to help every- one who asks for help. Saying no can be a great stress reducer by preventing a person from becoming over committed. Here, there are five points to remember:

3. Saying no should not mean rejection or putting down the other person. It simply means you are refusing a specific request. You should be able to keep the relationship with the other person, and the fact is, you might say yes to other requests in the future.

4. When saying no, be brief and direct.

5. Do not diminish your refusal with elaborate explanations, apologies, or excuses. You can give a brief reason, such as "I'm really too busy right now. Maybe next time." Excuses only provide the other person with ammunition for trying to make you change your mind.

6. If you really mean to say no, stick to it. Don't be swayed or coerced by the other person, who may plead, compliment you, or make you feel guilty, particularly if you have been manipulated into saying yes in the past. Remember, although the other person has needs, wants, and desires, so do you. And you have a right not to meet all the needs of others. A person is not obligated if they can't do it.

7. Use assertive body language when saying no. Make direct eye contact, speak clearly and distinctly, have good posture, and use appropriate gestures for emphasis. Avoid whining, slumping, and looking away.

People who get caught in the trap of overwhelming demands are likely to become prisoners of the routine of saying yes. They may not take time to notice other opportunities, and their habitual routine prevents them from taking the first step necessary toward harnessing their will to say no.

Most people are overwhelmed by the demands put on them, not-so-much in the actual work situations, but from how they deal with those situations. How does a person know whether there's a problem with the way they approach life? Some deem other aspects of life more important than others and that is natural, but a person may have a problem when they never find time to really see what is going on in their life and relationships. Or they might feel under constant pressure from all of the above. The danger sign is when a person believes they are indispensable, and have problems developing the capacity to dream an idea into existence and transforming it into a concrete intention.

People, who fall into the trap of overwhelming demands, typically fail to actively deal with the influences and demands, and they let them take them under. There are some people who take demands for granted, or simply don't respond to them. They rarely question what they are actually doing about their demands, or does it make sense whether they could reshape them. They are always feeling, "Under the gun," and never finding time to ask themselves, "Am I too busy or am I doing the right things?"

The simple fact is that being busy is a way of life, and some people do it as a way of escape. Most people cannot admit that a fragmented day could actually be an excuse for being lazy. When the demands of the day require the least mental discipline, it will show up in the amount of nervous energy spent on the situation. Responding to each new demand, or chasing after a new quest, or complaining about the overwhelming demands. The next step is to look at your priorities and then find a solution.

Fortunately, most people can overcome their habitual fire-fighting. However, they must first clear the most difficult hurdle of personal demands, the belief that they can change everything. "Change the things that can be changed, and understanding there are some things you can't change and have enough sense to leave the rest alone." People who complain about having too little time often thrive on their sense of importance and that generates their life. They enjoy being at the center of frantic activity, and people continually ask them for help, information, or advice. If they are honest with themselves they need to reflect on what is important to them and what needs to be done. Take on the problems for that day and don't let them build up over time.

To minimize the constraint of overwhelming demands, a person must develop a clear personal agenda. That means coming up with a precise idea of what you want to achieve in life. For example, when you aim in a general direction you may go in any direction, aim at the target, "growth" and "doing the right things." Try crafting a vivid mental representation of your objectives that includes ways to achieve them.

While reacting to demands can be distracting or constructive, everyone needs a personal agenda that creates a productive healthy outlook, and a sense of what they want to archive. It allows a person to integrate with the diversities of life while relating to goals for the short-term and long-term, while dealing with the responsibilities in life. Broaden your outlook and master the demands in your life. You can, therefore, relate to immediate and short-term priorities with a long-term purpose in mind. Which ultimately is much more helpful than merely responding to the mere demands of the day and life?

Some people constantly worry whether they are meeting or pleasing others' expectations. Trying to please everybody, people tend to get absorbed in what others are doing, rather than what they expect of themselves. The best strategy in meeting those expectations of others, ultimately, people fail because they don't meet their own expectations, they don't find time to pursue their own agenda, and in some cases they end up pleasing no one.

Warning signs

Let's deal with the warning signs, and where do they come from. There are stresses relating to demands. Sometimes these stresses cause a crisis, however a person may not see the warning signs along the way. They may say they thought everything was alright, and nothing could go wrong. When a person or family feels everything is all right, did they miss the warning signs? They may have thought we will deal with these problems later.

Watch for the warning signs. They may come in the form of everyday situations building up over time. The basis for my self-help studies is to help a person look for the warning signs and the way to do that is by measuring the stress. Understand the role that demands play in their life. A crisis is an alarm signal, and is much more severe as it relates to extreme stress that affects a person's life. Stress is an interaction within the situation. Demands involve every aspect of a person's life and situation. All of these can affect a person's health and well-being.

I will deal with the amount of stress and show you how the warning signs work later, and how alarm signals are relevant to the crisis. It could point to future trouble.

The first thing a person needs to do is pay attention to the warning signs because they are a part of the CRY for HELP! There are warning signs on the roads and highways, and the same is true in life. I like to think of signs that have BIG CAPITAL LETTERS that gets a person's attention. Unfortunately some come in small print and those are hard to define. That is also true in life.

In the meantime, a person may say something like "leave me alone, while I bare this alone." When I needed help "I didn't ask for help," but in the mean time I was saying, "leave me alone, I will be OK." Are you at that point?

There is a danger here when a person does not pay attention to these signals. Be careful. Watch for the breaking point, the point of no return in a situation is identified as a crisis.

Crisis

This will give me a chance to relate some of my other personal experiences. I have a male sensitivity, but it does not mean I don't understand others, because I am aware of the different sensitivity levels in others, and how people relate to their problems.

In my life there were seven health crises times. I think of them as being "down for the count seven times," but I never lost hope. Each time I had a major health problem and each setback brought about another crisis to deal with.

It started with a major arthritis attack and eventually I end up with high blood pressure and some slight heart problems over seven years.

This will give you some idea of what I am going through, and this gives me a chance to explain my feelings at the time, I will let you know how I failed in the process of dealing with my health.

I had to deal with some personality health traits at the same time. I loved the stress and pushing my body to the physical limits which helped create and added to my health problems.

I had to deal with the personal side and the human side of my health. Each attack was worse than the last, but I like to think I was never knocked out. Each knockdown only brought about another crisis to deal with. There was a series of health crises in my life, and dealing with divorce probably added to the severity of the attacks.

The arthritis would get better, I would think everything was all right, and then there would be another arthritis attack. Each attack was pretty similar in nature elevating my blood pressure. My arthritis has never gotten any better during the years. Stress caused the high blood pressure. In each set-back I was able to get the high blood pressure under control, but I would get better and think it wouldn't happen again.

It may seem odd when my heart would speed up I would feel better, but in the fourth set back it was different. My heart didn't slow down, it kept going faster. It had created an erratic heart rhythm, my heart liked going fast. This kept the blood pressure under control, I felt fine, but the trouble came when my activity slowed down. As the heart gets old it doesn't work as good and it takes longer for it to level out. In the mean time I could have a heart attack. It would take weeks for my heart to settle down, and it became harder each time to get my heart to slow down. As I stated earlier, I would feel better and do more and that is what caused the ups and downs in my health.

I would just get my life in order and think everything was fine. Then, BOOM! Each health situation brought about an even worse health problems, I know this may sound incredible to some, but it is true. You would think I would have learned from these experiences.

These health crises almost destroyed me, and the inward influences created problems in my last relationship and consequently another divorce.

Now let's take a look and see what I did to turn things around. Let's take a step back and see how I was dealing with things back then. I think this was the most important part of step one.

The very first thing I did was find out why I kept making the same mistakes!

I had a bad identity of who I was and who I wanted to be I had this need to be successful and accomplish things, and that related to who I thought I was, I also thought of myself as a bad person, why else would this be happening to me I took on a terrible personality identity.

When that is going on inside, if a person doesn't have a good foundation to stand on and do the right things for the right reasons, life will not go in a good direction. It doesn't make any difference what a person does if they are going to make the same mistakes over and over again. That is just what I had been doing. If a person doesn't understand what they are doing wrong, and why!

How can they change?

In my case, it took several crises for me to take a serious look at my life. In my case I had gotten to the end of human endurance before I wanted to change. It took a series of crises to shake me up over a period of years, and believe me when I thought I was going to have a heart attack that got my attention.

That gives me a different prospective as to how to deal with my health. When I finally saw how bad my life had gotten, I decided to change.

That change has brought about a fitness program, dealing with common sense guidelines in my life, and that has brought about the healing process that gives me sound judgment to base my health decisions. Sound principles and values are the beginning of change; I took things for granted because I thought I would get better with- out having to deal with my health.

I found that the motivation to change my life came because of a crisis. Then I used principles to help me understand my health problems. How does this fit into human behavior? I learned that if it didn't fit into good heath guide lines, it was wrong for me.

I found myself getting better day by day and week by week, and after a year and a half I was beginning to see my physical health getting better. Then, I understood why I needed the right kind of help and guidance. I have learned how to take control of the inner person and deal with the outside influences.

I feel that there is a reason for everything that happens. Let's look at it this way and see if this makes sense. I think a person needs to look for the treasures in life whether they are good or bad.

The important thing is how I dealt with these health crises. It is important how a person deals with each crisis because each failure can lead to an ultimate downfall. Now let's look at how to deal with stress, demands, and crisis.

In summary

Alarms are built in inner thoughts and feelings that tell us there are personal limits. I call them alarms, because, in reality they are busy signals that cause a person to be alarmed. It sets up personal limits within a situation. When someone is hurt or has been abused the safety devices in the brain are at risk and want to take over and in some case they are unable to help them. When that happens, a life is altered. If life does not go back to normal or a person can't overcome a problem they need to look for normal limits and boundaries. Still, a person may not be able to accept the hurt and abuse. A person may not like it, or choose not to do anything about it, or they are not able to deal with it. That is one of the reasons why that person's life is not functioning.

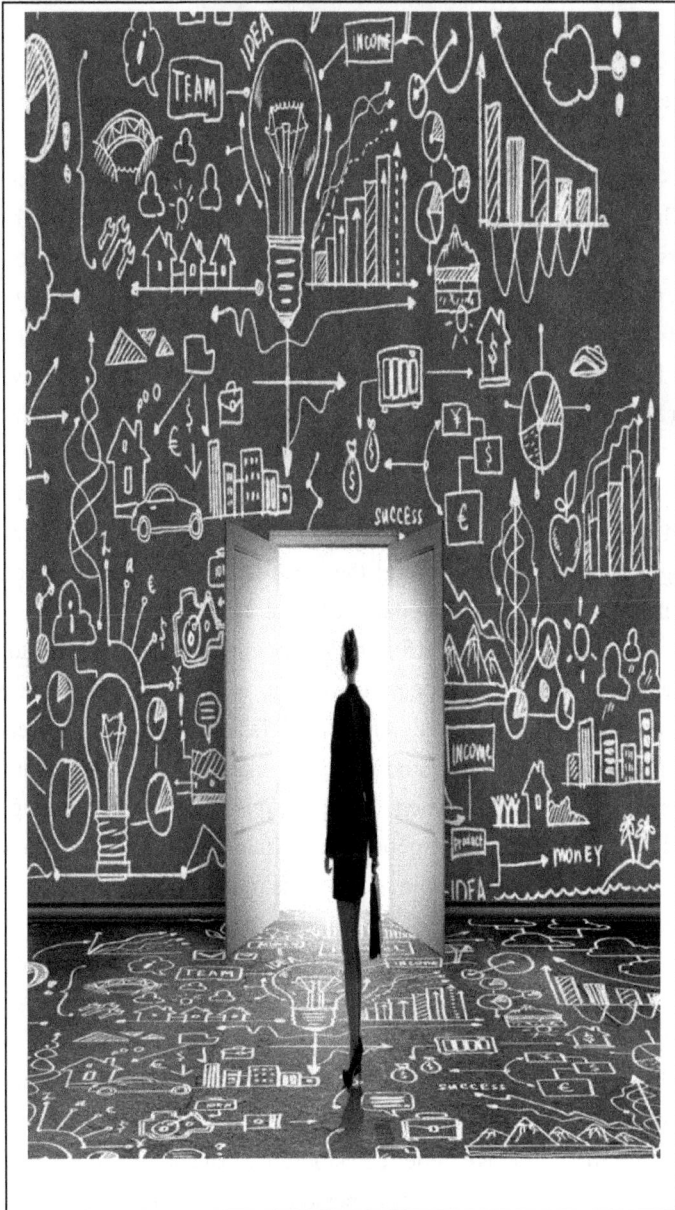

Chapter 3

Step 3
YOU'RE CONSCIENCE & IDENTITY

Door 2. Personal-Awareness Identification

The psychological aspects of the mind and behavior, door 2 is an awareness of your emotional state of mind. Now we are going to reflect on how you deal with your feelings, and the events that happened to influence your feelings. It is crucial to your psychological insight and understanding of one's self. There is a sense of false feelings when you think things are all right. An inability to notice your true feelings is a direct collation of the conscience and what you think. People certainly should learn more about how to understand their feelings. Not having a better sense of how you really feel leaves you at the mercy of the situation. A situation may dominate a person's feelings as to who they are going to marry, to what kind of job they take, rather than what is best for them.

It is in decisions such as these that a person's feelings may over- ride their good judgment. The role of the amygdala in our brain is pivotal in the sense of letting the amygdala scan the experience for trouble. This puts the amygdala in a powerful position of influence with regard to fear, and fear is a part of the process of making a decision. There are other physiological aspects in decision making. It is like a psychological sentinel challenging your thoughts and decision making. It brings fear into perspective, and this is when a person questions their thinking and conscience; which results in good or poor judgment. The amygdala reacts instantaneously. It is telegraphing a message to all of the other parts of the brain to be aware.

A person is autonomous in that a person has the power to self-govern. In a sense, there is a definite need to reassure a person's own boundaries. If their feelings are in good shape they are able to insure good judgment and make better decisions. This will result in a healthy psychological balance, and those who do that tend to have a positive outlook on life and make better decisions. The psychological aspects of a situation begin to occur before a person is consciously aware of their feeling.

The psychological phenomena is manifesting itself in the form of feelings and allows a person to control their emotions. Passion is always followed by impressions of pleasure if good decisions are made, or pain when bad decisions are made. The result is satisfaction or disappointment, liking or disliking, joy or sorrow. This is only possible if a person enjoys the positive attitude, and is able to understand the negative influences in their feelings.

When I say: "I feel affection for someone," am I expressing love, or tenderness or emptiness. The psychological phenomenon is manifesting the emotion into feelings. Passions are always followed by impressions of pleasure, satisfaction, liking someone, joy and happiness. They are derivatives of affections, etc. When I say: "I feel affection for someone," I'm expressing my feelings. There are degrees of love that results in affection, but the emotion can be just as strong when it comes to anger or fear. Emotions and feelings can be both positive and negative and there are various degrees of emotion. The physiological feelings can create organic and chemical imbalances in the body and the disturbances may go together in the sequence in how the brain processes the situation.

The mental aspects of both feelings and emotions are used as interconnections in this life study. However, I think each of these words have to be taken in light of what is happening, because of the mental state of a person at the time may well affect the situation.

The mental aspect relates to the mind, to become aware of what a person thinks at the time, to organize conscious and unconscious feelings, the mental recollection, remind, and memory. The distinction between the "heart and soul" is the act and emotion that follows. The heart aspect is knowing something is right in the heart/conscious, and then there is a conviction in the mind. All of this is a part of a person's thinking in relation to what they do. There is a reasoning process in every situation and the mental aspect comes through controlling your emotions over what the mind has perceived by past experiences. The more intense the feelings the more or less the dominance is when it comes to the mind. There is likely going to be interactions that relates to the mind. It is going to be harder for a person to overcome their emotions in relation to the mental aspects as they are dealing within the situation. The more ineffective the mind is in a situation, the harder it is for a person to perceive how to deal with it.

There are some that believe women deal with things from their emotional make-up. They are more intuitive for the most part in their decisions. Sometimes intuitions rule their thinking and mind-set.

A person needs a mental awareness as to who they are. The intellect and intelligence of a person, their mental state of mind, is vital to the mental well-being of a person in this section.

Then, a person needs to be able to respect themselves, their mental well-being. In other words be kind to yourself, and don't feel sorry for yourself at the same time. Hidden somewhere in your emotions and feelings is the ability to overcome a problem. A person may have a tendency to feel dejected and ask, "Why did this happen?" Sometimes the help comes when a person least expects it, while they are going through a situation; the circumstances are interacting with their emotions and feelings. The best response is to wait for the right answer while life goes on.

Since 1997 I have dedicated my life to writing my life story and developing my life skills study guide. This is the key that unlocked the door to the different studies and programs. When I opened that door in my life I was able to deal with a person's mental well-being and the mental attributes in a person's life. I didn't understand why things were happening at first. Now I understand how a person has to deal with their mental mind-set and how it could affect every aspect in their life.

What does Mental-Awareness means?
- Mental-Awareness means working together daily with others in having meaningful relationships.
- Mental-Awareness includes the Mental, Emotional, Physical, and Social skills, and the ability to handle stress.
- Mental-Awareness means evaluating your principles, values, and standards of belief.
- Mental-Awareness also means using guidelines that help a person make good decisions that are right for them and others.

But, on the other hand, wrong decisions / choices tend to cloud and cause a person to feel confused and uncertain about their self-concepts,

and that becomes the major influences in their life.

How dose Mental-Awareness interact with the emotions?
- Mental-Awareness interacts with the emotional and physical needs.
- Mental-Awareness supports each other as it affects the well-being of each other.

The over-all well-being of a person involves all interactions working together in a positive manner and promotes a positive attitude. Above all it improves a person's well-being.

I believe a good healthy mind-set is vitally important for everyone.

Taking care of one's self is a responsibility, and should not be taken lightly. The mental aspect can get mixed up and out of balance. I am spending some time dealing with the mental aspect of the person, because this is where a person starts to get off track. I think this is a common problem, because I see so many others not dealing with the mental aspect of decision making, I see a person's failures that they don't see.

When the mental aspects of the emotional thought process gets mixed-up and out of balance, a person needs to look at their thought-process and why they made the decision that influences their well-being.

The physical-energy and health comes from the body's-chemistry, such as adrenalin's, and the nervous-system comes from what the brain sees and feels.

The mental process can get mixed up and out of balance, and therefore a person may need to look at the personal, social, and human behaviors involved. The next part of these studies is based on real formulas, axioms, and profiles. Hopefully you will get a better understanding of your emotional and logical reasoning as to why you feel the way you do and are able to understand those feelings.

Our Conscience Being

Another area that a person has to deal with is their conscience being. I want to emphasize at this point it is important for a person to be able to live with their conscience feelings. More than anything else a person needs to be able to discern what they are doing, and see if there is any evil or bad intent. A person's mind and conscience reinforce their values set forth, most of the time without thinking, sometimes even if they are happy or not happy with their conscious decision-making and personal choices.

It is even more complex if a person lets their conscience form their guideline. It is not always what is best, because it is the right thing to do, even if it is not what they want to do. That is where guidelines come in and that is only one aspect that has to be dealt with. There are other interactions that go into a situation. This part of the study in itself relates to the reasoning process, but I could not go on without discussing this aspect of the conscience as it relates to a person and the situation. When the mind and conscience brings out the emotions of a person's conscience, there is a need for the mind and conscience to work in harmony, otherwise a person can make the wrong decisions/choices.

When the mind and conscience cannot get together, or when a person's mind is made up, the conscience always has an interaction and can be overruled by the mind-set, but a person may do some- thing without considering either one. Then, in that case, the mind and conscience have given into the reason a person wants to do something. The mental process has failed, because they have failed to use proper guidelines.

When the conscience and the subconscious kick in together in any given situation or if the problems seem too big, and if a person doesn't heed the warning signs, they may suffer tremendous damage to their well-being and state of mind. The two are supposed to work in harmony. The conscience is there to remind the person of what could happen, but when a person bends the rules of the mind and heart there can be consequences.

A person has to acknowledge the desire to do something, but what is wrong if they have the wrong desire or they make the wrong decision. A person can wound and cripple the human spirit as well, even give themselves a sense something is wrong. If they are not careful there are a couple of other things that can happen: (1) suppose the human spirit has suppressed their well-being, they may have met the challenge or they fail to meet the challenge, (2) what happens when the well-being takes over? One of two things happens: one, they feel good because they met the challenge or two a person's spirit is broken because a person's ego and self-esteem is lowered.

I am talking about the rules of the heart and conscience, the inner part of a man or woman. The heart and soul of a person lives with their conscience decisions. The mind also relates to the subconscious, which signals many of the responses, a person has to pick up on these responses, but a person can be fooled by their wants, needs, and despairs, when pride and lust enter in they may fall into temptation.

Although, a person may not be conscious of these things, which could be leading up to him or her going astray. They take the chance of doing something wrong because they think it is worth the risk or don't take in consideration the consequences.

May I say one more thing, a person can get so mixed up sometimes by all of society's rules and standards, and even religious beliefs, that it's hard to live up to all of them. A person is bound by their conscience, which is always there, and the conscience can become non-responsive in certain areas, or in such cases of abuse and other things that have happened.

What have I been talking about when I say conscience? Let me go a step farther and talk about the rules of the heart and con- science. Here are some quotes from the Bible: "As a man (he or she) thinketh in his heart, so is he" (Prov. 23:7). "Search me, oh God, and know my thoughts: And see if there be any wicked way in me, and lead me in the way everlasting" (Ps. 139:23 & 24).

Look at Luke 6:45, "A good man out of the good treasure of the heart bringeth forth that which is good; and an evil man out of the evil treasure of the heart bringeth forth that which is evil: for of the abundance of the heart his mouth speaketh."

Let's say someone criticizes a person or doesn't agree with what has been said or what has happened. There is going to be a reaction, usually negative.

What if the person did not mean to be critical, but the other person observes what has been said as criticizing or even thought it was criticizing. They may not say anything. How can a person say something they really didn't mean, they didn't mean for it to be criticizing a person?

It has to do with the way a person perceives what has been said! If a person is a very critical person or a person has an argumentative nature; they will feel like the person is criticizing them because of something they have done in the past and they are going feel hurt.

Let's take a minute and see it in another way. Say a person is trying to get their point across. There are two people trying to solve a problem. Can that be done? Of course, if both are in agreement about coming to an agreement, but during the discussion someone says something they don't agree on or didn't like, what happens?

One: we start with a person who gets their feelings hurt, the hurt applies to some degree with how many times their feelings had been hurt in the past. If it starts with a person's hurt feelings it is hard to get through the agreement without bad feelings. What about a person who gets angry when someone says something to intentionally hurt them.

This can be just the beginning of a more serious problem. The hurt can get out of control when it lingers, and a person can't get over what has been said or done. In that case they could get angry at the time, and it is forgotten in a short time. If it happens over and over again it becomes a bigger problem/deep seated, most of the time a person learns to live with it or they began to dislike the person for doing it to them. They may get angry or they just take it while the hurt goes deeper. When it reaches the anger stage, the other person may become angry too, now both are unhappy. This is a good example of the anger stage and how to meet the psychological aspects in a person's mental well-being.

When a person has been hurt, the anger stage may set in, there will be evidence of a conscious hostility stage, which may only last for a short time, but the bitterness stage is long-term, and in some cases lasts for a lifetime. When all these have set in, a person has some deep rooted problems to deal with. Not only to the one who is hurt, but, as a result, they have their own set of problems, because it hurts them in the process. When it comes to criticism, constructive disagreement can be good, if it is taken in the right way.

Now let's deal with the angry stage, and how this affects a person's feelings. Anger is a very strong emotion when a person has any major situation in their life, the hurt and anger may come into play. This leads to hostility and then bitterness, which plays a big part in the emotional level and balance. Another problem is when they don't want to talk about these emotions or do anything about the hurt and anger stage, and now the hostility has led to bitterness. A person tends to bury things in the subconscious because it hurts too much, and if this goes on for years it will take a while to heal.

These emotions of hurt, anger and hostility build to bitterness, and they are devastating when all four of these are going on at the same time. Sometimes the reality of these are hard to detect because they are under the surface of the person's inner feelings, and most of the time they don't realize how bad it has gotten, and to what degree it is affecting them. Even worse, when they don't realize any one, or all, they become dominating factors in their life, which also affects their conversation. This can influence their relationships, because of the severity and degree it has taken over time, and finally, it affects their personal-well-being. Let's look at each of these four emotions.

The Hurt Stage

When a person has a problem in any given situation, which of these emotional stages are they in? The point is when someone or something hurts a person they are going to react in some way, which brings out more hurt that started somewhere in the past, and in some cases it becomes a way of life. As it develops over time it gets rooted in the mind and it becomes a way of life. It either changes or they become unhappy with themselves or with the other person. Each of these axioms has to be dealt with in combinations as we deal with mental breakdowns.

What about when these hurt feelings have not been dealt with? When someone says something to hurt a person how do they react? If they are letting those hurt feelings linger and fester like a sore, this can bring about a breakdown. At this point a person's reaction has triggered the breakdown. In that case it may be forgotten to some degree, but it is still a breakdown.

There is a positive and negative side to every situation in life. When a person gets hurt, they may react in different ways. They may yell, or they may not say anything, but, the fact is, they are hurt. This may show up in outward forms of aggressiveness or in- ward by showing remorse, unhappiness, and depression. When a person has a problem in a relationship, the good and bad elements are mixed together, and if they are not in proper balance and con- trolled they will show up in how a person reacts sooner or later. A person is reacting in some way even if nothing is happening in an outward expression.

Let's break down the conflict even farther. If the person has a problem dealing with a situation, how they have been hurt will determine how much anger they are experiencing. Another thing to look for is how many times they have expressed their anger. The way to identify it is when it shows up in a person's hostility and sometimes it affects other situations. Let's say they may have argued about a situation in the past, and when it comes up over and over. Now it becomes too much for a person to bear, the result may be they don't speak to each other or they are yelling at each other. This is a good indication it has become an outward manifestation of each other's feelings. Each time it is an emotional expression of their hurt feelings. Another, is when a person gets hurt and says they want to get even. They usually want to hurt that person because of what they have done to them. Sometimes when the hurt gets so bad they are out-of-control, and they may not always take it out on each other. This can result in hurting others.

There is another problem at this point when a person takes out their anger on another person (for instance, their children, other family members, or at work) because they don't want to get into another argument with the person who is hurting them. When a person is in the hurting stage it will affect their children, work, and other relationships.

This is the start of a chain of reactions that affects the spouse, and especially children who pass on their hurt at school, their studies will suffer, and in some cases they will take it out on classmates. In each case it can lead to the use of drugs and alcohol as an escape. A person must realize that they are hurting their children by letting their hurt feelings dominate and these feelings are usually passed on in some way.

When a person doesn't go back to a normal pattern, or rhythm, the hurt is still there. Now let's look at it from the child's point of view: they are caught in the middle sometimes. They look at it in a different way because they feel their rights and wishes have be infringed upon. This is a good example of how the hurt and anger affects relationships.

When a person has a reaction or a combination of reactions to what has happened, in many cases this will affect their children and the family, because everyone takes one side against other. At the same time, hurt, anger, hostility and the bitterness sets in the children, and it will affect their relationships in the future.

Now let's look at a major hurt in a person's life. It could be that someone lies and misrepresents something. It could be that someone has cheated in a relationship, or they have been abused by someone in some way. Now the person has a major hurt to deal with. A major argument could lead to hurting someone and causing a separation, or a divorce. All of these major hurts fit into this category.

Now a person has a serious situation to deal with, and as I have previously discussed this can really affect their children and family. The one thing a person has to watch out for is how the children are reacting to the situation. This is a warning sign and a guide as to how to deal with the situation. They are hurt, and it shows in their anger when they get mad over nothing, and it is going to show up in many other ways. This is not considered a short-term stress; a person is going to be dealing with this kind of hurt for a long time. Remember, this comes under the term long-term stress, demands on life, and could lead to a crisis; and it may result in a long-term breakdown. As long as a person is hurting they are going to be dealing with this hurt in every situation taking place, and this usually affects their attitudes in their relationships.

Now, it is going to affect every aspect of the different stages of growth. This can take months or years to resolve depending on how long a person has been dealing with a particular stage of hurt, anger, hostility, and bitterness. When someone hurts a person, either the husband or wife will suffer. In this case it is someone they love who has hurt them.
It could be some other situation that could lead to bad undertones. When a family member has a bad attitude it affects all of their relationships. The couple usually has a control problem. It affects their parents, their uncles and aunts by those bad feelings, especially if they never get resolved. It could also be a friend or a business partner that has gone bad. Remember that children get hurt so easily, and they can be so judgmental depending

on who or how many they feel have hurt them. This will leave a scare to deal with and in most cases there is a major hurt that effects their own life.

Another, thing about these hurt feelings in a marriage; this can even prejudice a person in the way they think and in their attitude toward life. This can affect their proper emotional balance and control. It is like an operation, it leaves an emotional scar afterwards.

What is the anger stage?

Now let's go through the sequence of dealing with the anger. It is a very strong emotion when it gets in the anger stage. A person gets mad at someone for whatever reason. This can be a short-term reaction, much like a normal reaction, but very emotional in nature, and anger can also turn into a long-term breakdown reaction. In this case it affects every situation, and they will have a problem dealing with it. The anger they feel from within may be the biggest problem, or the person who they are angry with. When a person has major anger problems, it will play a big part in their emotional level and affects their proper balance and control. That is usually when a person says things and does things they may regret later.

I have found, at this point of discovery, it is very important to deal with the anger stage. Every time the hurt is brought   up, a person gets mad or angry all over again or the hurt feelings get worse. The question is "do you see that pattern and are you doing something about healing the hurt feelings before it gets to the anger stage?" When a person reaches this stage where they don't want to talk about it or do anything about it, they get angry and disappointed just thinking about it. A person tends to bury it or this becomes a barricade in the mind. The subconscious doesn't want to deal with the hurt it is too much to talk about at this point.

What is the hostility stage?

The hurt feelings and anger can also be displayed by a person's hostility in the situation. I think hostility is a very good term in showing how a person is reacting, because it measures the degree of hurt and anger in a person as it relates to the situation.

First, it may be caused by a hostile environment a person lives in, and in this case it is usually passed on from one generation to another. In the worst cases it leads to abuse, violence and/or domestic abuse or violence. A hostile emotion is not healthy for the person, and it shows up in their relationship / family. This can also lead to some of the more drastic behavior patterns usually brought on by strong emotional behavioral patterns, contributing to the violent actions such as out-of-control, or uncontrolled temper out- breaks. In extreme situations a person may want to hurt or even kill in this kind emotional state of mind. When the arguments are hostile in nature, they have serious problems to deal with.

Personal hostilities

When prejudices and biases go beyond the norm for the most part, or when a person can't think of anything good about another person or situation. All of these elements of hurt, anger, and bitterness are reflected in hostility. They come together and form a pattern, and a way of life. When a person is more than angry they have become hostile in their thinking, but even worse is when it shows up in their actions with extreme negativism. When hostility shows up in a relationship it is because a person is out-control, as a result a person has a bad attitude toward the relationship.

There is another saying that comes to mind: "a hostile environment" This term is used a lot in sporting events where a team goes into another team's hometown, school or home court. The fans go crazy for their team. This term can also apply to a hostile environment in a family or home life.

What is the bitterness stage?

When bitterness sets in over a period of time, this can become a major factor in your well-being. The underlying problems are usually hard to detect, but they will show up in a person's attitude. In the meantime, they are hurting this is like a cancer eating away at their very soul, it affects their mental-well-being, and in some cases causes physical and even mental problems and it affects their emotional-well-being. When a person is angry it shows up in everything they do. It is so important to understand why they are hurting and why they are experiencing and expressing their anger.

It usually shows up somewhere in some form in their relation- ships, and it reflects in what they say and do. It also comes out in the form of bitterness. The problem they are facing is their own grief for what has happened, while they are expressing the hurting that others have caused them, and they think they feel better while expressing their anger. I have gone through all of this in my life and I know what kind of pain a person can be going through.

The bitterness is a part of the emotional anger, it is deep-seated. When anger is added to hostility it has become deep seated and bitterness sets in. It affects everything that is happening at the same time. The worse thing all four are continuing to the buildup and add to a person's feelings in the different stages of the problem.

This is where adults and children really differ:
- Both have a hard time sorting out their true feelings.
- Bitterness is always a long-term malice of the heart and mind- set.
- When the anger stage sets in, the bitterness usually sets in too.
- When bitterness sets in it can go on for years and even for the rest of a person's life.

Sometimes bitterness is the hardest to detect because it is deep-seated in the heart and mind and it is the hardest to deal with. Most of the time a person doesn't realize how bad it is because the emotional level is either too high look for anger or if it is too lower look for depression, other than that it is like the other three. Even worse, a person doesn't realize it dominates and influences each situation in their relationships.

Bitterness is the root form. It comes grounded in the thought process. A good way to describe it is when you think evil thoughts. Those thoughts are detrimental to the soul of a person.

I have been there and I know the agony of the hurt, anger, hostility, and bitter feelings. I believe there is only one person who can change what is happening in their life:
- It comes from the challenge inside,
- A person has to want a change.

I believed I could change things in my life, and yet I still had those old feeling. Believe me, I'm still the same person I was before all of the bad things happened. I have said the same thing to my- self. The worst thing about being hurt I felt like I deserved the bad things that happened. I had a guilt complex and thought I deserved to be hurt.

I never became angry. I blamed everyone else but myself. I guess, in a way, that is a form of anger. I never thought of myself as the angry type, because I kept it inside. I did take things personally, and again I felt I deserved everything that had happened to me. I did not blame my family or God. It happened to me and I didn't like what happened.

All of this did not happen overnight, nor is it going to change overnight. Again, the worst thing about bitterness it gets deep-seated in the heart and mind-set. It took a lot of effort on my part, and then the sticking-to-it was the hardest for me, because I had blamed myself for the bad marriages. I really didn't blame the other person, because I was disappointed in myself. It made me feel better when they blamed me. I felt better when I look back it wasn't always my fault anymore, but I did blame them for their part in contributing to the divorce. This brings me to an interesting point, being able to get over what has happened. I was able to see I wasn't to blame any more. I do not know how they feel because both of us have gone on with our lives.

The Conscience

The conscience relates to how a person sees the human experience it is complicated by a person's will, When the mind and conscience says what are you going to do, the other side says why are you doing it. There is a different conflict in what a person is going to do, and it could be that a person does not know what to do. This may mean no decision is made, or no development in what to do. A person has a conflict of the mind and will that creates a problem. How does a person know how to deal with a person or situation? I will give you some reasons why people do things.

Frustration

Frustration lets a person deal with what threatens them. What happens when a person is overly disappointed or stressed this can be direct or indirect. Frustration is expressed in one of two ways; aggressive or passive behaviors, or outside influences. Aggressive behavior results in doing the opposite of what the other person wants them to do. Passive behavior is saying I don't care what you do. This is due to the inside pressures a person puts on themselves. When a person feels within their conscious mind that they think they have done nothing wrong, they can't understand why they feel frustration, or why they have aggressive or passive feelings. This may vary depending on the situation or the personality of the person. But, in either case they are not proper responses at the time. Aggression usually causes more problems than it solves.

A good way to understand frustration is by the degree of anger felt. First, ask the question, "Why am I so frustrated or feeling so angry? What caused me to become frustrated? What can I do to change the anger?"

Sometimes this is enough to cause a person to think how silly it might have been to feel that way, but on the other hand it may be very revealing as to their true feelings if a person still feels hurt, anger, hostility, and bitterness.

A person may need to talk it over with a person or persons, or a counselor, and come up with a solution as to why they feel the way they do. But, if a person still feels aggression or anger they may need to take on counseling, a support person, or seek professional help.

Methods of controlling frustration:
- Control the anger!
- Talking about your feelings can help manage feelings!
- Staying calm is another way to control your feelings!
- Self-talk, talk it out with yourself / think it through first!
- Take in deep breaths, and breathe out slowly, and relax!
- Redirect your focus!
- Take a walk, exercise, or listen to relaxing music!
- Take all these actions seriously and think it through before taking any adverse action, consider the consequences and feelings of others before making a decision.

The precedent set here is how to deal with frustration or anger. It affects a person's inner feelings of inadequacy and not being able to control their feelings. This is another case in point where a person has a tendency to take their frustration out on someone else, such as a fiancé-spouse, family members or a friend and even co-workers. The frustration is there and a person tends to transfer the blame to someone else.

Sometimes the frustration comes at the expense of a loved one, because a person thinks they are supposed to understand, and forgive them because they love them. What is wrong when a person feels that way? A person can have the mistaken idea that because they love them, why they don't understand the way they feel and they have done nothing wrong. A person may not realize they are releasing their frustration out on someone else, and that is wrong, too. In many cases the damage is done to a person who thinks they are bad and they take it because of their past bad experiences. When this happens it can do damage to a relationship, and to another person. On the other hand a person may not think it is their fault. The real problem is the person creating the problems needs to deal with their own frustration first.

A person may need a way out because they are frustrated in the first place. The frustration is a very strong indicator in any situation or relationship. Another common problem is when they don't face the truth, or they are afraid of the truth, or afraid of the consequences and what is going to happen, or when they don't do anything to help the situation. It may be worse than they think and they may need to get out of the situation or relationship! Another thing they need to do is check out the damage and what is causing their frustration. They need to repair the damage before it goes any farther.

Anguish

The most excruciating pain of any of these is anguish, because it signifies a deep seated pain. In some cases people don't even know who they are and where they are going. There is a real danger at this point when the pain is so severe the person feels numb.

The best description of anguish is losing a loved one or dealing with a traumatic experience. People who go through these traumatic experiences get to where they can't think of anything else, because of the pain involved or when they are missing someone. At this point they can't make their own decisions, they can't stand up for their rights as a person, and/or they can't stand on their own two feet, so to speak. They are beaten down or they may feel trapped.

The anguish can come from physical pain, sometimes emotional pain is even worse, and sometimes they can't escape the pain of a situation. In extreme cases they feel they deserve the pain. The worst is when they don't want to deal with the pain; this is when it is really bad. My hope is that I can encourage a person to do some- thing and deal with one or all of these symptoms that come in the form of depression, anxiety, or panic.

What can a person do if they are caught up in a bad situation?

Disappointments

The disappointment relates to conscience feelings. There are some things a person should live with and some things a person should not have to live with. In some cases nothing can be done or changed. What are some of the consequences if a person can't see past their disappointments, mistakes and failures? A person should always look at the whole picture, but if disappointments rule a person and take over a person, then what?

There will be negative causes and effects in any situation. When disappointments become deep-rooted, they will add to a person's depression and other aspects of a person life! A person has to look at their own circumstances to see if the damage can be repaired or not, and if they can live with the situations or can they change the situation.

Remember, a person must be able to overcome the negative disappointments and commit themselves to dealing with the situation, and not let disappointments get them down, and let this become a way of life and don't go on living with a misconception of what is important. What happens if a person wants something so-badly they will do anything to get it. This may not be good for them, and the same is true as to how far they are willing to go to change things?

That is up to the person if they are disappointed. They may be able to live with the disappointments, but the big thing is to deal with those personal feelings and don't hide from them. The great thing about a disappointment, it does not have to involve another person directly, but they may disappoint you, and not know they have disappointed you.

Sure, I've had my share of disappointments, and my attitude about being disappointed was a destructive force at one time. I had to find a way to cope with the previous situations and I began to see how bad the relationship had gotten over the years. My true feelings show up in the fact I am afraid of another relationship, and it creates many apprehensions in a new relationship. I actually feel defeated, but now I have hope and believe it could be a good sign. I have tried to find a way of overcoming these kinds of fears. This is a question still unanswered in my life up to now.

Guilt

This is probably the worst feeling. There is a conscience feeling when you feel you did something wrong. That can be devastating if a person doesn't conquer their guilt feelings. The important thing about guilt it comes from the inside. It is usually not seen. In some cases the person feels the guilt because of what they did to another person or what someone has done to them, or they feel guilty because they feel responsible.

Sometimes a person shares in the guilt and the damage done. The problem is when a person feels so guilty that they want to be punished. This usually takes on some form of a guilt complex, and sometimes this is brought about by abuse in the past. The guilt can reflect in a person's pride and ego. They may feel guilty for what someone has done to them, which is also a bad state of mind for a person. This is a very devastating characteristic when a person feels guilty. Does all that sound familiar? Or not!

There is another thing about guilt in the way it hurts a person. Some may feel they deserve to be hurt because of their guilty feelings. There are a lot of relationships that have to deal with guilt. I will go into the guilt in a relationship in another study.

I had guilty feelings because I am a very caring and sensitive person, "Soft hearted." As my dad would say, "I was not hard enough." Another thing is that I took the divorces very personally and I felt responsible. When I was growing up I felt worse when I had done something wrong. I felt guilty while others seemed to blame someone else. This brings about an improper balance and this carried over into my adult life; I had to find some way to control those guilt feelings. I think I am better because I try to balance them without losing my caring heart.

This is a situation everyone has faced many times: Guilt. A person is going to have to dig deep inside if they feel guilty for things they have done. A person has to lay aside prejudices, self-guilt and personal desires to control their guilty feelings. This is when one of the many defensive mechanisms kicks into gear, it is meant to protect a person, but the big thing is being able to control-your-guilt. All of these play on a person's emotional-balance. When a person thinks of themselves as being guilty, and when others blame you for something. Both parties may be equally responsible and usually feel guilty at some point, but some don't.

People tend to become adolescent in nature and selfish rather than being a mature adult. They may want to shift the blame on someone else and not accept any of the blame. It still leaves the question unanswered if they don't feel some guilt. Guilt feelings are OK, but does the person have some idea of the magnitude and gravity of the situation when they are involved, and how they deal with their problems is the answer?

A person can wind up with a crippled spirit as well as a broken heart and mind that could be a death warrant in the way they live their life, if they do nothing about it. There are a couple of other things that can happen when a person suppresses the spirit of guilt. It will create a negative feeling over a long period of time. There can be a great deal of damage because guilt carries over into their attitude in dealing with a situation.

For instance, if there is a prolonged stigma concerning an affair? I know of people who are crippled by the guilt over other things as well; it can lead to psychological problems. That is when a person may feel the need for help to overcome their guilt.

The Subconscious Mind

We have dealt with the conscience and now let's look at the subconscious, when guilt takes over in regard to how the mind works. Who rules in the situation or does a person let the brain work? If it is an automatic response the brain rules a person thinking, but a person may need to take control of thinking and emotions. They must have the knowledge and then the desire to make it right. They may not want to take responsibility for someone else's guilt, but their own. If a person can't make the decision to forgive, then it is left undone.

At this point a person needs to understand and know a little about the human spirit and how it is affected. The fact of guilt is a driving force and must be dealt with. What can be the equalizing force in guilt? It is a very important aspect in some relationships. How does the human spirit work, if a person has been wounded, in the case of guilt, don't be surprised if a person does something to cover up the guilt! Sometimes doctors and psychologists cannot understand or predict what a person will do under the stress of guilt.

I was not happy and felt guilty about the things I had done, but I didn't feel I deserved all of the problems that came my way. I didn't feel that I was to blame either, but I felt guilty for all of the things that had happened. At times I felt out-of-control because of the different situations, and I had some pretty bitter feelings. I didn't want to go on and have all of that bitterness, pain and the hurting inside. The mental anguish and grief was an overload on my mind and body, and my soul was burdened with guilt. I cried within myself because of the pain I had brought on myself.

There had to be a better way of dealing with my guilty feelings. I had to do something to get my life straightened out and get the pressure of guilt off of me, and get my life back on track. Finally, the answer came when I stopped feeling sorry for myself. I listened to what was going on inside. I was creating the conflict from within because in reality I was feeling sorry for what had gone wrong.

It was a process of filling my life with other things rather than self-pity. I had a problem because I blamed myself for everything that happened, but fortunately I don't carry the guilt around any- more. I've put it in the past, and I let it stay in the past. Now I look to the future and it looks much brighter.

Up to this point I have discussed two primary components of getting help, one is when a person tends to think they need help, I have been majoring on how a person feels. This has to do with (life & self-actualization needs) and, two, in reality it boils down to a person's (innate nature and character in seeking help).

When a person deals minor things (their innate nature and character) shows up in how they are welling to get things and how they go about solving a problem. Sometimes they tend to ignore or dismiss the things they don't like to do or have to deal with, and put them off, (procrastination is a good term and fitting). This usually makes a person (feel) unsuccessful and unfulfilled and I want to deal with those feelings.

When it becomes a problem in actuality, a person is actually majoring on minor issues within themselves, not the insignificance of the issues, and in most cases they are not able to prioritizing the problems in their importance. But, what they could be doing in **actuality is doing them in-** the-wrong way, and for the wrong reason. That can cause bad feelings in a perfectly good situation, these feelings are brought about feelings based on a false sense of values and morals. It makes a person feel good because they think they are right, and they think they're making progress, when in reality they are not. (Feelings are good, but can lead a person in the wrong direction) yes they can be misleading, when they are not based on true principles and facts. It makes a person feel better knowing they have done the right thing for the right reason. That is the right kind of feelings we want you to look for.

Chapter 4

Step 4
Unlocking Control Mechanisms

Abuses

This is a key step, so let's start by defining a person's feelings. Again, this is a major issue in understanding who you are.

In this crazy world we live in people use the term "Crazy" pretty loosely and it has many different meanings? I'm not sure how far we have to go to be considered crazy in the realm of good mental health. There are some "crazy people" in this world and that does not mean they are mentally off, but it could mean they are out-of-control of their feelings. But, in this case we're talking about mental health and well-being.

There are lots of myths and misnomers about mental health to say the least. But, the days when people were locked up in rooms for having mental problems are in the past for the most part. Mental-well-being and mental stability is not an exact science.

We have come a long way since the middle-ages. When people were considered to have demons and devils; they were tortured in order to cast out the demons and devils. Today we have a way to deal with demons and devil worship, but we don't lock people up, because there are ways to deal with demons. A book I recommend is Neal Anderson's the *Bondage Breaker*, which deals with spiritual warfare.

There are people who need to be in Mental Institutions. Now we have treatable means when it comes to dealing with mental illness. In our life enhancement studies we talk about a person's well-being.

When we talk about mental illness, for the most-part we're talking about people with extreme behavioral problems and mental disorders. This is where people usually need professional help.

Counseling is another way of dealing with the mental-well-being of a person. The following gives you an overview of bad and good mental health patterns:

Symptoms and Characteristics of Mental Health.

Symptoms of abnormal health include self-defeating behavior habits, and patterns. Abnormal level of competency and abnormal relationships are a bad indicator. They often feel rejected, insecure, and introverted.

Normal people with good mental health have problems, illnesses, and behaviors problems, but they are able to adjust without going over the edge of reality. Normalcy is meeting needs and reaching goals and includes liking one's self and has some in-dependency and self-assurance. Now let's look at the warning signs in bad mental health and well-being.

Anxiety

Anxiety brings about feelings of uneasiness, and fear. There is a sense of insecurity that brings about apprehension that something bad is going to happen. Anxiety will bring about unpleasantness and escapism that may lead to using drugs and alcoholism.

Defensive mechanisms are used to hide anxiety, and to protect one's self. Defensive mechanisms are used to defend one's position and feelings, and prevent the hurt and misgivings about one's self.

People suffering from repressive mechanisms refuse to think something is bad, and often fail to deal with something that upsets them.

People in denial refuse to take a threat seriously. They consciously forget something bad, and deny guilt for wrong doing.

Protection mechanisms

Sometimes people accuse someone else for their bad attitude and bad feeling. They project their anger on someone else for their misgiving's, and transfer of guilt to someone else.

Displacement mechanisms

Emotional rejection will bring a shifting their anger to someone else or thing. This is usually a normal reaction to hurt and anger. This hurt and anger may be ignored or forgotten in a short time.

One of the biggest parts of a dysfunctional relationship is low self-esteem and loss of confidence. They are usually filled with conflicts, and are not self-fulfilling. For the most part, they are not functional. There are poor communicators and poor communications. There is a lack of trust, respect, and confidence in each other. The result is usually a withdrawal and shutting others out when this process takes place. At this point two people are living their separate lives.

There are demands on the emotional and physical aspects   of a person, expecting someone else to make them happy and finally expecting love when it is not there.

Phobias

Phobia is an irrational fear of something you cannot see. There is an irrational sense of close places, an irrational apprehension like hearing something that is not there. Often there is an irrational emotional reaction to normal situations or problems that can lead to health issues. Mental anxiety leads to hurt and pain.

Mental disorders

Bipolar disorders

Bipolar sufferers often experience a wide shift in feelings with extreme mood swings. They can't tell the differences between fantasies and realities and are overly depressed. They may need professional help and in some cases medication.

Hallucination disorders

People with this disorder see a situation or thing that did not happen, and make up a fabrication of the truth.

Delusion disorders

They might think or believe they are someone else which includes a combination of twisted ideas and beliefs. They are out of touch with reality and are living in a dream world. They are sometimes odd, or peculiar in nature. This behavior can be frightening and dangerous.

There is a twisted system of false ideas and values, usually very negative thinking—I'm right, everyone else is wrong. This can include serial killers and mentally disarranged people.

These people are going through what is called mental illness, and the same is true when it comes to alcoholism and drugs. Not only mental health professionals, but many other support programs are available today, and all of them can treat many of these disorders and diseases.

With professional help many of these people can be helped in today society. There are some cases where people can respond to treatment and live a fairly normal productive life. Others live with these disorders with professional help and medication. Some people don't respond to treatment and continue to have these problems for the rest of their life.

Three kinds of eating disorders
Anorexia affects more females than males and includes:

- extreme dieting
- food rituals
- compulsive exercising
- frequent weighing
- intense fear of becoming fat

It is usually treatable with medication and psychotherapy when found early. It can lead to:

- low malnutrition
- menstruation stops
- low metabolism
- heart problems
- even death

Bulimia disorders come from emotional problems with symptoms of eating large portions in a short time, and then reverting to vomiting and laxatives. There is a feeling of being out of control and depression. Bulimia is treatable with medication and psychotherapy

Compulsive overeating includes continual snacking between meals, which results in a feeling of guilt and shame, feeling out of control of the situation, with the inability to control binges

Eating disorders are attempts to cope with psychological and emotional needs. People think that appearance is everything, which brings about eating disorders. Not everyone fights and struggles with weight problems, but in some cases people have to deal with extreme cases of eating disorders. If you know someone who has an eating disorder, encourage them to seek help. Let them know in a kind way that their well-being is at stake.

Society is gradually changing their view of mental health. Very few people think today that a person cannot be helped in some way by professional help. However people have a problem excepting mental illness without being fearful. People tend to fear the un- known, and what they don't understand. Others have prejudices against metal illness, and this can influence their attitudes. Even if it is a friend or relative, they may still use the word sick or "crazy."

Mental-well-being:

Just as the mind works with the mental aspects, and just as your emotions deal with the thought process, your well-being depends greatly on the function of your body systems. It is just as important to maintain a good healthy body.

Summary

In summary, take a close look at yourself. Are you the person you wanted to be and why not?

The BODY, HEART, and MIND are crying out for help! People of this generation use pills, hot lines, self helps, the quick fixes, and some use alcohol and drugs to meet their physical and psychological needs. People even think they can beat the odds in these cases and try all sorts of things to satisfy those cries for help, and there are other alternatives out there. Which direction are you going?

While a person's stress levels are an indicator of their overall health; the real indicator is when a person wants to be happy, and if they are not happy that is a warning sign. This is in reality is an alarm. When alarms go off, and the way they know something is wrong they are unhappy and a person knows things are going in the wrong direction. A person can be a time bomb ready to explode, and feel trapped, and even confused. This is a cry for help! A person's life can feel pretty mixed up at times.

There is always double and triple jeopardy in a person's mind- set because there are three elements to deal with:

1. The fleshly desires,
2. The personal wants / selfishness,
3. The need to belong or be loved. Even worse is when a person

accuses God and blames God for what Satan has put in their heart and a person yells at the temptations of the flesh. Everybody faces those kinds of battles in the thought process every day, and the conflict between right and wrong.

The problem is when these influences control the mind, when things become a warfare from within and sometimes from without. A good indication of the failing process a person can't see the bottom, or why the situation is not getting any better. When they are in the middle of a problem all they can see is their world falling apart. Life is passing them by, and they are engulfed by the situation. They feel helpless and they can't stop their world from spinning. It seems like they can't get the situation under control. That is the defining point!

Another thing is when a person can't see the end! In some cases they don't look up until they get to the bottom, and their only hope is to look up and make changes in their life. I call this tunnel vision! When a person can't see anything but darkness, this becomes a way of life and they feel trapped.

They know they need a change in direction, but they can't do it because the problem has probably gone on for years. This will affect their emotional and rational thinking, and the result is the amount of increased frustration and stressful feelings, and the levels of uneasiness in their life. Again, these are warning signs. The mind is confused and a person keeps coming back to the same old problems they started with.

Then, on the surface, common problems become more pronounced, and a person in this condition may need some help just to get through their daily problems. Don't despair at this point. It can be the beginning of wisdom in the healing process when a person looks for a new life. This is not the beginning of a problem I knew I was in trouble because I had reached the bottom and I could not go any further down. I knew I needed some changes. At this point a person needs a way out and up! A person needs a way to let the air out of the situation. I call it pressure-relief. When a person is feeling down, they may need to examine their self-worth and a way of expressing themselves.

No matter what had happened I had to try it again, because I thought a new day would be different; could I out do myself, and could I do better than I did yesterday? There was always that challenge inside of me. It seemed like my life had no room for error and I kept on running. Sometimes I didn't know why I was running, or what I was running from or to. I was running because I was supposed to be running, I guess! I had to try and reach that goal, but sometimes I didn't know what the goal was or why I needed help. All I knew things couldn't get any worse every decision should be better than the last, and I felt I had to be right, or did I? I knew what the consequences were for doing the wrong things, because my life seemed wrong. But, why did I do those things? Because I was supposed to be running, and as long as I was running, I thought I was "OK." "WRONG!" I was running in the wrong direction, and I created my own kind of lifestyle because I'm me! I have always liked me, and I have enjoyed other people.

There was "The Cry for Help," and there was no one there to help me. I felt alone, not knowing which way to turn. There were many cries for help from every part of my being. I heard the cry from within, and I didn't understand it. I looked for help in my life, and tried to satisfy the different needs in my life. My desires changed over time because I was getting older, but it was more than that, I was learning from my mistakes and begin to understand why I made those wrong choices.

Now, I am talking about a new way of life, those kinds of things. I wasn't confused any more when something went wrong, and I began to understand why? Is there a way of communicating within myself and being able to learn lessons from my heart and understand what my heart and soul is telling me, and the role of the mind plays and sets the way to change?

We are not a creation within ourselves. The person inside us wants to be revealed, finding our identity, and now we are able to understand and know what is going on inside. The outside influences are some of the strongest factors to deal with, but our mind-set plays an even bigger role in life. A person has a tendency to ignore the inner person because it is so quiet at times and unassuming, but when there is a cry from within it can be like the thunder and the pounding of a thousand horses. The dilemma comes from inside, and it can be demanding and get very confusing when it comes to understanding why someone does something.

Another thing to consider it seemed the circumstances keep changing. Just when you think you've got it figured out, it seems like the rules change. It really wasn't quite that dramatic, but things were changing all right. There is enough information within a person's mind-set for them to discern what is happening if they listen to their heart and mind, but the mind-set doesn't always have the answers. There are many problems when that happens. There are also so many demands, voices from within, and a person can get confused. A person has their own opinions about the situation. Sometimes there are not a lot of choices, and a person has to do the best they can to get through the circumstances.

We have to be taught to discern how to deal with our feelings, but on the other hand a person has to be sensitive to their inner feelings at the same time.

In my case, I learned "The Cry for Help" turned out to be something special, because I learned to listen. Now I have a pretty good idea of what to do, but I didn't always see my problems as a problem. When I learned to accept the answers in my life, I began to grow again, and understand my life. I had to use some common sense, and put some new guidelines in my life to help me. Now I understand myself, and what I want to pass on to you. So stay with me and see what happens. One way of doing this is to write or talk about your problems and define ways to deal with your inner-being. Then, a person needs to see and hear what they are saying, and what it sounds like to others.

You might be very surprised to learn how wrong you are! I have had people say, "Make a list of the good things and weigh them against the bad things." I am saying, weigh the situation, and add up the pluses over the minuses, and that will give you a better idea of the situation. The right answer might be that still small voice inside that says it's right or wrong. It takes all of those things to get to know yourself and understand the person inside you. Then you can start to discern what is best for you.

I want you to look at the major pieces of the puzzle. I know you may not be able to relate to some of the technical terms about the brain, but you will be able to relate to how a person may act and react in relation to the functions of the brain.

The brain is a vital part of the function of a person's behavior, and another is how the function of the body works in harmony or discord between the brain and body. It depends a lot on a person's background and childhood, but there is one interesting fact most don't consider, the brain cannot reproduce its own cells, so you can't start over. You have to work with what is there. Any other part of the body reproduces and can reproduce new cells. Every seven years the body reproduces new cells.

The brain is the center of all the functions, the brain supplies energy and healing to the body and mind. The brain functions never change, but the cells in the body do change. You have to take that into consideration. The brain cannot reproduce itself or medical advancement still cannot transplant cells into the brain. That is the reason the brain is able to retain a person's memory if it is not damaged or has been blocked by some event. Therefore, if it is damaged, it can't regrow new cells, but the body can. That is why there is a need for psychological counseling and therapy. The only way the brain can change is by retraining it.

For instance, when a person has created a bad habit, the brain remembers and responds the same way almost every time. You need to know how the brain works, and I have tried explained and have studies how the function of the brain works as it relates to other aspects of a person's life and behavior.

What do emotional feelings have to do with your thinking?

Emotional feelings are a signal of the action or reaction. How do different emotional feelings relate to shame, embarrassment or unworthiness?

The feeling of belonging equates with your stress levels, also social acceptance, peer pressure all play a role in strong belonging behaviors and needs.

If a person can or cannot recognize any or all of these personal characteristics, if they can they will better understand their feelings in regards to relationships with others in a better way.

How can a person manage their emotional feelings?
- Emotions can signal (drives, needs, and desires).
- Emotions drive the nervous system and the emotions may be characterized by yelling / screaming / shouting

- Emotions cause impulsive reactions like (hitting, slapping / retaliation / out of control)
- Emotions cause reactions and if a person does not control themselves in the situations.
- Emotions can be controlled or managed by controlling their reactions toward another.
- Emotions must be considered if the other person is out-of-control and causes you to react badly.

A friend of yours gets a new haircut. You may think it is too short. What do you say not to hurt your friend's feelings? You may say, "I see you have new hair cut or perm. Do you like it?" This lets them react and then you can respond.

You have not hurt their feelings, but they know you have seen the new look.

The dialogue may proceed from there.

There are even more to emotional feelings when your emotions are out of control, the brain is refining the input. In a sense everything starts with the brain circuitry, such as an automatic response, it is connected to the interactions to the degree of emotional involvement in a problem or situation. At the same time the brain sends signals causing glands to act and they secrete chemicals into the body and nervous system, in some cases causing emotional and chemical imbalances. That is reflected by the energy or lack of energy. Another indication is joy or depression. There are three ways to deal with these emotional responses:

1. Counseling / psychological methods,
2. Psycho-therapy / therapist and medication,
3. Is by behavior modification, which we take up next.

Controlled Person

There is the controlled person, and the one who is controlling the other person. Which is your situation? How do you feel about a person who controls you?

Let's take into consideration a person who is being controlled, and one who is out-of-control. I confess I have been out-of-control, it was an inward feeling and things seemed to end in disaster at certain critical times.

There is something out of balance when a person is controlled. I believe these are some revealing aspects of a person who is controlled. If they are dominated, the act is important to the controller. Usually being controlled comes short of mental and physical abuse. It does border on some forms of excessive abuse. It is very revealing to others, but usually not readily accepted by the person being controlled. The real issue is to what degree of abuse is involved and Why?

There are many reasons why a person is conditioned to controlled behaviors. There are two sides, the one who controls, and second, the one who lets it happen. The controlling factors are usually brought about from a family's background of abuses and cultural backgrounds, and yes, even religious beliefs can be carried too far.

Where does a person draw the line in their life and relationships? There is something wrong when a person is afraid of what the other person may say or do, when it comes to the point of hurting the other person. When the other person has to smooth over what the other person has said or done. I know that jealousy can play a big role in a person's insecurities from within themselves and how they treat others.

Yes, jealousy and abuses are two major problems in relation- ships; jealousy is one of the major problems in a relationship and can lead to the controlling of another person. Another factor is being possessive and controlling.

Being super-jealous of a person's time may lead to abuse. A man should respect the position of the women in a relationship and the wrong kind of love is never a lasting love. This kind of relationship will result in an unhappy marriage. A man should want her to feel comfortable with herself in public places or when going out with her friends. At the same time, she must respect her place as a woman, and not provoke jealousy. If he or she is too jealous, they will not be comfortable in any of these situations. He must want her without being possessive and controlling.

One example is when one person in the relationship is overly friendly to the point of flirtation. Sometimes it makes a person feel good to know that someone else likes their looks. The point is, when they like attention to the point that it borders on sexual attractions and/or even worse, lust. This could be one of those cases where they have crossed the line of proper conduct, and it even happens as a Christian! I know there is a point where any person can cross the line, and Christians need to be protective and responsible because of their testimony.

Controlling Behaviors

A short temper or being impatient causes aggressive or passive behaviors. Another is when a person has dominating or controlling behaviors, when a person acts violently, or when they get angry, or mad. This very typically shows up in every aspect of their life, relationships, families, etc. When a couple gets married, usually they have dated, or maybe they just fell in love, and decided to get married, or they could have been sweethearts for years. In any case, they are not used to seeing each other all the time and dealing with all the decisions that go into a marriage. The things they overlooked before have become sources of friction. When they were dating and fell in love with that person they may have been able to overlook those little things, but what if they are big things? The human traits and behaviors have become a problem.

I knew of a young lady who said, "All my husband wanted to do was sit and watch TV, play games or computer surfing; while I do all the work around the house." She worked a full-time job, helping to support and raise her child. She ended up divorcing this person. Was she right or wrong? There must have been more to it than that to cause a divorce. I know the lady, and I believe there was?

There is a point when degrading the other person is wrong. This usually leaves the other person with low self-esteem, and it can be a direct or an indirect influence in their relationships. I liken it to taking total control of a person.

Let's take into consideration this question, "Who's the boss?" That is usually a big question in any relationship. Some people who are controlled are afraid to give the other person any credit or authority in a decision, when that happens they don't trust their own judgment, but stay in the relationship, or they don't trust themselves because of what has happened to them in the past.

There is another type of person, the one with a super-ego, who will not give in, they are always right, this kind of person gives demands, usually doesn't like to receive demands, and there is another type of person who has insecurities. All these behaviors can lead to control abnormalities, an imbalance of power. None of these look for the common ground in a situation. Both types of people are headed for disaster in a relationship.

I would like for you to look to see if the giving and taking in a relationship is the same. In some cases some people are givers and some are takers.

Another problem I recall from my past. At times each of us wanted control. That caused conflicts, but I was unable to control her feelings and behaviors? The big difference between the two of us I was willing to give in when things got bad. I hope you will be able to understand the difference. I hope I have pointed out the differences, the ability to use self-control is up to each person, and being able to control their outrages, impulsive actions and emotional out-breaks, and how to deal with each of these behavior problems.

To share love is one of the greatest privileges a person can experience. The more a person gives in truth, the more they should be able to get back, if it is true love. When a person is controlling, they are taking away from person's dignity, and the less they are going to get in return. When a person is controlling another person, they are suppressing the other person's feelings and their ability to share openly, and for them to give from their heart is what makes a relationship. The giving of one's self comes from the heart. The little things are probably the most important, for instance, when a person gives and gives and it is never enough. That is the wrong kind of love in that relationship.

Out-of-control

Every person needs to understand how to get his or her feet on solid ground, and realize that there is trouble when the other person is out-of-control, when the relationship has gotten to the point where both of them are out-of-control. Being able to get a handle on their life before their relationship becomes a serious problem, or a series of problems that are insurmountable to deal with. It is much easier to deal with something before it gets out-of-control. One of the problems with most people they have a tendency to procrastinate. They think, "I will handle the problem tomorrow rather than to face it head on."

This brings us to self-discipline. It is not really two-fold as you might expect. There are many aspects of self-discipline, just as there are many forms of expression and emotions in a person's love and passions. Any of these may enter into the equation of being out-of-control. A person's thoughts are expressed in their actions and deeds.

In a good relationship, a person expresses their opinions about different subjects or things without major problems. The important thing is failing to express their love for each other. When a person expresses their emotions they may come in many forms and it shows up in their outward expression of their feelings. If it becomes a violent emotion, the person is out-of-control. It can be an expression of the stress in the situation, too. When a person is out-of-control, it can affect their love for another person, which builds walls and makes it difficult for the other person to able to express their love. Some people do have problems expressing their love.

I would like to take being out-of-control a step farther, and kick it up a notch if possible, and relate it to the emotional needs, and then deal with the emotions from the other person. A person has to deal with the need to express their love, which shows up in their feelings toward the person. This love can be expressed in many ways.

The out-of-control person may not be able to show their love, for selfish reasons; therefore, their needs may show up in many other forms of selfish desires. If a person has bad feelings this will also affect and destroy their relationships and can destroy their joy and happiness.

If the other person becomes too dependent on the other person, they can feel the loss of joy and happiness, and that does have something to do with their ability to love. This could affect the relationship. It may come out in some form of self-denial of their wants, needs, and even despairs. This will leave a void, an empty feeling, a real need for self-fulfillment. It may be lacking from with- in and show up in their relationship.

If these needs for self-fulfillment don't balance, or they are dominating a person, the relationship may be out-of-control. Neither person is going to have that real joy and happiness. If a person does not have either, they are incomplete and so is the relationship. May I bring this down to a practical application and use an- other illustration? There is a saying: "We are what we eat." This saying has to do with what a person takes in food to feed the body's system. What a person takes in mentally is likely going to feed the mind and what a person does and what a person says works the same way. This also comes out in the way of personal expressions, their views and opinions, and is very evident in their actions. It affects a person's prejudices and biases, and is likely to show up in their attitude. This person is likely going to be out-of-balance if they are not careful they are out-of-control at the same time.

Now, there are several ways to help a person who is out-of-balance. My hope is to help everyone deal with self-control, and to help people get back on track, and add some new dimensions to their life.

Three Types of Control Disorders:
- Uncontrolled
- Controlling
- Out-of-Control

The psychologists and counselors spend much of their time dealing with the different personal conflicts, struggles and warfare's from within and in their relationships.

Life is made up of conflicts, struggles and in some cases war-fare! The book of Job is based on a man's conflicts and struggles, and deals with spiritual warfare. We read in Job 14:1, "Man *that* is born of a woman is of few days, and full of trouble." And Job 5:6, 7 says about the same thing. "Although affliction cometh not forth of the dust, neither doth trouble spring out of the ground; Yet man is born unto trouble, as the sparks fly upward."

What is uncontrolled anxiety?

We all know what it is like to feel anxious. Most of us experience anxiety when we're faced with stressful situations or traumatic events. Our heart may pound before a big presentation or a tough exam. We may get butterflies in our stomach during a blind date. We worry and fret over family problems, or feel jittery at the prospect of asking our boss for a raise. Anxiety is the part of our nature called "fight-or-flight" response. It's our body's way of warning us of danger ahead and, for the most part, anxiety is adaptive. It gears us up for life's challenges, and spurs us to action when we're faced with a threat. However, if anxiety is preventing you from living your life the way you'd like, you may be suffering from an anxiety disorder.

What is an anxiety disorder?

According to the National Institute of Mental Health, "anxiety disorders are the most common type of mental illness in the US, with approximately 40 million people over the age of 18 affected each year." Anxiety disorders can take many forms. You may experience free-floating anxiety without knowing exactly why you're feeling or why. You may suffer from sudden intense panic attacks that strike without warning. Your anxiety may come in the form of extreme social anxiety or in unwanted obsessions and compulsions. Or you may have a phobia of an object or situation that doesn't seem to bother other people.

Despite their different forms, all anxiety disorders share one thing in common: persistent—and often overwhelming—fear or worry. The frequency and intensity of these fears can be immobilizing, distressing, and disruptive. Characteristics of an anxiety disorder include:

- Anxiety which is constant, unrelenting, and all-consuming!
- Anxiety which causes self-imposed isolation or emotional withdrawl systems.
- Anxiety which interferes with normal activities like going out- side or interacting with other people.

The toll an anxiety disorder can takes over your life and lead to other problems as well, such as low self-esteem, depression, and alcoholism. Anxiety can also negatively impact your work and your personal relationships. But the good news is that anxiety disorders are highly treatable. With the help of a qualified mental health professional, you can get relief from your worries and lead the life that you want.

What is an anxiety attack?

Anxiety attacks, also called panic attacks, are unexpected episodes of intense terror or fear. Anxiety attacks usually come without warning, and although the fear is generally irrational, the perceived danger is very real. A person experiencing an anxiety attack will often feel as if they are about to die or pass out symptoms include:

Shortness of breath
Palpitations or pounding heart
Chest pain or discomfort
Trembling or shaking
Dizziness
Nausea or stomach distress
Fear of losing control or going crazy
Hot or cold flashes

What are the symptoms of anxiety disorders?

The primary symptoms of anxiety disorders are fear and worry. However, anxiety disorders are also characterized by additional emotional and physical symptoms:

Heart palpitations or racing heartbeat
Chest pain
Hot flashes or chills
Cold and clammy hands
Stomach upset or queasiness
Frequent urination or diarrhea
Sweating
Dizziness
Tremors, twitches, and jitters
Muscle tension or aches
Headaches
Fatigue

Insomnia

Because of the many physical symptoms involved in anxiety disorders, anxiety sufferers often mistakenly believe they have a medical illness. They may visit many doctors and make numerous trips to the hospital before their anxiety disorder is diagnosed. In fact, according to the Anxiety Disorders Association of America, "people with anxiety disorders are 3-5 times more likely to go to the doctor than non-sufferers." Therefore, it is very important to be aware of the unexpected, physiological forms anxiety can take.

What are the types of anxiety disorders?
There are several major types of anxiety disorders, each with its distinct profile and set of symptoms. Look below for help in-depth and overviews of the different anxiety disorders, including treatment options and self-help tips:

Obsessive Compulsive Disorder (OCD) – OCD is characterized by unwanted thoughts or behaviors that seem impossible to stop or control. You may be troubled by obsessions, such as a recurring worry that you forgot to turn off the oven or that you might hurt someone. You may also suffer from uncontrollable compulsions, such as washing your hands over and over.

Panic Attacks and Panic Disorder – Panic disorder is characterized by repeated, unexpected panic attacks. These panic attacks strike without warning and usually last a terrifying 15 to 30 minutes. Panic disorder may also be accompanied by agoraphobia, which is a fear of being in places where escape or help would be difficult in the event of a panic attack. If you have agoraphobia, you are likely to avoid public places such as shopping malls or confined spaces such as an airplane.

Phobias – A phobia is an unrealistic or exaggerated fear of a specific object, activity, or situation that in reality presents little to no danger. Common phobias include fear of animals such as snakes and spiders, fear of flying, and fear of heights. In the case of a severe phobia, you might go to extreme lengths to avoid the thing you fear.

Separation Anxiety – Separation anxiety is a normal part of child development. It consists of crying and distress when a child is separated from a parent or away from home. If separation anxiety persists beyond a certain age or interferes with daily activities, it may be a sign of separation anxiety disorder.

Social Anxiety / Social Phobia – If you have a debilitating fear of being seen negatively by others and humiliated in public, you may have social anxiety disorder, also known as social phobia. Social anxiety disorder can be thought of as extreme shyness. In severe cases, social situations are avoided altogether. Performance anxiety (better known as stage fright) is the most common type of social phobia.

Facts about anxiety disorders from the National Institute of Mental Health:

- Most people with one anxiety disorder also have another anxiety disorder.
- Anxiety disorders frequently co-occur with depressive disorders or substance abuse.
- Nearly 3/4 of those with an anxiety disorder have their first episode by age 21.

What are the causes and risk factors for anxiety attacks?

There are a number of complex factors that contribute to the development of anxiety disorders. Your environment, personality, family dynamics, brain chemistry, and genetics all can play a role.

In addition, major life stressors such as financial difficulties, marital problems, or bereavement often trigger the onset of an anxiety disorder. It is important to realize that no single factor causes an anxiety disorder. The various anxiety risk factors are interrelated and can interact with and impact one another.

A person's environment can play a huge role in the development of anxiety disorders. Difficulties such as poverty, early separation from the mother, family conflict, critical and strict parents, who cause them to be fearful and anxious, this is passed on to their children, and also the lack of a strong support system can lead to chronic anxiety in children too.

Personality differences can affect whether or not an anxiety disorder develops. People with anxiety disorders often view themselves as powerless and the world as a threatening place. This pessimistic perspective can lead to low self-confidence and poor coping skills.

Brain chemistry

Some studies suggest that an imbalance of neurotransmitters such as serotonin, GABA, and epinephrine may contribute to anxiety disorders. Abnormalities in the stress hormone cortisol have also been found. Many medications prescribed for anxiety disorders aim to readjust the brain's chemical balance.

Heredity

Anxiety disorders tend to run in families. People with anxiety disorders often have a family history of anxiety disorders, mood disorders, or substance abuse. Although this is often due to the home environment, researchers also believe that there are genetic factors which represent an inherited risk for anxiety disorders. One risk factor may be a biological vulnerability to stress.

Trauma

An anxiety disorder may develop in response to a traumatic event, such as a car accident or a marital separation. Anxiety may also have its roots in early life abuse or developmental trauma. Trauma in infancy and early childhood can be particularly dam- aging, leaving a pervasive and lasting sense of helplessness that can develop into anxiety or depression in later life.

How is anxiety disorders diagnosed?

If you've experienced intense anxiety or worry for six months or more, you may be suffering from an anxiety disorder. Worry that interferes with your work, relationships, and activities is also a red flag that is an indication you've crossed from normal worrying into the territory of anxiety disorders. If your anxiety and fears have become so great that they are causing extreme distress or disrupting your daily routine, it is important to seek help.

First, you should consult with a doctor to rule out possible medical conditions. Some medications or diseases create anxiety-like symptoms such as rapid heartbeat, dizziness, nausea, and nervousness. A change in medication or the correct diagnosis of a medical illness may take care of your anxiety problem. Your doctor will give you a physical examination and may also run some laboratory tests.

Medical Conditions Which Can Mimic or Cause Anxiety
- Thyroid Disorders
- Diabetes
- Hypoglycemia
- Asthma
- Sleep Disorders
- Adrenal Disorders
- Epilepsy
- Certain heart conditions
- Migraines

Other psychiatric illnesses
- Medications and Substances which can Induce Anxiety
- Caffeine and other stimulants
- Drugs such as heroin, cocaine, and amphetamines
- Over-the-counter medications such as decongestants
- Steroids such as cortisone and prednisone
- Weight loss products
- Hormones (birth control pills, thyroid medication)
- Inhalers and other respiratory medications
- Herbal remedies such as Ma hang and ephedrine
- High blood pressure medication
- Withdrawal from alcohol
- ADHD medications (Ritalin, Adder all, Dexedrine)
- Withdrawal from benzodiazepines (Xanaxansa, Valium) Anxiety can also exacerbate many pre-existing medical conditions, such as ulcers, hypertension, and respiratory conditions including asthma and chronic obstructive pulmonary disease. Furthermore, anxiety is

associated with mitral valve prolapse, chronic fatigue syndrome, sleep apnea, irritable bowel syndrome, and chronic tension headaches. Because of the many medical issues that can cloud the diagnostic picture, working hand-in-hand with both a physician and a mental health professional is critical.

Natural and Herbal Treatments

Herbal remedies such as valerian root and have been used to treat anxiety for many years. However, the effectiveness and safety of these products has not been well-documented.

Other Anxiety Disorder Treatments

Relaxation techniques – Relaxation techniques such as progressive muscle relaxation, controlled breathing, and guided imagery may reduce anxiety.

Biofeedback – Using sensors that measure physiological arousal brought on by anxiety (such as changes in heart rate and muscle tension), biofeedback teaches you to recognize and control these body processes.

What self-help treatments can help me control my anxiety?

A healthy and balanced lifestyle can help you control and reduce your anxiety. Here are a number of things you can do to keep anxiety at bay:

- Exercise is an effective treatment for anxiety. To learn more about how moving your body is good for your state of mind.
- Lack of sleep can exacerbate anxiety.
- Healthy eating can help you in your battle against anxiety and stress. Make sure your diet includes plenty of fruits and vegetables. Relaxation techniques such as deep breathing and visualization can help reduce anxiety. Relaxation Techniques for Relief of Anxiety & Stress describes a variety of relaxation exercises you can practice on your own.
- Don't use substances to cope with your anxiety. They can make the problem worse, and eventually will cause problems of their own.
- Stop drinking or cut back on caffeinated beverages, including soda,

coffee, and tea. Caffeine can increase anxiety, cause insomnia, and even provoke panic attacks.

• Spend as much time as possible with people who make you feel good and are emotionally supportive. The more social support you have from friends and family, the less vulnerable you will be to anxiety and stress."

• There is a natural harmony in life for the most part, and yet there are conflicts between any two personalities. For example: a man and women have their own will, and the earth has its conflicts (tornadoes, hurricanes, and earthquakes). I guess the greatest of all conflicts is the warfare between God and Satan, the battle between good and evil. Every person is born into that conflict and warfare.

• There can be struggles in relationships too, but when there is warfare in the relationship, they are in real trouble. This can lead to a number of problems which will be dealt with in the next chapter.

Scriptural Warfare

Ephesians 6:12-18 says, "Put on the whole armor of God" and pray, because we're in a warfare mentally, physically, and spiritually."

Chapter 5

Step 5
Behavior Identification

The following Graphics will be helpful in evaluating your actions. The reactions are multiplied by actual feelings of stress in the situation, as they are taking place at the same time.

Behavior Identification Chart Layout

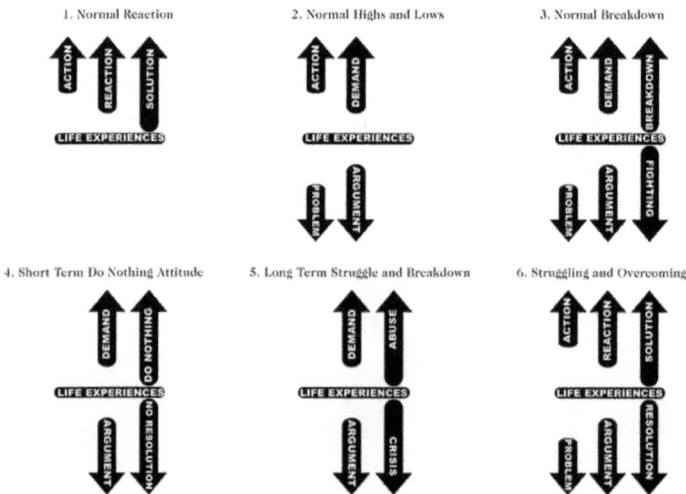

All of the reactions in the chart are based on a person's "Life Line"

represents things that happen in your life. Every person's life has intersecting movement and we want to keep you in your comfort zone. The life line introduces six kinds of reactions in a person's life. We are going to allow you to apply the axioms 1 through 6, and build on them based on your Meta Cognition, mental-well-being and awareness. The idea is to be able to understand what is happening, while being able to distinguish between the kinds of patterns that are repeated over and over again. The psychological term is called cognitive behavior patterns, which are based on the ups and downs in a person's mental attitude. Our goal is for you to get to know how to create a conscience effort in changing behavior patterns, and live a better life.

This may look like a line, but it actually represents a person's life in chart form, this part of the study will allow you to see what is actually happening and for how long. Following the chart will make it more realistic. It really helped me when I saw how a simple chart could actually demonstrate these aspects in my life.

Personal-well-being and feelings

1. Normal Reaction

Now let's look at the diagram 1: Normal Reaction, and how it relates to the normal reactions actually taking place. This is a normal reaction in relation to how we deal with stress, demands, and a crisis. Also, when looking at the diagram, we are showing you normal everyday stress levels to take into consideration. A person should have a good understanding of what a normal reaction means. The demands in a person's life happen when someone expects them to do something or tells them to do something. The best way to describe diagram 1, a normal reaction is when the pat- tern and rhythm go back to normal in a short period of time. The one thing I want to emphasize is that there are both positive and negative reactions happening in a situation. Both have occurred at the same time.

2. Normal Highs and Lows

ACTION DEMAND

LIFE EXPERIENCES

PROBLEM ARGUMENT

Diagram 2: Normal Highs and Lows, deals with the psychological, mental, and conscience reaction, when a person says, "I can't do this anymore!" This does not mean that life does not go on, but the person may suffer at a cost to themselves and their relationships. This is a normal reaction, where the personal problems are resolved without needing to feel any despair, and while they are going back to a normal routine in your life.

As a person relates to Diagram 2, there is the hurt, anger, hostility, and bitterness, which are emotional experiences which relate to frustration, anguish, disappointments, and guilt in a person's life. As I drew the Chart in different aspects of life, I began to see how much of a reaction is taking place. I created the Life Line to demonstrate what is happening; the ups and downs level out and they are short in duration. The chart reminded me of how a reaction looks and feels in real life.

During a normal reaction, life going on with little or no consequence, and after the normal reaction, life goes back to normal. This is evident because nothing changes as a person looks at the diagram. The normal reaction is a very slight movement up and down, and a person's life goes back to normal fairly quickly, or in a short period of time.

The mind and conscience sorts things out rather quickly and the decision is made, and the person is happy, or even if a person is unhappy with what happened, life goes on as before.

Now, let's see what happens when it happens over and over again. At the least a person is looking at an annoyance over a short period of time. But if it happens over a long period of time it may become a serious problem, but usually normal reactions are of little or no consequence.

The goal here is for an individual to try and accept their actions and reactions, and to respond to them as they take place in- stead of ignoring them.

Identifying Personal-well-being and feelings

In Diagram 3: Normal Breakdown, what happens when someone has crossed the line this relates to a moderate conflict in a situation or circumstance and how a person feels afterwards that counts or something has happened they can't control beyond their control. This is clearly a reaction, not like the reaction in diagram 1 in the "Life Line," where the experience goes back to normal, there is an underlying problem that continues.

3. Normal Breakdown

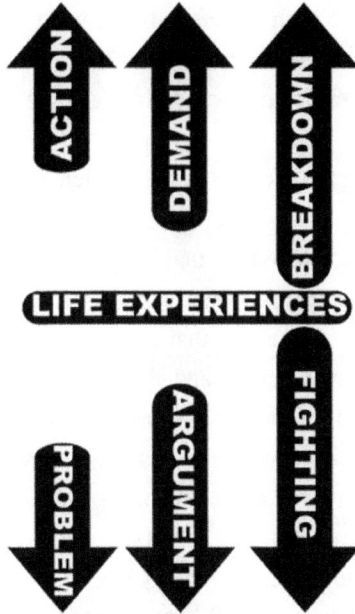

ACTION DEMAND BREAKDOWN

LIFE EXPERIENCES

PROBLEM ARGUMENT FIGHTING

These emotional experiences are normal, but because of the intensity, a breakdown has occurred, there is a reaction, where a person does not go back to a normal pattern. It could be a matter of trying to deal with several normal conflicts at one time.

This could be a matter of going through a normal amount of stress in the conflict. May I emphasize that life goes on; even if it looks normal to others involved the issue may not be completely settled.

The pattern shows a pronounced problem, and there could be some turmoil and a disaster headed their way. Again, the longer this conflict goes on and is repeated, the more the conflicts will increase with each ensuing situation, and as this relates to the everyday normal reactions that don't get resolved, a person may have a major problem to deal with later.

Now let's say the conflict increases, the stress and demands go up at the same time. It probably has not reached a crisis at this point, the reaction is still in the range of the normal highs and lows, but nevertheless it is a series of the highs and lows happening over a period of time. If they become a problem, what needs to be done? It could be situations that relate to such things as a marriage or job. There is also the emotional experience that has to do with a person being happy and their personal feelings reflect an emotional reaction. Let's look at a highly emotional experience, where there is an extremely negative reaction and the emotions are not normal.

The person does not go back to normal, which is a sign they have problems to deal with.

This has a lot to do with a normal reaction with highs. It is not a good sign if there are excessive highs of anxiety set forth in a person.

There are stages in a situation that can add more stress. The time and effort should be short in nature, and should not make it harder to get back to a normal pattern, but when things go wrong a person will have problems if there are too many highs and lows in any given reaction. Especially when over reactions are taking place, a person may experience anxiety, nervousness, exhaustion, or even fatigue.

All emotions are good when there is a proper balance and control, but where there is improper balance and control in a situation a person will have problems.

Now, I am going to introduce some more new terms that you may not be familiar with in relation to the emotional experience. What do all of these new terms mean?

When there is an over or an under reaction to a particular situation the term is imbalance that has occurred.

The next term is dealing with what causes crossover tendencies. What do I mean by crossover tendencies? A readiness to change a particular kind of thought or direction that causes an action having to do with behavior changes within the person's feelings. When actions and attitudes are affected by some other behavior there is always more than one reaction taking place at the same time. A person or situation may have different meaning to different people at the same time.

A decision is a choice of action. It can be difficult to understand why a person said something, or did something, without knowing what were their intentions at the time. It is not unusual to take it to be one way, and someone else could take it to be another way. A person may base their reaction simply on their emotion, or what they thought the other person meant. It is even more complex than that. The mind and conscience can get confused and interpret wrong feeling, and make a wrong decision based on what they thought was happening.

Let me illustrate this point. When a person sees a red light and doesn't stop, and they go ahead as if the light were green, that is a wrong reaction. Now that person could have thought the light was going to change and they wanted to get a head start. It is a different situation when a person sees a yellow light and they think it's okay to go through the intersection. I would like for you to think of a flashing yellow light, which means caution or warning. I call them warning signs and alarm signals.

Identifying Personal-well-being feelings as it relates to Stress, Demands and Crisis

A breakdown could have started as a normal reaction, and a normal pattern leading into a breakdown. In this case a particular incident brought about the breakdown. We use the term "red flag," which means there is a problem in the situation?

How a person deals with their reactions determines if the person explodes over what has happened, followed by an emotional breakdown. Now let's see how it relates to the amount of stress, demands, or causes of a crisis. The stress point is the first thing to look for. How a person reacts to stress is one of the most common denominators in the problems a person faces. When a person has demands put on them, there is a stress point, and when the problems get bad and reach a point of a crisis in the situation there is a negative breakdown. The stress point has gotten too high. That is not a good sign, but the reaction is going above the line. That can be an indicator of anger or being out of control. How a person reacts is very import- ant. That will determine whether it is a major or a minor problem they are dealing with and we want them to look at what is occurring during the breakdown.

There are so many demands in life that a person cannot count all of them, let alone deal with everyone in a day's time. That is where the brain comes into play. It will signal previous patterns and will account for most the decisions being made. There are ways to make the emotional experiences easier, but on the other hand a person's life is complicated by their feelings. Again, it is important how a male and female approach an emotional experience. Most of the time there are two different views of the same situation. Then, you have two different emotional sensitivity levels to the same situation.

A Normal Breakdown has little or No Consequences

4. Short Term Do Nothing Attitude

DEMAND · DO NOTHING · LIFE EXPERIENCES · NO RESOLUTION · ARGUMENT

There could be any one of three reactions taking place in a breakdown. You need to realize how an experience relates to the "Life Line." When there are multiple reactions taking place, look at the reactions that apply. It is important which ones apply, because it gives you a look at how to deal with life's experiences.

There are three major events in life; there is your birth, marriage, and raising children. Whatever the experience, people are most likely to look at it in light of whether they made the right or wrong choice, and how successful they were in the decision. Sometimes it is based on how bad a person fails in their marriage, or raising their children.

The situation is usually set up by some decisions they made earlier.

However, these reactions are normal reactions in some form, but when it comes to a breakdown after breakdown there is a pattern that forms. This is usually the one that gets a person in trouble, and is the hardest to recognize, because it starts out as a normal problem, and then the breakdown occurs.

There are several reasons for trouble after the breakdown, a person may think everything was all right before the breakdown, and everything should be all right after the breakdown, so why worry about it. Maybe they just hope everything will work out because it is normal to have a breakdown every once in a while. That is the philosophy of the day, and that is why some people don't say, "I'm sorry." When they hear another person say, "I did not know anything was wrong." How many times have I heard that statement about bad relationships?

It could be any reaction that caused the breakdown, and they don't see the warning signs. A person doesn't see it because nothing has happened like this before, or they choose to ignore the problems of the past, or even worse, they don't care. Sometimes a person doesn't realize there is a breakdown occurring, and it will be too late when the other person has said, "Enough, and it has gone too far." It could be a marriage problem, short-term illness, or a short-term problem gone too far, or a relationship that doesn't work out.

Another thing a person has to deal with is when they think it is all right now, as the person waits to see what is going to happen. They may think everything is all right when it really isn't. The other person may be hurt and angry, and they don't realize how bad they have been hurt. The first person doesn't see the anger, or why the breakdown occurred. This adds to the complexity of the situation. I always find they are caused by personal feelings from their past experiences. Nothing seemed to be wrong before, and that can be an underlying problem in the future.

In my observations, you never know why or when a person has had enough (the breaking point). Sometimes that person does not know in themselves what triggers a breakdown. As you can see in this diagram, the person does not go back to a normal pattern in life, after the breakdown happens.

My feelings about a breakdown

I like this saying, "You should not judge a book by its cover." In other words people should not judge another person "until they have walked a mile in their footsteps." This is one of the first lessons I learned. I know it is hard, but a person should not judge other people. Having dealt with all of my problems has given me a different perspective on life. I think that is one of the good things that came out of my life situations. I certainly have no right to judge another person.

There are certain contributing factors to any situation, as to how the contributing factors fit into the equation of what has happened, but it is much more important how they relate to what is happening in their life. I learned to understand how to relate to each circumstance in relation to the past and what I needed to do in the future. Some would say life is about providence and a person can't do anything about what happened, others may say that it was just bad luck. Some flip a coin, or say, "Whatever will be, will be." Each individual uses a different method when making a decision.

Again, when looking at it from the human side, there should be a logical explanation, or some use intuitions as a point of view. I am definitely concerned with how a person deals with their problems in a situation, but I am even more concerned with how they are going to deal with their own problems.

Long Term Struggle and Breakdown

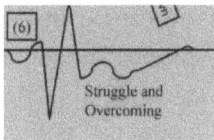

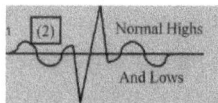

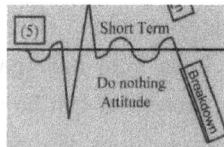

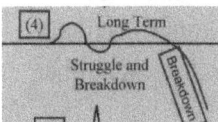

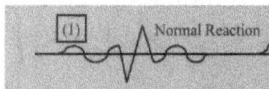

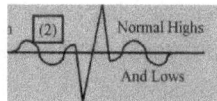

5. Long Term Struggle and Breakdown

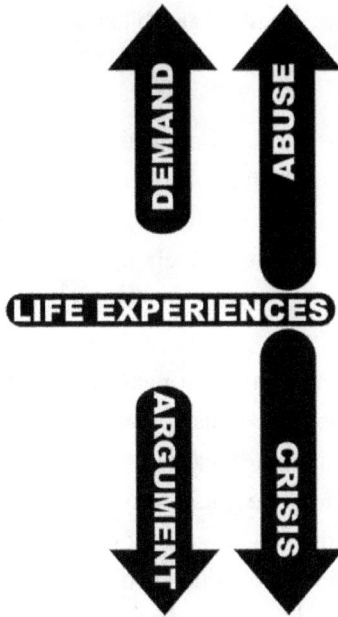

DEMAND **ABUSE**

LIFE EXPERIENCES

ARGUMENT **CRISIS**

There are three major elements in the negative aspects of Long Term Struggle and Breakdowns in the Life Line.

Every situation is measured by stress, demands, a crisis breakdown and the emotional experience. There are normal reactions taking place all the time, but a breakdown takes place at a certain point. Look for what caused the breakdown, what happened when a traumatic experience has brought about a breakdown. It could be a series of normal reactions, and then a breakdown after a long period of time. These are some of the things that could have caused the Breakdown: a job, marriage, or illness. A long or short term illness can fit into this category.

For example, a person in the armed forces who has been on the battle front for a long period of time fits into this kind of long term breakdown, or Post Traumatic Stress Disorder (PTSD). This kind of breakdown can be some of the hardest to deal with. A person may feel helpless at the time, depending what has happened up to this point. It may take years before a breakdown occurs or to get over a traumatic experience. This kind of trauma, in some cases, is a life-long battle.

The worst thing that can happen in a long term breakdown is that the person does not realize it is destroying them day after day, and year after year. When the hurt, anger, hostility, and bitterness set in; there can be various degrees of stress. That is another way to understand the stages a person is dealing with.

A lot can happen when you put all of those elements together in a situation while dealing with the hurt, anger, hostility, and bitterness, and add to it the everyday stress of a family and job. Yes, a person can go to church with all of these elements in their heart and life and still have major problems.

Add Frustration, Anguish, Disappointments, and Guilt

Add these elements to a relationship; now let's say for instance the glass is 3/4 full of bad elements. It leaves little room for good elements in the glass. I compare it to the glass, so you can see how much it's affecting your life. Depending on how full of good or bad elements there are, the glass is always full of something. If nothing else, the glass is full of air, and so it is with life. It is a matter of what kinds of elements are filling your life. I am talking about the heart and soul of a man or woman. There are motives behind why or why not?

Our Life Enhancement studies deal with the aspects of a long term breakdown and how it affects a person. Some of these axioms include frustration, anguish, disappointments, and guilt relate to how bad the breakdown has become. Where did they come from and how it could have been prevented at the start of the problem. There is a direct result as a person looks at the factors in this breakdown. Identifying these breakdowns will play a big part in the rest of these studies.

It may take years to get over any "Long Term Breakdowns." In some of these cases people need professional help before they can go on with a productive happy life. Support Outreach Services web links can help anyone find the right kind of support-help. Even with professional help you can find a support partner that has gone through the same experience.

This also applies to short term breakdowns. The one thing I want to point out here is that when an adult gets hurt they feel and react, and so do children. Sometimes a person feels down because they are suffering. The problem may not have been dealt with properly before the breakdown.

The brain sends the warning signs

This part of the chart has to do with a short term breakdown. This is usually another one that gets a person in trouble, especially when they don't seem to think they have any problems coming from their reaction. In this case, life does not go back to a normal pattern. When there is a short term breakdown a different kind of reaction has taken place. The reason it might give a person some trouble is that they are not expecting any trouble, or maybe they are just hoping everything will work out by itself, and they have the do-nothing attitude.

I always use stress as it links to any breakdown. At this point a person can do several things; the problem can become dormant, or resurface at a later time. In any kind of long term breakdown there can be a crisis time in the situation before it goes back to normal. It is a problem when a person can't get over a situation. The demands can be short term, but when linked to other types of demands they can take on different stress levels.

Any normal reaction can lead to a breakdown, but there are warning signs just before it happens. Sometimes, in these cases, it is too late. It could be a short-term illness, or a short-term problem that doesn't work out in their life.

Another thing a person deals with is their feelings. They know something is wrong, but they can't put their finger on what caused the problem. While they are waiting for an answer there is an explosion. Next they have to wait to see what is going to happen after the explosion. That might be all right in some situations, but that is why it is complex in nature.

A breakdown occurs when a person knows something is wrong and life does not go back to normal. That can be an underlying problem until the breakdown is resolved. No person can ever know when they have had enough. Sometimes that person does not know what will trigger a breakdown, and in some cases it is simply too much for the person. The normal pattern has been interrupted and causes a breakdown.

Built into the nature of the brain there are limits which cause a person to look for danger or the fear factor. When someone abuses, or causes abuse, or causes domestic violence they have broken a person's limits and safety devices are altered their life is changed. That can be one reason why a person has problems living a normal life after a breakdown. They usually live with the fear of it happening again. There is another influence that is just as devastating; knowing someone has wronged them.

Because there has been some disruptiveness in their life, some people deal with the breakdown by using what is called selective memory. This person remembers only what they want to remember. In some instances a person may have a faulty memory in the way they see things, and hold bad feelings. I believe that within certain limits and boundaries there is an ineffective participation that reinforces a person's belief. This happens when a person thinks they have done nothing wrong. Giving over to the day-to-day experiences can facilitate some bad behavior patterns. Nevertheless, when things happen above the normal limits and safety devices are not met, emotions are hampered and sound reasoning doesn't work. This throws off a person's ability to evaluate the situation

Some choose to think, "The devil made them do it." I choose the position that there are many strong influences in a person's life including the devil and we will deal them later in this Life Enhancement study. These influences can lead to abuse by someone else; it could have been something as far back as their childhood. The warning signs and limits are there, and the safety devices have been threatened and altered before the breakdown. However, they just don't see them, because they are not in proper balance or don't want to deal with them.

That is when someone says: "I can't take it anymore." Too often people permit only a narrow range of attitudes concerning their behaviors which is based on what other people think, based on bias, prejudice, hasty generalizations, or limited past experiences. Think of those statements like, "I can't believe (he or she) said that," or "Imagine (him or her) doing that," and so on. I recall these proverbial saying, "My life is not about living up to someone else's expectations, but being able to live up to mine."

May I say at this point that every person and ever family has problems and there are problems in everything a person does, the important thing do they really want to do something?

This next section is going to help a person even more as they understand how to deal with their struggles.

Emotional Struggle and Overcoming, The stress, demands, and Crisis Time in Life.

Finally we come to a good reaction when a person is struggling to deal with a situation after a breakdown. The chart shows how a person relates to an emotional experience, and also relates to how they deal with their stress, demands, and crisis.

A person needs to understand the thought process, and how they are reacting. Again, may I emphasize that this is not how society has programmed a person to react? Everything is all right be- cause a person didn't do anything wrong. That is not a true statement, because everything does not work out in life.

A situation is only bad when a person doesn't come up with an answer or a solution. Let me say this; with every decision a person makes there is going to be good and bad decisions taking place.

A person usually doesn't see or think about the reaction taking place; as a consequence many reactions are not consciously observed. A person doesn't understand why they do or say certain things. They tend to think of themselves first, and not in relation to the events happening, but they should be more observant of their attitudes at the same time.

By looking at all these diagrams maybe a person will be able to relate to things happening.

Chart II, diagram 5 has to do with **short term breakdown**.

This is usually another one that gets a person in trouble, especially when they don't seem to think they have any problems coming from their **reaction.** In this case life does not go back to a **normal pattern,** but when there a **short term breakdown** a different kind of reaction has taken place. The reason it might give a person some trouble, they are not expecting any trouble, or maybe they are just hoping everything will work out by itself, and have the **do-nothing attitude.**

Chart 5 I am always going to use **stress** as it links to any **breakdown**

at this point a person can do several things. The problem can become dormant, or resurface at a later time. In any kind of **breakdown** there can be a **crisis** time in the situation. The **demands** can be **short term**, but when linked to other types of **demands** they can take on different **stress levels**.

Any **normal reaction** can lead to a **breakdown**, but there are **warning signs** just before it happens. Sometimes in these cases it is too late. It could be a short-term illness, or a short-term problem that doesn't work out in their life.

Another thing a person deals with is their **feelings**, but they know something is wrong and they can't put their finger on what caused the problem. While they are waiting for an answer there is an explosion, and they are saying what happened. Next they have to wait to see what is going to happen after the explosion. That might be alright in some situations, but that is why it is complex in nature.

As a person can see in the "**Life Line**", their life does not go **back to normal**. That always defines a **breakdown** when a person knows something is wrong and life does not go **back to normal**. They could have thought nothing was wrong, and that can be an underlying problem until the **breakdown** is resolved. No person can ever know when they have had enough, sometimes that person does not know what will **trigger** a **breakdown,** and in some cases it is simply too much for the person. As you can see in **diagram 5** the **normal pattern** has been interrupted and caused a **breakdown**.

Built into the nature of the **brain** there are **limits** which cause a person to look for danger. When someone abuses or causes abuse those **limits** and **safety devices** are altered, their life is changed. That can be one reason why a person has problems living a **normal life** after a **breakdown**; they usually live with the fear of it happening again. There is another influence that is just as devastating knowing someone has wronged them.

Because there has been some disruption, there are several way a person can deal with a **breakdown** they use what is called selective memory, a person remembers only what they want to remember. In some instances a person may have a faulty memory in the way they see things because of their bad **feelings**. I believe that within certain limits and boundaries; there is an ineffective participation that reinforces their beliefs. A person thinks they have done nothing wrong, giving over to the day-to-day experiences facilitating bad behavior patterns. Nevertheless, when the above **limits** and **safety devices** are broken their emotions are hampered and sound reasoning doesn't work. This throws off a person's ability to evaluate the situation.

Some choose to think "the devil made them do it". I choose the position there are many strong influences in a person's life including the devil. These influences can lead to abuse by someone else, or it could have been something as far back as their childhood. The **warning signs** and **limits** are there and the **safety devices** have been threatened and altered in a **breakdown**, however they just don't see them because they are not in **proper balance** or don't want to deal with something.

That is when someone says: "I can't take it any more". Too often people permit only a narrow range of attitudes concerning their behaviors based on what other people think of them. Which is based on a bias, prejudice, hasty generalizations, and their past experiences? Think of those statements like, "I can't believe (he or she) said that," or "Imagine (him or her) doing that," and so on. I believe this to be true, "my life is not about living up to someone else's expectations, but being able to live up to mine".

May I say at this point every person and ever family has problems and there are problems in everything a person does.

Now let's look at **Chart II diagram [(6)]** I think this section is going to help a person even more as they understand how to deal with their struggles in life.

6. Struggling and Overcoming

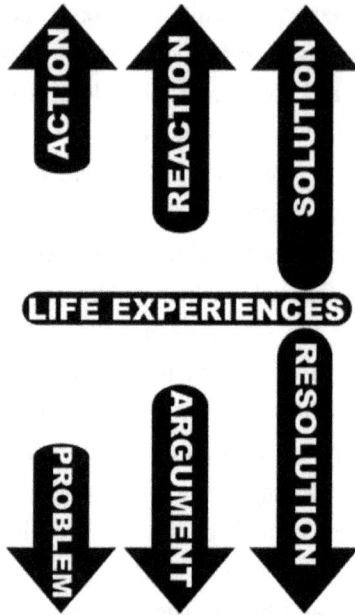

ACTION

REACTION

SOLUTION

LIFE EXPERIENCES

PROBLEM

ARGUMENT

RESOLUTION

This chart lay out may really help a person in the future. A person may let things pass or say, "It will be okay." Let's face it, most of the time everyday situations do work themselves out. Should every problem be a real problem? Of course not!

A person should not get alarmed at every problem. If they do, they may be an alarmist, and they may need to deal with an alarmist attitude because they are over-reacting. It is just as important to know how to handle problem solving as it relates to proper balance, and control.

Let me say this, if a person second guesses themselves in every decision they make or think, there is something wrong in every situation. They don't understand what is happening when a reaction is taking place, or how to deal with it. The problem is actually being perceived as something that is not true or good for them, which makes the problem look out of focus. It is in the way a person handles difficult problems. In some cases people don't realize a problem exists.

That is where some critics may say, "Why worry about it?" There are some who may take the doomsday approach "everything is wrong."

Another thing, while a person is dealing with a problem, they usually don't spend enough time to get the victory over the problem. This will show up more as we go into problem solving, later.

It may take weeks and months, and lots of study to get the victory over just one problem. After all of that, a person will still have new problems come up every day. As you can see, a person keeps all of the old problems, plus all of the new problems that come into their life. That is why life can be so hard to deal with.

Another question a person should ask themselves is why? If a person can find the reason, or why it happened and look for the root of the problem, it makes it easier to live and deal with. A person may or may not blame themselves. When they see the real reason for their problems, they should have a good idea how to deal with it as they identify with the problem. It is not always easy to see and do. Even if something turns out bad there is something to be learned from it.

The point I am making, there are some good reactions taking place. This can represent struggling within the situation, while dealing with the problems. That is where family and friends can help, if they are not critical by saying, "Something is wrong with you" or they may say, "I wouldn't worry about it if it were me." If it is a problem to you, they are not the ones dealing with the situation. You should not let it pass without coming up with a solution. That is another reason why small problems become major problems.

While a person is struggling and dealing with a situation, they might ask a friend for advice. They may ask for prayer and advice from a pastor or Sunday school teacher. Always think it through before taking action on your decision.

When a person is struggling coming up with the right answer a person's outside influences may affect their decision-making. Another thing, when a person is struggling with a problem, they usually don't spend enough time to get the victory over the problem.

I have found it to be true, in my personal life and studies, that struggling comes before victory in any problem. When a person keeps all of the old problems bottled up it makes it much harder to deal with the new problems that come, and that is why their life can seem so difficult.

Some say life is a struggle, and it's true, but how does a person overcome problems in a situation? If it is a problem, then why is it a problem? There may be a reason why the problem has developed. Face the issues. I believe in most cases a person chooses to be victorious or they choose to be a victim. I know it is not always easy to find out why. Overcoming is certainly the best alternative, but it may mean taking on the responsibilities in your life.

Either a person takes responsibility and does something, or, in many cases, they blame someone else for their failures and unhappiness.

Those who choose to overcome don't find life to be a struggle, but instead of thinking of it as a problem, they think of it as a challenge. They find life to be exhilarating. They don't encounter problems without having a positive attitude. They merely face the challenge as a chance to do better. When they find something blocking their way they look for a way to overcome it. In other words, they look for, and find solutions.

On the other hand, those who choose to be victims are experts at looking for excuses. They almost always delight in finding others to blame for their misery. Let's take a look at two principles.

One: the amount of difficulty in a problem should not be impeded when overcoming the problem. This is a part of the quest, but there is a need for, dedication, determination, and discipline.

Two: success come through overcoming a problem. It may be measured by the difficulties and challenges, or whatever choices a person is called on to do. This should not stop a person's progress.

Rather, it should cause a person to ask the following questions.

1. What do I want from life and can my goals be accomplished?
2. What obstacle or problem is preventing me from reaching my goal?
3. What will I do if I fail? Is the cost too much if I don't succeed?

The answer to all of these questions is directly pointed at the very purpose and meaning in a person's life, when they know what they want to be and do. They have goals to achieve, and that will be one of the keys in climbing their mountain. Then there is the challenge in overcoming the problems. The struggling is the challenge. It should be the natural thing to do. Why is it so hard for some people to overcome a problem?

Although, a person may want to improve their life, why can't they, or why do people expect immediate success? They may experience temporary success, but real success usually doesn't happen that way. The discomfort and struggle is usually accompanied by making changes. When a person finds themselves hesitant about a situation they should not get discouraged. Rather, understand the cause of their hesitancy and focus on the benefits that change will bring. In some cases a person is forced to take steps they don't want to take and cause them to step out of their comfort zone.

When a person begins to change, they must answer the question, "Who am I, and where am I going?" This relates to the changes needed, and how to make preparation for these life-changing decisions. In this stage, a person should outline the needed approach for reaching their goal.

The implementation means carrying out their plan of action instead of a plan of reaction, and then they can take on the necessary changes.

Maintenance is when a person checks their progress from time to time, makes corrections when needed, and makes sure they stay on course, and are headed for the target.

This is a good feeling when you have these tools; knowledge, materials, and ability to do anything. Some might think, "Why try?" People are trained to rely on other people for the most part people who think small limit themselves. But, can they interact with the world, and become a complete person with their abilities to do things.

The ability to be constructive is the enjoyment of the challenge. Creative people are eager to test their own limits and eliminate problems. They are willing to work hard, and do not give up easily. Sometimes their discontent is almost artificial. They aren't really unhappy with the status quo in things they do or in some areas of their life, but, they want to find something better just for the challenge of it, and the opportunity to improve their own lives and the lives of others around them.

I hope you are able to distinguish what patterns are in your life, and how to deal with the personal challenges in the emotional experience. If a person is able to do that, they have come a long way in their life.

What actions promote Mental Well-being?

It can become a problem when the over-all mental well-being is threatened and doesn't work out, and a person is out-of-control. If a person is worried this may cause mental, emotional frustration

Anxiety:

- Promote Mental Well-being from within.
- Promote Mental Well-being through thoughts, feelings, emotions, and human behaviors.
- Promote Mental Well-being through physical, social, and psychological behavior.
- Promote Well-being with good peers and friends.
- Promote Mental Well-being through your own support group.

When a person says, "A person is crazy," are they talking about mental health, or does it really mean the mental well-being of a person? A person may do something "crazy." Does that mean they are crazy? No! It is never appropriate to call someone "crazy," but people do it in a joking way.

It is important to be able to determine the emotion and motivation relevant to a situation. My hope is that I will be able to establish some guidelines in the mental well-being of a person's life, but also in courage a healthy emotional person.

What is emotional health and Mental-Well-being?

1. it is an ongoing process
2. the ability to learn to create a healthy emotional atmosphere.
3. the need to accept change and be willing to change your mind.
4. it is a willingness to bend but not break.
5. to learn from life. Don't let the circumstance overtake you to a fault.
6. to be willing to learn from past mistakes. If the same mistake happens
7. admitting to failure and wrong doing, if you're not totally at fault.
8. doing and take pride in having a good relationship instead.

What is meant by a mental and psychological edge? When I think of a movie star or television personality, they are people with a highly visible life. They are very conscious of their appearance. That gives them an edge.

If a person looks hard enough, they will feel they have an edge in his or her life. Mine was dealing with health problems, without those obstacles, I would not be where I am today.

Chapter 6

Step 6
STAGES IN LIFE THERE ARE

The history of America can be tracked through stages of growth: the first century started with the American Revolution, the second century was marked by a Civil War, the third century by the Industrial Revolution. The turn of the 20th Century brought WWI. I grew up with the Stock Market Crash of the 30's, WWII, the fifty's unions and the exploitation of the middle class, the hippie generation, the sex revolution of the 80's & 90's, the technology age, and who knows what the 21st Century will bring.

Let me explain people change and so doe's society. The growth Stage from birth to childhood is a wonderful time in a person's life. They grow up under mom and dad's guidance and help. In some cases this is not a happy time in a person's life. Sometimes a child may feel helpless, especially when abuse comes into their life. Sometimes adults take advantage of a child's growth process and use it to their advantage.

I have come up with a formula that is relevant and that com- bines the age and stage during life. This formula applies it to the different emotional experiences during each stage a person goes through, and I will take it a step farther. I am still trying to unlock one of the doors to the meaning of mental-well-being in a person's life.

Formula for Age, Stage and the Life Cycles

A person has to understand there are certain things happening at certain ages that will have a direct bearing on the different situations, and how they relate to their age within the stages of life. The social and personal pressures may have a direct bearing on the timing in the life cycle. They are compounded by the circumstances surrounding the situations that make up the various aspects relating to the person. It is a never ending journey, and life can have its moments during the various stages.

These are some of the things a person has to watch for in a particular period of time. Each stage of development is important in a person's growth process, how they relate to the life cycle at the time, and how they deal with their own particular problems.

Stages in Life
- Conception to about Age 14, Growth Stage.
- About Age 15 to about Age 25, Exploratory Stage.
- About Age 26 to about Age 45, Establishment Stage.
- About Age 46 to about Age 65, Maintenance Stage.
- About Age 66 to about Age 75, Declining Stage.
- About Age 75 and above, The Golden Years Stage

Social pressures affect each stage of life. A person compounds their life by not dealing with the stages of growth. These are some of the things to watch for over the period of a life time, but also in each stage.

I have spent some time dealing with the patterns and attitudes that develop over time, and how they can become set in a person's life. The worst thing about dealing with the different stages is that a person doesn't always realize how many problems have built up during that stage, or at least I didn't.

The thing to look at in every stage is their maturity and personal growth, even if they are male or female, and this can vary depending on the way a person deals with their lives in different ways. There are many different problems surrounding the life cycles. How a person deals with each stage is also very important when facing their responsibilities and what happens during that life cycle. My hope is you will have a better understanding when we get through this part on stages. I hope this next formula will give a person a better understanding of one's self in some way, and it helped me to understand the different stages in my life. Now let's take a look at how the formula is going to work.

Age and Stage + Situations x Stress Factors=Pressure.

I think of it in terms of a mathematical equation, for those who like to think of problems in that way, but everybody will understand the language. When I say Age and Stage, the terms should have some meaning by now, and what is happening in relation to a time in a person's life. Now I am going to be adding a sign (+) as to how many situations have been added to the age and stages. Next, let's take X times the Stress Factors = Pressure. This is another one of the ways of evaluating how bad the situation is in a person's life. Now add all of their personal problems that relate to the situation, this multiplies the forces when there is too much stress in a person's life. When they are dealing with higher stress levels that will create more pressure in a situation.

For example, let's take the age of the person, and look at what he or she is going through at the same time their life has more problems as they get older. Then, look at the + side, and the – down side, measured by the increments of the stress levels. Let's look at what stage a person is in, what are some of the things they should be dealing with, mixed in with how they're dealing with their problems. Add what they are dealing with besides what is happening in their relationship, like problems at work or school. Now let's look at how many + situations there are, good job or school and see where the = pressures are coming from, and see what kind of pressures they are dealing with within the relationship.

I have an illustration that might help in understanding the equation better. Think of a tire on a car. If it is flat, you are not going anywhere! However, if the tire is inflated right, the car will run smoother.

Let's look at a person's life, and see if the pressure in their life is too high, or if it is too low. If there is too much pressure the ride will be bumpy. It could be that they don't have enough pressure which creates lows and negatives in their life. If the tire is low you will be going from side to side. If the pressure is right the ride will be smooth, but if it is too bumpy a person's relationship has too much stress, or if it is low, the relationship could be going from bad to worse. When there is either too much pressure or not enough pressure you are going to be dealing with problems, or you may be swerving back and forth dodging the problems, but sooner or later it is going to catch up with you.

This illustration helped me with the formula, and helped me understand what was happening in my life.

The age and stage of the personal experience is important to understand. A person may suddenly find out, despite their progress, that they will experience a setback or two. They may slip back into their old patterns. This is to be expected from time to time. Although, everyone does not experience the same problems in the stage, some have different expectations. Some people progress faster, while others falter at different ages because of problems.

When this happens, just pick up the pieces, and say, "I'm not going to get discouraged and give up now! I refuse to choose to be a victim! I choose to be victorious; I'm getting back to the program of change and regaining control over my life." But, while doing this, it is important to look at the age and stage you are going through. That may be one of the many reasons for your problems. Another is not reaching your goals, not realizing the simplest things may be affecting or controlling your life.

This is where some people need help getting past some of these obstacles above. My hope is that you will learn more about yourself and understand your possibilities, abilities, and qualities embedded/rooted in the mind, body, and spirit.

The instant a thought goes through the brain it is going to relate to the conscious – primary influences and subconscious – secondary influences, and then it brings about emotions of good or bad feelings. Thus arousing the past influences, setting up the actions and reactions. There are also direct or indirect feelings taking on some form of action. A person's feelings are influenced by their emotions, attitude, and motivation. This in return brings out how genetics and environment influence what a person does.

I had to learn how to define and understand why I felt the way I did and understand how primary and secondary situations influenced my character, genetics, and environment. At that point I started to learn how to cope with my character influences in relation to my problems.

Primary Influences

Attitude is also a reflection of one's self, and it is very much like a mirror into a person's life. When a person looks at their reflection there can be a problem because they tend to see only what they want to see, and in the way they view a problem. In a mirror they may not see the real problems, or their own personal attitude.

Let's look at the primary influences first. To do this I need to develop the precept of what is important. We must first examine a person's motives because they are a major influence. This is going to be a reflection of how a person is dealing with things. These primary influences will relate to their personality and, for instance, their family and moral values. These influences can eat at a person from the inside and destroy their life, and have a lasting effect on their relationships.

It also points out a good example of good patterns. I was determined not to make the same mistakes over again, but I did. I tried different ways, but I ended up with the same problems as a result. Look at the patterns in your life, and see them for what they are. Now I want you to see the primary influences, and how they are affecting you or may be how they are controlling your life. Break through those chains that are holding you captive.

There are also three other primary influences, wants, needs, and desires. How do you deal with them in your life? This happens regardless of what methods you have used in making a decision. I personally like to use these axioms, dedication, determination, and discipline. A person has to learn how to be happy with themselves not having a false sense of pride or being, but really knowing who they are and being able to relate and give to other people.

The answers are interwoven in the fabric of these primary influences, wants, needs, and desires. It even goes farther when a person uses dedication, determination, and discipline. How in the world is a person expected to understand and learn how to define their primary influences, by coping with their wants, needs, and desires. Because of the different variables in the formula, now we add age and stage + personal influences. Personal influences can get involved in a person's actions and thinking!

A person may be happy with their life as it is, and they may not think anything is wrong in their life, but when a person becomes too critical of others they have a problem. I came to that conclusion when I started to understand what I really wanted in life, and how to be happy with me as a person.

I think there is another way to understand these primary influences – wants, needs, and desires. Let's look at who that person in your mirror, these are reflections of one's self. Because a person tends to see only what they want to see and not the real person inside. They are looking at their physical appearance. The person sees the physical flaws because they see them every day. Another question is what do they think of that person in the mirror?

They are looking at an image of themselves, when a person moves, the person in the mirror moves and it reflects movement, but it can't reflect what a person is thinking, just movement. I think this is an accurate analogy of how a person sees themselves.

I want to go from there to looking at the primary influences in another way. They are there, but a person may overlook them because they can't see what is happening to themselves every day.

You must understand what is going on inside. Examine your motives; look at what is happening because this relates to your primary influences. This is usually a reflection of what is happening in your real life. The primary influences can also show up like a disease, the problems of the past can eat at a person and destroy their life and relationships.

Coping with primary influences

A person needs coping skills, and to be able to let the pressure out of the situation. I consider coping to be one of the primary avenues of being able to relieve some of the pressure in a situation. I use the word cope because it fits; it gives a person a good mechanism to deal with in the situation! Let me say this, I don't condemn any person for using things to help them cope. Without some kind of pressure-relief, life can become impossible to live with, and deal with at times. If a person is able to cope at every level they will be much happier. A person may not be able to see some of the real dangers if they cannot handle some of the pressures in a situation.

This is another thing I learned about myself, I like the pressure of setting a goal and reaching it, I liked working long hours, but the pressure brought about stresses in my life and body, and it affected my relationships too. That is one of the things that led up to and contributed to bad relationships.

When I was raising my family, those were the different kinds of pressure. There were a lot things to cope with besides reaching my goal and getting ahead. I tried to balance all of that in the relationship. When two people are raising a family; one problem is over doing too many things, like work, and not keeping personal ties to the relationship. May I say this as I look back, this probably reflects back to how I was raised, because I was brought up to work hard and put in long hours? It also reflects on how I am dealing with my life today. Has anything changed?

I want you to take a closer look and apply the formula we have just introduced. Can you agree that, while coping with everyday situations, you lose sight of important things? What does that mean?

How did I deal with the stress factors as they related to the pressure, and what kind of pressure-relief did I apply? In my case working was an outlet, and a lot of men fit into that category, because their job is a part of their identity. It may sound harmless enough as I think back, I thought I was coping in my own way, but this created problems in the relationship. It became the proverbial hot potato, because it eventually caused problems. The arguments became hotter and the problems got worse during that time. We spent more money, and that became a major concern to me, because we were not able to resolve other major differences. My way of resolving problems was to earn more money which meant I was away from home. Unfortunately, that was not her way of resolving the problems, which led to a divorce.

Those were some of the bad things that happened, as I look back, there were too many minuses in the situation they added up in my case. There was too much stress because we kept getting farther in debt, and it got to be too much in the relationship; the pressure got greater in each situation.

Situations like this can lead to a multitude of problems: another problem is eating disorders, drinking, drugs-pills, or smoking. These are some of the pressure outlets. Fortunately, I did not use any of these. As we look at the formula, do these indicators bring out a larger problem? When a person tends to overlook these symptoms, they do not see how they are affecting the larger picture in their life.

At this point, when things are going bad, a person may say something like, "I need a break," or "I need to get away from the situation for a while." When a situation is too much for a person to handle, they tend to over react in some way, and go in the opposite direction. This is usually a warning sign. This may be where a person looks for a way out, and when a person feels that way, be careful! I wanted her to stop spending money we didn't have, but this was her way of coping and relieving pressure.

Sometimes a person wants to get even, but it only brings a negative response and adds to the problems.

There is a need to find a constructive way of coping, handling the Age and Stage + Situation X times Stress Factors = Pressure.

There is usually a transitional stage in any situation. Be careful, this could be when a person tends to let their guard down. They need to relax, and yet be on guard.

An illustration is when a family plans their vacation so that they can get away, relax and have a good time, but this relief brings out a different kind of stress and pressure to deal with. It can be fun, and the stress levels can be higher in these situations. The family is in a pressure situation and tempers flare more easily, but the fun and excitement can overrule in this situation, because they are having fun at the same time. I hope you can see how the fun and excitement helped relieve the stress of the situation, and made the situation fun and tolerable.

A person or family needs to apply these same principles in their everyday situations. Life can get into a routine, and the excitement is gone. They come home and eat, turn on the TV, forget they have any problems for a while, go to sleep and get up the next morning and go back to work. The same old routine, I think this could sound familiar to most people and families.

When a person has to deal with their burdens and the every day cares of life that can get to be too much. It really gets bad when a person thinks they can get through the situation. One way is finding a pressure-relief. There are plenty of books and videos on these different subjects and information to help a person cope.

When it really gets bad a person may need to try and express what is going on to their spouse or friend, but what happens when the other person doesn't want to listen to why they are not able to cope? It could be how a person identifies with what is going on in their situation. Can they identify with others in the same situation? See how they relate to the circumstances and how they are coping with their situations and circumstances. Maybe look at why and how they may have failed. A person may need encouragement and then, the question to ask yourself is, "What could they have done differently by looking at it from a different point of view?"

This is where a person's hobbies and outside interests come into play. This is an area where a person needs to center some of their attention. There is another good source of pressure-relief in the right kind of exercise. Plus, there are all kinds of ways to meet a person's wants, needs and desires at the same time.

Dedication

At this point you may need to understand and know how to deal with the human spirit and will. I like to think of dedication as an attitude that can be a driving force. It can be the equalizing force in some situations.

There is a need to deal with the situation sooner, not later, but the human spirit has a part in every situation. What about a life threatening situation? It is no surprise what the human spirit and will, can do when dedicated to a task or problem that is life threatening.

Determination

Determination is a powerful influence that comes into play. At a pivotal point in my life I thought I was going to die. I was close to having a heart attack; I was under a doctor's care. This was no pre- tense on my part; it literally shook up my life. As I thought about death, the hereafter, and God, this experience changed my life, and the determination not to have a heart attack was a profound influence in my life, and the way I went about preventing a heart attack. Also, at that point I was really mixed up, and I didn't know which way to turn. It took several years to sort this out, and get the tools I needed to turn my life around, and get me to where I am today. That took determination to stay in there when it looked like I was defeated. That is why I call it the "7-year search" because

I had the 7 major health attacks over those years, but I never had a heart attack. In fact my arthritis almost destroyed me physically, and threatened my mental and physical-well-being. It is a testimony to my determination.

Discipline

First and foremost is discipline! Second is carrying out the discipline!

1. You have to be committed
2. You have to make a conscious effort on your part.
3. You have to be motivated.
4. You have to maintain good work ethics and work habits.

Here is just one aspect, self-discipline, which in turn can enable true development and build a foundation for a person's life. It took discipline to build a good foundation in my life. The foundation is self-discipline; the victorious life is based on self-control. This is a key to mental-well-being, and being motivated is a guideline for one's self, whether it's doing homework, to finishing a job, or getting up in the morning. Self-Discipline is the ability to control gratification and channel one's urges, to act properly in the situation based on the personal will of a person. A person needs to control one's appetites, passions, and do right by others. It takes will-power to have discipline under control.

It takes will-power to build self-discipline, which in turn enables true commitment to true standards, values and morals. The need to practice them builds essential skills of discipline. In that sense it goes hand in hand with good moral values, and also develops character. It is through self-discipline that a person builds their character even when things go wrong, but also at that time a person can build a disciplined life.

Secondary Influences

Let's look at the attributes of a person when they face situations, building on their habits, traits, and attitude. The secondary influences start from the inner person, and there are also other influences.

Forming good habits ensures good behavior and enables the safe functioning of the person. They are acquired after a very long sustained effort. At the age of thirty, a person tries to learn writing skills. It will take some time and effort if they are going to learn the skills of writing. It will be much harder as a person gets older. Every habit is acquired over time, and there is a history behind every habit. Some habits are like polite manners; others are deep-seated. Habits are in submission to the subconscious. The former are far more difficult to change than developing new or changing old habits. Still, even surface habits, like polite manners are learned skills as a child.

Habits, when acquired, are accepted gradually by the total being. A physical skill like writing becomes more and more perfect when a person takes an interest in writing, and the mental aspect becomes a way of life. The mind understands the process, and puts its energies behind the physical act of writing. A mental act like good behavior starts from the mind-set, and steadily passes through the mental and physical process. When a habit is learned by all parts of the being, there is a saying, "It is in their blood," it has become "second nature," or it has become a part of the mind-set. The whole life is vital to the mental. Once habits are fully entrenched, they are hard to change.

Let's look at another example; the family teaches certain skills, while the school and society add to the learning process. We start with a child. They learn to be social individuals; thus their character is being formed over the years. If earlier generations are trained in one line of work, the latter generations pick up those personal traits quickly, and yet a child is more likely to take on the same habits as their parents. But, the process can be changed from one generation to another.

Traits are also a part of the person's mind-set. The human capacity to function relates to the mind-set. This capacity of functioning is readily applied in a given situation, and it does not only belong to the mind-set, it also belongs to the inner being as well. Human traits also have the capacity to be developed from what a person thinks of themselves. They are innately inherited characteristics and also learned behaviors. In as much as a person has the capacity to learn, they have to learn to deal with the relevant traits and be able to use their capacity to function wisely. The person will emerge and act on his or her own knowledge. This becomes the training center as a person applies learned knowledge and applies those skills to change things.

How do you undo certain habits, traits, and attitudes? Your attitude has to change, and as difficult as that may seem, it is even harder to change habits and traits.

If a person gives up using sugar, and changes to an artificial sweetener, it will take some form of effort on their part to change the habit as it was originally learned. They learned the taste of sugar made food taste better. Some have no problem getting off sugar, some liked the original taste. A person may want to use the substitute sweetener, because they heard it is better for them. They learn to acquire a new taste. The body system will adjust to the person's taste. Some people change because they feel it will be better for them, you get the idea.

The undoing must start from wanting to change. In time the mind begins to accept the change. The change may be difficult for some, or it may seem impossible to others. Most people either suppress those feelings, or replace them with something else. Many of the habits and traits remain a part of their life as a useful function. Many others are not fully developed, but some remain alive and deep seated. They can come to the surface when there is an occasion that brings them back to the conscious mind. For things to change there needs to be personal energy put forth by the person as they try to identify with their bad habits and traits. It takes time and effort to recognize the need for change.

In trying to undo any habit, it is safe never to take on the challenge right away. Such an uprooting of old habits and traits will take a change of attitude. It may tilt the balance and create new problems such as nervous tension. The mind may send signals not to make the change or even think about the changes. A person may think there is no need for change.

It is safe to say that you must be aware of the changes in your-self. This goes back to the age and stage of the situation. Because people don't change over time the same is true when age and your stage in a situation come into play. One indication is when a person becomes cynical and overly critical without knowing it.

If a person really wants to give up a habit, they must have a change in their mental attitude and then it will take place. Their attitude must change first, but more than that, they have to undo the previous behaviors because they have become a part of the person and become a part of a person's nature. Many habits are generated from sentiments and emotions surrounding their behaviors. These are complex areas within the Life Cycle. It is equally true there are useful habits, while there are also non useful habits. Both are stored in the brain, and can create problems for a person. It is a challenge when a person deals with new changes.

Learn to watch out for bad habits. They are associated and are inner woven within the emotions of a person who may become rig- id or have a stubborn personality. It will be much harder for them to break away from a bad habit. The problem is to what degree is a person has become a slave to the habit like drugs, alcohol, and tobacco. A person can become dependent on them. This is valuable knowledge in knowing how to change things.

I believe people need to deal with their human nature and look at it from a Christian viewpoint, but with practical applications of good judgments. Everyone has to deal with "who they are." Built into a person's nature are limits, tolerances, and degrees of accept- able conduct. Of course social and Christian principles should help guide a person in prayer, Bible studies, and self-helps.

These are just some of the battles and factors a person deals with

Now let's go back to the influences that cause a person to over- react. Everyone loses control once in a while, but what if a person overreacts too often? A person should pay attention to why this is happening, because their safety devices and stress limits may be out of balance. Especially when and if the stress limits don't send an alarm for some reason, a person should have some reason for concern when they are overreacting. There may be other influences controlling them.

This is one area where I failed in my life. It wasn't hard for me to hide those bad feelings, and I didn't want people to know I was hurting, but when it came to the hurt, anger, hostility, bitterness, and disappointments, they showed up in my attitude toward life. This failure affected me and my relationships with others.

A person can be so miserable, even in the best of relationships. When a person is dealing with personal problems affecting them there is always room for improvement in that area. Also, pride and self-will plays a big part in relationships. Then, add insecurities and jealousies, and they can play a role in the relationship too. All of these things, and more, influence a person's relationships. This can bring about an improper balance and control. A person can be weakened, crushed, and even destroyed by these influences.

People seem to think if they can do things to change their mood or feelings that will be enough to solve their problems within the situation. It doesn't usually work that way.

For instance, some like to shop, while others might enjoy going on a trip. These are some of the ways a couple may deal with a problem or situation. They are much more likely to take their problems along with them regardless of what they do. This is a temporary fix. It goes back to the reflection in the mirror. It only takes the pressure off for a while, that is good, but if it is a real problem, it will go much deeper than a reflection. It hinders a person's ability to deal with the problem.

Some may say, "The devil made me do it. I could not help myself, and I really didn't want to do it." This is a weak argument for giving into bad influences that control their life. In some cases these influences have been out-of-control since their childhood. The same is true in abuse cases that go back as far as their childhood.

How to recognize the Issues in your Life

A person can create good or bad habits, but right now I want to look at the different issues in your life. Can you see them for what they are? Look for the good and the bad.

Now let's extend the boundaries within a person, and how their habits are affecting and controlling them. How is a person holding up under the stress factors, and what are they holding on to that they don't want to give up, and to what degree are these bad habits controlling and influencing their personal life?

Remember these habits have developed over a period of time, and sometimes a person doesn't realize how much real damage has been done over time. At that point they are in trouble, or are they? The main problem is when the habit is controlling them, and even worse is when a person doesn't want to change things or to get rid of the habit.

This is one of the steps in the healing process and dealing with problems, and the recovery time takes time to get victory and control over them. I want to help you in your personal recovery. Whatever way a person chooses, they need to look at their alternatives. We are looking at steps 8 thou 10 when we deal with the road to recovery.

There were times when I thought everything was fine; I had a tendency to procrastinate. This is a way of finding out how secondary influences relate to a person's inner feelings and are inner related to their habits, traits, and attitudes.

Dealing with the problems in the situation

I believe life is about the journey and trying to understand one's self is a part of the learning experience and the whys in relation to the challenges in any given situation. Certainly the degree of emotions and feelings have a lot to do with a person's actions and reactions in any given situation. It is much more important to solve personal problems because they do relate to the problems in the situation. Whatever else transpires during any given situation it is related to the cause and effect, of course all of this is very important in any given situation.

But, probably some of the most overlooked factors involved in the situations are certainly influenced by the outcome of any situation.

Here are some explanations as to some of the most baffling problems in a person's life. When their emotions overwhelm them in a brief span of time, or overtake them in the process of dealing with the situation. Understanding the interplay of the brain structures may in some cases give some insight into the passion and joy taking place in an emotional experience. A person's emotions reflect their feelings and can give rise or fall in a given situation. The big problem is when a person is engulfed by the situation.

There is much evidence that testifies to the fact that people who are emotionally inept, who don't know how to manage their own feelings, and who can't deal effectively with other people's feelings, are at a disadvantage in life.

Whether its romance, job, school, or a relationship, it matters if they are unable to have meaningful relationships with another person. People who are emotionally stable govern themselves, and are well organized in handling their emotional skills. They are successful in their personal life, and in their vocation. They are more likely to be content and happy, mastering the good habits, traits, and attitudes of the mind and body, plus being productive. People who cannot master bad habits, traits, and attitudes fail, to some degree, in everything they attempt. In these cases, they may not have control over their emotions of fear, anxiety, and are battling their ability to focus on life and their job, etc.

The extent of the damage is very important. I see this quite often in personal relationships and in bad family situations. This can bring about a lot of heartaches and pain. The next question, can the damage be repaired? Of course it can. But how much damage has been done is a very important question? How far should a person go in solving problems will be determined by how willing they are in solving their problems. Are you willing to go all the way through the healing process? If you are not willing to go through the healing process it may be better to leave things alone until such time when you are ready, and decide on what kind of help is needed.

How is a person going to stop the never ending merry-go-round? A person says, "I want off, and I want it to stop." There are people who have lived that way and they don't want to change their lives. They embrace the mess because they believe they deserve to be hurt. There are many ways to solve problems, but how a person builds on the resources from within and wants to repair and controls the damage is important?

How to control your habits, traits, and attitudes

I would like to explain how to control habits, traits, and attitudes and how they play a role in a person's life. There is a point when the occurrences of a particular habit and trait have a lot to do with the person's attitudes. A short temper is a result of aggressive behaviors, and/or dominating, controlling behavior patterns, when a person reacts violently, gets angry, or mad. This is very typical of the over view of a person's reaction, and revealing in their personality trait.

Built into life are the human habits and traits. Let's consider the genetics from a person's parents. We have discussed the family traits passed on generation after generation.

There is a saying, "One for all and all for one," and there are reasons for this philosophy. Of course built into each sex is an innate nature. The sexual side of a person's nature has its common desires and conflicts between the sexes.

Competitiveness is one of the purest genetic characteristic. I am going to explore the different sides of the competitive nature and spirit. I am talking about the kind of person who does not want to be out done. It does not necessarily mean pride here, and yet it enters into the picture.

In some cases people just want to be better than someone else, or stronger, prettier and mostly better than the other person or persons. I believe a person should strive to be a better person and improve. But there are some cases where there are no boundaries, and no shame, causing endless arguments over who is right or wrong, and sometimes it is not very kind in nature.

Both men and women have an inherited competitive nature, and they are very similar in nature.

But, on the other hand men and women have very different natures. No two people are alike, but how do men and women differ, and what makes them compatible? It is certainly a competitive world.

In men, competitiveness borders on childish games, and manly competition. Oh yes, don't forget men feel they are superior to women. They feel they are supposed to be the stronger sex, but that is not always true. Men do feel they are physically stronger. Men compete with men to prove their manliness. Sports are a good example of the competitiveness. Men and women are just as competitive and some women feel the same way about sports. For the most part men are easy-going until they get mad or upset, and then it's a different story.

In women competitiveness borders on vanity in some cases, a new home and family. That usually pushes the button for the women. Women feel superior to men in many ways, oh yes, believe it or not they are just as competitive, and in some cases more competitive than the men. It will show up in courtship and carries over into the marriage. When it does, in many cases, it causes problems. With women it is who's the prettiest. They take pride in their cooking, and some women like sports as much and more than some men. Women have an emotional nature, but can get upset just as easily, and some can be just as aggressive with a bad temper and bad language.

My second wife and I were on a bowling team. She got more pleasure out of beating me than the other team. I didn't like it; she was a better bowler than me. I thought it should have been a team thing in winning. I had played sports, mostly team sports, but there is an individual competitiveness in personal accomplishments. I could never quite understand that, but I do now, as I've gotten older and wiser.

It was personal to her, beating me was more important than winning, with me it was about winning. She did get a personal satisfaction out of beating me, more than beating the other team, although she did have her competitive nature, and she liked sports. In some ways she wanted to feel superior as a woman. In this case you would have thought the man would usually be a better bowler. So you can see it was very personal with her, and beating a man in a male situation made her feel very good.

What's wrong in these situations?
- Do women think they are better than men?
- Do men think they are better than women?
- Who's right or wrong?

The question will never be completely answered to either side's satisfaction as long as there are women and men. But, can two people come to a better understanding of each other?

Believe me there are times when a person needs a swift kick in the right place figuratively speaking. A person should be able to put down their petty jealousies and insecurities, and put them aside to some degree. When it became a personal conflict as in the case of the bowling competition, it created a problem.

What about a bad attitude

We kept adding other diminutions as to how a person deals with the areas that affect their attitude? That is why it is so hard to define who a person is. Their attitude will influence their emotions and love for people. I want to be specific in how a person deals with their attitude.

There is a very real problem because a person's attitude is going to affect their way of thinking regardless of what is going on in any given situation. People react in different ways because they are disappointed in some way. They say bad things about people, like "they don't care anymore," and their attitude can influence their will to live, get well, and even die.

These parts of the study deals with different kinds of influences that may help a person understand their attitude. How do interactions affect their attitude? How to handle this part of life is crucial because this will determine much of a person's happiness. How they interact to the outside pressures and influences will govern some of the principles we use to help people. My hope is that a person will be able to understand how to react to these outside influences.

Something had to change I had failed in the most important things like my marriages and that affected my attitude toward marriage.

This is one of the most important factors to understand. The important thing is to be able to make changes and not let them change you as a person. The important thing is dealing with these issues and how they are affecting you and to what degree.

These are some under lying problems that are just under the surface and they will not be visible. Those are the ones that cause real problems. The real problem is being able to determine what category they fall under. They come under the heading of secondary influences. There is a cause and effect and they need to be defined and dealt with. These problems need to be handled differently, because a person may have created some walls and barriers. They are real problems, and they are strong influences, indicates prejudices and blind-spots. They can also be warning signs of things to come. They may even become closed-doors in some cases. These skeletons will come back to haunt a person.

How to Deal with Walls and Barriers

Some people need to tear down some of the walls they have built. I think people build walls around themselves to protect their feelings. Much like the walls of a house, they also serve a purpose. I wasn't mature enough at one point to know how to deal with those barriers. This brought about some of the most dramatic changes, and in the process I unlocked a lot of closed doors. While some of this worked out as I dealt with each situation, in the process my feelings changed about some people. My rebellion caused me to build some unnecessary walls and barriers.

Barriers are useful in keeping out the bad, but they can also keep out good things that could happen. I used them to protect me. Unfortunately in some cases the same barriers might end up doing both. I realized the nature and presence of these barriers. I became more independent rather than using them as a protective mechanism to keep things out.

When I looked at those walls around me, I did not see the real me, I wanted to be a better person. If I am more comfortable and confident it is because I tore down some walls and allowed myself to go outside of those walls. Some people handle their transformation from one situation to another better than others. I could have handled things better without changing who I am. I felt like a "bull in a china shop." I liked feeling tough and not letting people in. It's hard to believe I enjoyed the protection of those walls.

At times I felt I was doing things inappropriately to keep people out. I failed to discern wisely, leaving the past behind me. I tried to overcome the walls that separated me from the realities in my life, and this brought about the changes needed to open those doors and break down those walls. That created a comfort zone and the happiness I had lost over the years. I don't want to embrace anything evil, but be able to wisely tell the difference. Some may understand what I'm saying, others won't. Some may resent me and some a little of both, and some simply just won't care. I can live with these facts of the past. More than anything I know the change must still come from within. It is the inward journey that will benefit me, and those around me.

Prejudices and Blind spots

Now let's get a clearer picture of what is happening in a situation, because prejudices influence a person's action and reactions, and the result is that they can't see things clearly. I am not speaking of racial prejudice all together, I have prejudice feelings about certain things, I personally like blue as a color, and I like certain car makers over others.

I try to look at my life with an open mind as much as possible, and not so much how others may see me, because I'm not going to live up to their expectations most of the time.

How a person sees themselves is important. Really, when a person gets down to it are they able to evaluate their strong points and their weaknesses? How can a person overcome prejudices without seeing themselves in light of others? Good question!

To get a clearer picture of what I'm talking about, it can be hard to do because there are so many underlying variables to deal with at the same time. Prejudices can influence the way a person sees things. I am influenced by my religious beliefs, and I am not prejudiced against other religious beliefs. Maybe in some ways I am, but it does not cause me any ill will toward them. So keeping that in mind I am not religiously prejudiced.

A person can have blind-spots and not realize what kind of person they are, or what has happened to them along the way. That is what happened to me, I was blinded by what had happened, and ignored what was happening because I believed I was right.

When a person is letting the past dominate, they may have lost their sense of direction, or accomplishments along the way, and where they are going? Each day should be a steppingstone! But what happens when life is a series of stumbling blocks? Without the right kind of help a person may be stumbling around in the dark. That is like "the blind leading the blind!" I know what it is like to stumble and fall. I had to look deep from within to find the answers in my life.

These blind-spots can happen with parents who don't see the things their children are doing wrong and don't correct them. They don't see correction as being good for the child. This is very prevalent in today's society. Children get on drugs and the parents are not aware of their blind-spot. I have taught in public schools in the past. When there was a teacher's conference some parents seemed to think their child was the only one in the class. They expected their child to be treated special because they were special to them and they are, but they had to get along with others. There were rules in the class room. They may not have seen their child's aggressive behavior as a problem, but it was a problem in a class of 20 other children. In this they were likely to have other blind-spots in their child's behavior.

What happens when a person doesn't see what is coming, they think everything is all right, or the past will catch-up with them. Sometimes it hits them from the blind side, and they are not prepared to handle the situation, then what? There is also "the law of sowing and reaping" and how to deal with the past in light of the present situation.

Sometimes a person thinks all it takes to solve problems is by ignoring them. I found that to be true in some areas in my life, not so much what I was doing. This is a major case in point when a person thinks there is no need to change. In that case nothing will happen or they think that nothing could go wrong. Now let's look at the reality of the situation if a person is looking at life with blinders on, or "rose colored glasses." Their prejudices could be taking over, or they can become too emotionally involved, that is the real test. It takes an honest view to be realistic. They are blinded by not knowing what is about to happen. For instance, a spouse says, "I want a divorce" or the other person may not have not been paying attention to how bad the circumstances had become in the relationship. Look at what happens when a person ignores the situations in a relationship, or the warning signs! They have not been paying attention to what has happened along the way. Of course the relationship has gotten off track over time, every relationship does, but they really don't see their blind-spots, or know just when or why it happened.

Closed doors

Now let's explore the situation where there are closed-doors and skeletons. Closed-doors could relate to the status of the mind- set. When something happens the emotions turn off and a person doesn't communicate in any way. A person has to listen, but if there is no response from the heart they are not able to understand what is happening. The person wants to be able to reveal themselves and let others communicate with them, it becomes more difficult when a person closes the door to the heart, and doesn't let anyone in. No one can cross those boundaries if the door is closed. If there is not enough information the mind can't discern how to deal with the situation. The real key is to be able to unlock those doors of the heart and mind.

When there are closed-doors it may be perceived by the subconscious will of a person, or they may not be able to comprehend because the mind has shut the door. The person has to decide whether to open or close the door. The subconscious presence in a situation can bring about unawareness in a situation. The reality of a closed door is not being able to identify with what is locked up. The emotion of a person can have a mind of its own. Let me explain, the emotions can overrule the mind. Someone can hold views quite independently of what they want to believe or what they think of themselves, and what they really believe to be true in their heart.

How the mind processes information or the lack of information is locked up in the knowledge relative to the situation. The mind observes and investigates the experience in itself, including the emotion. If the mind fails to explain or understand those feelings it may automatically close the door.

Worry, in a sense, is a warning of problems to come. In a positive sense warnings are not always pitfalls, the mind may be anticipating dangers before they arise and may close a door. When this happens and the mind does not work, anxiety overrides and threatens the situation, forcing the mind to be obsessed by the situation, and may ignore anything else at the time. When fear is triggered, any one or all of these can close the door.

A person, to a certain degree, has to discern the closed-doors, and be able to open the door for themselves, or get help. On the other hand, a person has to be sensitive to their emotions as the mind perceives the situation. In my studies I call it, "The cry for help" and it can be something special when a person does some- thing about it.

Skeletons

Skeletons are hidden secrets and in some cases it is better to let a sleeping dog lie.

However, sometimes a person just doesn't see the skeletons because they are hidden so deep and in some cases they are not dealt with, and they become dormant. At least they are not in proper balance from within.

Skeletons can be sins of omission and things a person doesn't want to talk about. They are remains of the past events in the family, or things a person wants to hide from themselves.

Character influences

My experiences help form my character! The choices I made in changing things were the backbone for changes in my character! What are inherited characteristics?

As I look around there are people just like everyone else we are unique because of our heredity. No two people are exactly alike, including identical twins, who have inherited some of the same characteristics, and have many of the same genetic traits. I have twin girls who are not identical. They are nothing alike in looks or in temperament. The one thing I see in both of them is the bond within each other, not like any other sibling. I don't feel it with my brother and two sisters. They are opposite in almost every way. I see features that make up their personality differences.

You are going to identify with some of your genetic and inherited traits, some from your mother and others from your father.

You will need to use some of this data as you trace your own family inherited traits. Those you are most likely to notice you look like your mother, or father, or even in your grandparent's. There will also be traits you do not associate with and wonder where they came from. Make a list.

There are so many things that individuals inherit, some of which can be diseases and health problems. The physical traits you inherit come from your family members, and can't be changed unless through plastic surgery. You have the nose that comes from your mother or father, or some close family member passed on from one side or the other. Before that, you may be able to discern who the inherited nose comes from. That is what I want you do, make your list of inherited personality traits. I use the Genogram to do that.

You have memories, for instance, of your family history, cultural information, and unique historical anecdotes and perspectives. It is a gift with a purpose. Give something from your heart, something that is priceless and impossible to duplicate. Create a new family heirloom, and pass it on may become a personal treasure that will last for generations to come?

It is important for you to know how to deal with inherited behaviors and emotions. Are you controlled by them unwillingly? These are questions you have to ask yourself. The family blueprint you inherited was passed on to you. So you can read it just as plainly as you read this information. You may need some help in under- standing why you do certain things.

Our study guide provides you with opportunities to develop in the areas you had previously neglected. Select new areas to improve. Perhaps you need to develop the art of forgiveness, understanding, compassion, determination, courage, or any number of those qualities. Not all of your feelings actually originated with you, many are learned from your family's background. It is those very thoughts and feelings which are the underlying influences I have been talking about, and some you don't want to talk about, because of the emotional entanglements of others.

The Genetic makeup of a person

The range of a person's emotional temperament is biological in nature, which adds to the different aspects in a person's personality. The background of a person's basic disposition is tempered by their feelings of right or wrong. Temperament can be best defined in the terms of mood that most typifies a person's emotional make-up. The big question is this, "Can the biological demeanor be changed? Of course change comes by dealing with the cognitive relearning process, and recovery methods can create temperament changes.

- Does that change the biology of a person? No!
- Does a person's chemistry change? No!
- Can a person's emotional-make-up change? Yes!
- Of course not, or in some cases, Yes & No!

Can a person change their personality? (Maybe/Yes), or more than likely No! Why not Yes? Only, if a person learns to manage their emotional-make-up, and puts learned lessons into practice.

According to some, there are three biological components which interconnect and retain the emotional-make-up. You can temper them, but you can't change the chemical biology in a person. There are also three particular types of intelligence, subjectively speaking. The sense of time and space, and the biological / mental mobility of a person as it relates to other less specific functions of the brain, which interacts with a person's personality.

This should lead you to believe that the brain is designed from the beginning to respond to specific emotional expressions such as empathy. That can happen when the biological make-up stays the same in a person's temperament, but there are personal changes in life that affect a person's temperament.

Despite many social constraints, a person may be moved by passion or fear; each or both may overwhelm a person at the same time. The fear of something or some person may have developed over time.

In terms of biological design, the basic neural brain circuitry in some cases works for the good, but if something bad has happened the brain will react on previous reactions. For better or worse a person's attitude and responses to their behaviors are based on rational judgments or emotions, but emotional judgments can create good or bad changes mentally and physically.

All emotions are, in a sense, impulses, actions or reactions. Emotions are also at the root of impulsive actions. The repertoire of each emotion plays a unique role when the inherited-biological signatures influences the reaction.

Research has found new ways to peer into the body's biological signatures, such as DNA. The brain plays a major role in the physiological details of how emotions prepare the body and mind for different kinds of responses. The best way is by cognitive behavior changes.

There is also another aspect to the body system that goes into action, which is equally as important, known as the Adrenal Glands, which create additional energy to the body system. That needs to be accounted for in dealing with personal problems.

This brings about emotions like happiness and/or depression. An increase in activity in the brain center can bring about positive or negative feelings and an increase or decrease in the available energy. In that case, it might result in quieting down the stress, or increased anxiety. This is likely going to bring about a physiological shift, or recovery caused by an emotional changing of the mind. The body and mind needs general rest for personal-well-being, to handle the tasks ahead with enthusiasm, and strives toward vitality and reaching goals. The biological makeup may have an influence on the psychological aspects of happiness, joy, love, surprise, and fear, sadness, hurt, anger, disgust, bitterness, guilt, and remorse. The emotional level can be inherited biologically and can be learned, which will bring about a controlled reaction.

Let's dig a little deeper into the physiological changes that can be measured by a person's response to the stress revealed, or hidden by the biological subtext of the mind and brain. When a person is dealing with difficulties or a level of emotional response is released, that is typically interrupted by the mind-set and is carried out by a person's emotional response.

Let's make it very clear that a person needs to pay attention to the potential dangers and influences affecting their life expectancy, and the quality of life. To be sure, a person needs to know more about why they behave the way they do. Be specific in the ways of dealing with a person's feelings. There may be a medical significance, even if the biological mechanisms do show up, or don't work.

Childhood Development

A person also needs to fully understand the process that un- folds according to an innate biological clock in each stage of development over the entire course of childhood, early adolescence, and dealing with a child's emotional make-up into adulthood. Every child is different and should be dealt with according to their temperament and personality, and disciplined to meet the correction needed according to the child's temperament. The timetable for emotional growth is intertwined in the development of their growth stage in relation to their learned cognitive development. On the one hand the brain's biological make-up and maturity is different with each child.

Now you can begin to see the significance of emotional growth. It is the hallmark of a person's biological signature and growth patterns.

During this time, there can be sweeping changes and patterns that are formed, and they interact throughout the emotional growth of a child's life. They are related to a unique set of cues to the mental maturity and the body growth process. For instance, the brain automatically sends out signals as the person or child tries to deal with a situation. Intense emotions may have been triggered by the situation before it ever came up.

While it may seem evident that the body growth process and the mind have to grow in harmony, it is not necessarily true that a person can or will develop their own patterns. Now let's see how a person's life has, or has not been affected by the psychological and physiological changes of the body, and mind. During this time unique patterns of behavior have taken precedent in the way the mind accepts things that happen.

What is genetics?

The genetics of a person are physical in nature. There is a mental make-up in the genetic formation of life, for instance in the hormonal make-up of the sex of a person. The social environment within which a person lives is called cognition, the perennial relationship and family relationships, and in relationships in general.

There is a more revealing argument that has to do with genetics that is in relation to IQ. Some believe that the IQ cannot be changed, because IQ is a fixed factor in genetics. A more likely aptitude to life is more revealing than IQ. When you look at a person, you will see how they are influenced by these aptitudes from their social, ethnic, and family environment.

The mental-make-up is tied to the genetic make-up and is just as important. Looking at the learning process, the ideal here gives a better chance for change as a child grows up. The question is what is related to the personal potential of a child or how much is genetic? The challenge of each generation has been passed on. Beyond this lies an even greater host of moral and social issues that have to do with their environment. A child raised in a backward environment may not do as well as a child who is raised in a socially healthy environment, but in some cases a child who comes up under a bad environment supersede their expectations.

So much for being able to alter genetic patterns. But what about those responses that are genetic in nature from birth. Can they be changed? That can be done by learned skills and cognitive behavior moderations:

- How, does a person go about changing the habitual reactions, and to what degree are they genetics?
- They are highly charged with extreme or moderate behavior, or low-keyed volatile reactions, such as shyness?
- There is a wide range of possibilities in the genetic constraints of behaviors.

Behavioral genetics are not only passed on by the genes alone, but by:
- determined behavior,
- their environment,
- their experiences,
- the learning process teaches a person how to grow, and shapes their temperament.
- their passion expresses their emotional capacities, and are very influential if given the right guidance
- the relearning process is vital in changing and improving temperament.

It is amazing how much can be accomplished as the human brain evolves. Of course, many of the opportunities fall under the genetic role in who a person is, but the genetic role and background can be overcome by hard work and perseverance. The will to do something bad enough, is the power of positive actions and thinking.

The age I lived in had a lot to do with the way I lived my life. What I did or why I did things were pretty clear cut. The social standards were set, and it was a much simpler time. A person is a product of their genetics of course, but also of their social environment and parental guidance has its influences.

My parents had a very limited social exposure, because of where they lived and their family unit. They lived in the same geographical area, and my social exposure was much broader than theirs. Today there is more social exposure because this country is militia cultured, but one thing still stays the same, the genetic-make-up has had to adjust some because of the social environment.

It is so important to understand the dynamics of your health and physical presence. The role of "The Life Cycle" is complex. Genetics is probably one of the strongest avenues in your health and life system. Also, it has its major influences in who you are and how you deal with your life and health, and who you become. In fact, it can affect your mental and physical-well-being. There are several sides to your personality, as you have seen in who you are. But, the way you deal with your life system is very important.

People are so busy and preoccupied by life that they forget to take care of certain areas in their life. Some people never think of their health when they are young because they have good health. But in my case I had health problems in my 40's. That is young for most people. It became a major concern, but as I have gotten older my health is much better.

Characteristics of Genetic Influences

A person has to deal with their ideals in a situation, and also in their mind-set. Say, for instance, love is supposed to make a person happy, that is the ideal. The ideal person is supposed to come along and make them happy for the rest of their life. That is an ideal situation of course. That is a storybook setting and ending, but it doesn't happen because people are not perfect. When a couple has children come into their life that adds to a couple's ideal of wanting children in their marriage. Realistically there is the sharing in a relationship, and I am using the term, "Who is the one that is going to wear the pants in the family?" Don't ask me who that should be, because I know it is different in each marriage. In some marriages it's the man, and some cases I see the women being the dominant person. To me marriage is "like a bed of roses." It can be beautiful, but you have to watch out for the thorns. The ideal should not be classified as perfect, but being realistic. The real truth in a situation or relationship is working together, and not pulling each other apart. I hope we can agree!

In theory, the ideal is a hypothetical hypothesis set in principle for being a good person.

The value you place on yourself

This can bring about joy and happiness. Another way to help a person is by describing their feelings about themselves and others, and another way to feel good is by doing volunteer work.

1. The Spartans trained their young boys/men to believe in physical strength as an ally in defending themselves and in war."

2. The Greeks believed in development of both body and mind. The arts, culture, sciences, and the intellectual.

3. Most societies/cultures follow the Athenians traditions similar to their culture.

Idealism

Here is another factor a person has to deal with: their idealism's of one's self and others. It is the ability to fight against self and self- will. Everyone has to deal with the ever present "who am I"? There is a problem when a person lets you down, and when you end up having to live with the situation and relationship, whether it's good or bad. Why not try to make things better?

The psychology behind idealism is not complete because of the nature of man. Their make-up is about the character of a person. Their past creates a mixture of behaviors, but to be more specific a person's nature does not necessarily fit the criteria of what some people think. Some believe God is the final authority in a situation, while others believe what a person wants is their right to choose in the situation, but never-the-less, a person is faced with choices. If a person could be right more than half the time and play the "Stock Market," they could become rich, while another person can become rich and never play the "Stock market." I hope you make the right choices.

There is a twofold approach to rational thinking: idealistically right always wins, and wrong always loses. But what about the third area, the gray area where people often have problems deciding how much is right and how far can they go before it becomes wrong? This is the functional side and makeup of a person's character, and how they deal with the different aspects to their being.

I think there are basic differences in how much a person relies on the psychology and physiology of patterns and routines. Some believe in medications, while others believe in natural foods and supplements for a solution to a health life. How do these beliefs relate to the physical problems within? Others may rely more on the psychological aspects of a problem as they go about trying to solve their problems, or the combination of both physiology and psychology. Ideally most people use both methods. The ideal is having a proper balance of the two.

That is why our study guide will make the difference in how a person tackles a problem. It is very important in knowing how to fix or mend the broken pieces in a person's life.

You need to have the ability to understand your feelings for others, and, at the same time, to see how your feelings affect others. Look at it from their perspective and respecting the fact that there are differences of opinion, and how they might feel and think about things. Relationships are a major focus including learning to be good listeners and asking good questions, distinguishing between what someone says or does, and what they meant. Look at your own reactions and judgments toward them, not being assertive at the same time, or pushy. Trying not to be angry, upset, or not being too passive at the same time; be caring and respectful of the other person's viewpoint without getting hurt or getting mad.

The art of learning and cooperating without having conflicts make resolutions that are negotiable, without compromising your- self ideals and values. Sounds good, but it is hard to do, do you agree?

What does embedded mean?

Embedded means, things that are deep inside. What happened to cause an embedded influence? How does a person change those influences or sometimes find it hard to change a person's mind? I have given you some of my background to help you understand what kind of studies you will need to enhance your life. It took a change in dedication to change those things in my life. I had to look at all of my experiences and expect them to bring me to where I am today. I found it took years to change things, because change does not happen overnight, especially when it took years for things to get embedded into my life.

Some would lead you to believe that there is an overnight

transformation in your life. No way! There are definite changes that start with little decisions one step at a time. It starts with a change in attitude. I found that it takes time and effort for the healing process, and it can be a wonderful experience. It is a daily process of growth with setbacks. There are even good times in bad situations. It's unrealistic to expect someone who has lost control to be calm and rational when they are up-set. So here are some techniques that will help:

- Think back to what caused you to lose control?
- What triggered the event?
- What signals did your mind and body give off that you were aware of before you lost control?

With these three questions, you should be able to come up with some good answers. You can engage in a mental exercise like counting to ten to help you prevent losing control in the future. Picture the same circumstance, and imagine in your mind if the same signals and you were about to lose control. Then, imagine yourself doing something else constructive. Imagine this happening over and over again until you have formed alternative behaviors that are firmly embedded in your mind. You will find that the next time you begin to feel rage or anger your mind will already be sending you the message. You have a choice to make, but some people don't. I say you don't have to lose control.

Next, begin examining these three questions. Start with con- trolling your behaviors. I will give you some suggestions. By doing this I will show you the psychological process of change. One person may be able to guide their own thoughts, feelings, and behaviors. When it becomes embedded, you have a powerful dynamic to change when it comes to explicated behaviors. Two is by not taking action to control your thoughts and feelings. These are powerful dynamics not inherently positive but negative. Can both be true? NO! The controlling of someone's behavior allows for a more enjoyable life. Also, embedded in modern thinking such as the cultural beliefs, a person can enhance their values, if they are based on opinions that are not arbitrary, but based on changing social standards and cultural backgrounds. A person has to change the bad embedded behaviors. You cannot change who you are any more than a Leopard can change its spots, but you can learn to control your behavior.

The courage of one's innermost character is embedded in the innermost part of the brain, and it is a vital part of a person's character. The inherent characteristics are the construction of a person's disposition, temperament, and can be a creative tool in controlling their inner feelings. The sum of such forces is within an individual, and is usually distinguished by the fundamentals of self-control and discipline, which are essential characteristics. The psychological, mental, and physical constitutes your drives, despairs, and wants. These functions are spontaneous, and are reflected by a person's attitude; also by the genetic makeup of a person. The inner sanity of a person is originated in the very nature of a person. Are the genetics controlled qualities of your environment? No! They are physical characteristics. Now focusing on personal feelings, and dealing with the inner being, a person should begin to realize relationships are complex, compelling, and often puzzling.

Mirroring is a term used by some therapists. They act out the way the patient acts to get them to see a reflection of them, and get them to look back at how they are acting and how they may have felt at the time. The important thing is understanding your mental-state at the time, such as a mother who does not comfort and empathize with her infant, or someone who is describing a bad accident.

These inner feelings are referenced by a person's expressions of personal remorse or lack of control. These are measured by the hid- den biological subtext of the brain, and the critical level of the reality in a given situation. These inner forces and thinking are what holds the key to holding on to relationships, or destroying them.

There are other inner forces from within a person that need to be taken into consideration. When there is a problem, why does a person go on, or can they stick it out? They need to understand what these inner forces are doing, and what is happening.

There are some inner forces and idealism's a person may have to fight, or can't deal with, such as uncontrolled wants, needs, and desires. The good or bad of these inner forces can drag a person down, and they need to take all these factors into consideration. My question is what to do about these inner forces? Next let's look at different types of identity and see which one fits your best.

How to tell a Type A from a Type B behavior?
Here are descriptions of Type A and Type B behavior:

TYPE A:
- Sharp, aggressive speech style
- Easily bored
- Eats, talks, and walks quickly
- Impatient with those who dawdle
- Does many things, for example, eats, shaves, and reads at the same time
- Selfish; interested only in things that relate to him or her
- Feels guilty when relaxing
- Not observant of details
- Aims for things worth having, not things worth while
- Feels challenged by other Type A's
- Assertive, tense; leans forward in chairs
- Believes success comes first
- Measures success mainly by numbers

TYPE B:
- Not characterized by Type A traits
- Seldom feels time is of an urgency, but can be as ambitious as a Type A person
- Easygoing, not hostile
- Plays a game for fun, not just to win
- Can relax without guilt; can get as much work done as a Type A
- Often more efficient and succeeds because of steadiness and economy of movement

If I'm one of those Types A personalities, what can I do to reduce stress?

Much of the Type A behavior causes undue stress, a Type A personality can be changed to healthier behaviors. A sense of urgency is one of the most common traits in a Type A personality and one of the most easily changed. Try the following techniques to help you relax and get your life under control:

- Decrease the pressure of always being in a rush by learning to organize your time. Allow more than enough time to get where you're going or to accomplish a particular goal, and enjoy the results with relaxed confidence.
- Learn to be assertive instead of having an aggressive behavior.
- Recognize when you are doing two things at once. Type A people think this is efficient, but it is usually less efficient and often causes accidents and errors. Concentrate on one action at a time and do it well.
- Get up earlier in the morning. Your body and your mind will appreciate having enough time to do everything calmly.
- Don't waste time and energy by getting angry at things or people you have no control over and cannot change such as being late or someone dawdling in front of you in line.
- Avoid confrontation with other Type A personalities. It can only serve to increase aggressiveness and competition. Spend more time with Type B people.

Type A persons should do things to slow themselves down and find things to let them relax. For example, listening to music for a half an hour, reading a book purely for pleasure, or taking a leisurely walk to get away from some of their responsibilities and challenges.

The elements of the body create high emotion, and this should constitute the individual's identity. The realization is embodied in the abstract of the individual's type A or B character and behavior.

Personal awareness is related to a person's identity as well, and how they see themselves. Their emotions have a mind of their own and they can be controlled, one which can hold views quite independently of their mind-set. If a person follows this logic, the person's identity need not necessarily be defined by their objectivity or purpose in life. It does matter how they perceive themselves, or how others see them. What may not be revealed in a situation is what they think of themselves, but what is more important how they perceive their identity.

If a person has lost their identity, how do they go about trying to find who they are? Identity is usually not independent from their problems, it is a part of their problems, but usually it has an indirect involvement in any situation.

There are many ways to deal with a person's identity problems, but the first thing is to choose which direction a person is going, and who they are. There is a depth from within and sometimes a person has to look deep to find their identity, look for something special from the inner person, and identify with it.

I can identify with someone that has written a song, a book, or a poem. I would like to think of myself along these same lines. There is a curiosity within a person, and the need to create from within. My hope is that some will identify with my feelings.

Each person can identify and should bond with other people. That is a great feeling, when a person knows their identity and is able to share it with others. To find a person's way is so important, and then to get on track can be exciting.

The identity crisis can be characterized by turmoil!

Every person has some form of an identity problem from the time they are born and from time to time. The problem is when it gets mixed up with who they are. If you are suffering from an identity problem, one way to know this is by not being able to focus on your life, and where you are going. It will show up in different forms and different stages of a person's life. A good example is a teenager trying so many different things to find their identity. The rebellion and defiance of authority is an aspect of finding their identity, and it drives the parents crazy. Just when they think they have found their identity, they get married and lose it again!

Another good example is a woman with her husband and children. It is perplexing, because they seem to lose their identity as a person. They are a wife, a mother, and, at different times, known as the children's mother. It all gets tangled up in who they really are.

I have spent some time dealing with moms going through these times in their life and how they can deal with these personal influences. This also relates to the pressures as a person, and how they identify with themselves. How they feel as a person is revealed in their identity. At the same time, how does a person meet their own personal needs, and are they able to share their life with someone else and still keep their identity? That is where a person really starts to get confused as to who they are.

Next, how do you deal with your spouse? It even gets harder to identify with your spouse. A person needs to be able to identify with what is expected of them, at the same time there are a lot of other things involved. How do you identify with your personal needs, wants, and desires? When your personal needs get pushed aside or put into the background, how you are meeting those needs when they are not met regardless of which sex? There are identity problems in many of these cases, but the real problem is how to identify with them.

At this point, a person may not know who they are, but where they are going. There is a real danger at this point, especially when another person is dominating and controlling. A person may feel isolated, especially when they don't know how to deal with it! They have lost their identity and it shows up in low self-esteem, and rises up when depression sets in. They feel inadequate, helpless, and un- sure within themselves. In most cases they feel the need to be hurt, and they become disillusioned in the situation. They can't move without the other person's approval. They are no longer able to deal with the other person's anger and disapproval, and even worse their violent out bursts. They feel trapped. Does this sound familiar?

"The cry for help."

This brings us to the next section about mental-awareness. These aspects were important in my cry for help. I had some health crises and there was also a mental crisis.

There are so many ways to help a person. It all boils down to what is the best way to handle the cry for help. The cry from inside will let a person know something is wrong, and if they look close, a person will know something needs to be done. The same is true of the mental aspects. It doesn't always allow for the awareness, but the mind is telling them something is wrong. They don't know why, they just know something is wrong. My goal is to help you find the information and the right kind of help:

1) The mind will cry out in confusion.
2) The soul will cry out in anguish.
3) The body will cry out in pain.

There are all kinds of stress or stresses; some are good for a person, but a person will have to be careful. Some kinds of stress can bring about disastrous reactions. Also, be aware of the stress levels in a situation or relationship. When the stress is too high it usually brings about a crisis.

A person has to stick it out until they get victory over the crisis as they deal with a situation. The recovery process will take time for a person to get victory over the crisis. Remember, at any time, when a person stops going forward in recovery, they are falling back into an old pattern. A person is defeating the purpose of changing a habit, trait, and attitude. A person can do things to change their life. Believe me; I could not have changed without having a way to deal with my personal problems, and with the help of God. Some of these axioms I have talked about will provide more questions than answers, but that is a starting point. It is up to you to do something about crisis within the situation. Also, nothing can happen until you move and do something for yourself. You hold the key that unlocks the doors, and there are three keys to unlock those prison doors in a person's life.

Sometimes going in the right direction didn't seem right because my life seemed so wrong for so long. There were times when I was wrong, and I knew it, but "I did things my way," as the song title, sung by Elvis Presley. Even when it seemed the worst, I believed the best was yet to come. In that case I was living in hope, when hope didn't seem possible. In my life I found that it was important to be true to myself. "Pride comes before a fall" is right, also "low self-esteem is a down fall." There were other factors that went into my decisions and choices. I have dealt with the primary and secondary influences. I do not consider myself a failure, but I do believe I have made some bad choices, and yet I have turned my life around.

The panic attack

Stress, demands, crisis, and other things can bring on a "panic attack." When that happens, the "stress levels" are going to go away up. A person can be out-of-control emotionally. It may be just the demands of having a bad day, or needing some loving care and understanding. It does not have to be a serious problem to be a crisis in a person's life and for them to call for help. The president has "The Hot Line." Support outreach Services has "The panic button." That is when a person may need to call us or talk to their partner.

When I looked at the reflections of myself in relation to the demands on me, and how my personal problems related to the situation, plus dealing with some bad relationships, I found that the real problem was relating to the causes within the demands. The effect was another thing in the situation itself. The real solution was inside of me and how I was going to deal with the stress and demands.

As I looked at the stress factors in the different crises, I saw how these factors influenced the crisis in my life. I did not have a proper balance and control of my life. How I dealt with a crisis, in some case it was not good, but it turned out for the best at the time.

A person needs to examine their motives and attitude. They need to look at the primary influences and secondary influences, because that tells them more about how they are doing, and if they are not dealing with the real problems. This will determine what a person needs to do to solve a problem. It will show up in how they are dealing with their problems leading up to a crisis.

Furthermore the need for change:

- What is a person going to change and for what purpose?
- If there is a need for changing a behavior how does a person go about it?
- If you go deeper and attempt to change in attitudes and belief's?
- If the answer is yes, who and how does a person insatiate change?
- Which changes need to be modified?

For most people, however, changes come in the form of the process and application of principles of behavior patterns. In most cases change may be like taking two steps forward and one step back. Most people are willing to change, but don't because they don't see the need for change, but not until they feel there is real need for change. A proven strategy is moving from a problem to setting goals, this is helpful when a person is seeking changes, but moving on in *where they have been to where they want to go and be.*

The rules of change

- *Be an advocate of change* –be able to motivate and move past fears
- *Be a teacher and plan for change* –have a plan and work the plan
- *Be proactive in change* –encourage, support, and challenge the change
- *Be equal to the change* –appraise and discern the changes that need to be made
- *Be committed to change* –call upon others and use the Holy Spirit to empower the changes needed.

The Road Map to Change

Most people have a tendency to seek external changes first, but it is usually more import to start with internal changes with one' self.

DISCOVERING THE REAL YOU?

Chapter 7

Step 7
TURNING YOUR LIFE AROUND

T he honesty of a person is a quality in which tells a lot about their character and it points out their integrity and their success. How does a person develop these principles, values and standards? While a person may want to get the victory, in the process they may have difficulty trying to overcome a problem. They must establish certain principles, values, and standards set forth in their life by what they have been taught and learned from their experiences.

This is an important step in a person's well-being as a person relates to how they make decisions and may not entirely be based on their conscious and subconscious mind, but a person must base their life on sound principles, values, and standards. In respect to their social acceptance, cultural-background, and family values. This section is probably the most controversial in nature, because there are so many different beliefs, and values.

Let's take into consideration what I believe as a person. This may help you to understand your conduct, ethics and values which are reflected in your daily life. A person should co-exist within religious and social boundaries. The fundamental principles laid down are very important guidelines and should not conflict with a person's Christian principles and beliefs.

What a person has been taught will greatly influence their beliefs as a person. A person's parent's probably has more to do with their standards than any other influence. A person is socially influenced by their nationality and the country they live in. It can even be divided geographically in some regions of the country or state. A person's race, color and ethnic background may have a lot more do with their personal and Christian values, their church preference, or religious preference too.

The principles are some of the vital links from within. I want to encourage you to go through these profiles. It will be worth your time and effort to look them over. If not now, do it as soon as possible, to keep the continuity of thought and purpose. I know these studies are very lengthy and it will take some time.

To refine and set new principles and guidelines are very important, but a person needs to understand the basis for setting up new principles and guidelines. These two must be firmly set in a person's life. Adapting to good principles and getting rid of bad adaptive principles, this can be done according to the amount of time and effort, and willingness to adapt refine or set new principles. How does a person deal within those guidelines?

I'm a firm believer in asking questions, and finding the best tools to work with in any given situation. The tools a person has to deal with are governed by principles, their values; these guidelines have helped me to see things more clearly. The Bible sets forth principles, and deals with a person in light of whether it is a sin, but I am dealing with social behavioral issues, relating to principles.

Knowing how to use these principles does not guarantee success, but they still can lead to a better understanding of what a person should or should not do. What is meant by that kind of statement? Good question, here is a case in point about a principle.

Profile Part I

There is usually some kind of principles involved in any decision-making. For the most-part a decision is conditioned by the mind-set in-so-much that a person doesn't take time to choose how much is principle or how much is the mind-set. The third part is reasoning and emotion. There is usually some logic involved and intuition involved, to some degree, in every decision. The application is putting the principle into action, but more-than-likely the decision is determined by the mind-set, and the decision is put into action without thinking.

I think you may be getting the idea that most decisions are based on personal whims. They are built on a foundation, but what if they are negative responses? Most are reactionary in nature, when a child asks to do something, most of the time the reply is no, because they have not thought about it. When a person gets the facts, they can make a good decision. Only then, can you know for sure the outcome of a decision.

Example Part 2

A person goes through a situation or crisis. They know with- in themselves whether they can do whatever they are called on to do. Their reasoning, knowledge, background, ego/etc. will influence their decision. They will say to themselves that they can handle the situation, because in principle, they know they have made the same kind of decisions before, but what about blind spots? It is much harder if they have made bad decisions. It only works when they start to put these principles into practice.

It may sound easy at first, but what if their best friend says it's a bad decision. When a person has prejudices and unresolved problems it does not come as easy, and when there is no clear path to take, a person may become uncertain about the decision they are going to make. Now it is important to reflect on principles that work, but what if it is wrong then a person needs to think it through before making the decision. If the principles you use are wrong can you make the right decisions right or wrong you have to believe you made the right decision for your own peace of mind.

I would like to explain how these skills work, when applied and used in the right way, then show you how important motivation and determination is in the interaction with these methods. Some of these personal principles I use every day as a basis for my direction and decisions:

- I believe in starting every morning as a new day.
- I clear my mind and reflect on the positive aspects of a situation.
- I try to accept the new challenges while dealing with the old challenges.
- I reinforce those values and standards that have helped me.
- I am not going to give up on what I believe in or compromise my belief in myself.
- Now I am ready to take on the day.

But, there are different stages in any process. A person's age will have a direct bearing on the circumstances, for instance, when a person is younger they might make a different decision, and yes, what has just happened might be a bigger influence later in life.

The challenge of each generation has a lot to do with a decision, and there are social and economic changes. There are generation-gaps between teens and adults. Parent's deal with challenges different that their kids. Teenage years are the best time to set the right kind of principals to guide your life. I feel that there is a perpetual challenge from generation to generation. Each generation wants to have more than the previous generation. This is nothing new from the beginning of time; every generation has had to face different challenges.

Without principles to guide a person, the values and standards change. Each generation brings out a new set of values and standards. Each generation sets their own morals standards in relation to the present social and religious values and standards that go along with the social changes.

Applying these methods, a person should respect an individual's goals, and how they deal with their life. I would like to give a little bit of a profile on how a person can approach these principles:

- I believe in a healthy mind free of past mistakes!
- A good wholesome healthy attitude!
- And maintenance of the body!

Sound principles are where our studies begin and end. Our studies place a value on the person.

Everyone needs to have patience, compassion, encouragement, love and understanding in their life. They need to use these same principles, because the wear and tear on a person's life can get to be too much at times. Can a person restore the damages, and can a person change things that govern their principles?

When I put these principles into practice and set guidelines, then I understood why I needed the right kind of help and guidance.

That has given me a positive direction when I make any decision. First of all it has to fit into my common sense guidelines. That gives me sound judgment on which to base my decision. This helps me to understand the emotional pull from within. Sound Principles are the foundation of wisdom. You can let your emotions guide you if they are based on sound principles.

Let's see how a person meets their needs, wants, and desires they can deceive their perception of what is going on, or why things don't balance. There are several kinds of check-ups and I will discuss them in step 8 in the study guide. But for now my purpose is to set some "Common-sense-Guidelines" to go by, and help you.

Common-Sense-Guidelines
- Don't go overboard. Use good judgment, don't OVER REACT
- Don't get in a hurry, WAIT. Take your time and THEN SOME!
- Don't give up too soon. Look for the RIGHT ANSWERS
- Don't ever say I won't. Be willing to accept the RIGHT ANSWER.
- Don't get discouraged. In well doing, accept the CIRCUM-STANCE.
- Don't forget to acknowledge. Personal responsibility, in the SITUATION.
- Don't forget the wisdom. In understanding both sides of the SITUATION.
- Don't forget the wisdom. In discernment of the RIGHT & WRONG.
- Don't forget the wisdom. In knowing, when to STOP, LOOK, and LISTEN.

"WAIT" can become one of the longest words in the dictionary! When a person breaks these cardinal rules, the keys don't fit, something is wrong. Don't break down the door to get in. These keys unlock the doors to the heart and mind.

Those are some good principles to go by. Another thing is hard work and sound principles. If a person doesn't have good basic principles to go by, life doesn't work. If a person does not base those basic principles on sound values a person will not make good decisions. A person is not going to be successful, and solve their problems.

Values and Morals

A person has to deal with and establish values to build their character. Parents are the first to help establish a set of values. The schools, society and the church also help in setting personal values. Next, is how to apply those values to the situations? That is going to give a person the insight to make their decisions.

How important is it to establish good values and morals? What happens when those values and morals are compromised? When a person changes their morals and value system, in all likely hood they have compromised themselves. Of course there are other things that forge a person's character. Sometimes the circumstances forge a person's character or a simple twist of fate changes a person's life. There are disasters to deal with, and that creates a fallout from the things that happen.

The outside influences, such as good relationships, help form a person's character. It used to be a hand shake meant something, a bond of paying back a debt. What a person says and does is so very important in a situation. All of these things mold a person, but probably the most significant is their values set forth in their life.

Where is a person going in their life? The next question, what is going to be the next step? Are they really the architect or artist that forms their life? Of course, but the circumstances are simply the materials a person has to work with.

Say one day a person looks at their life as I did, and sees nothing has changed over the past few years. People have a tendency to make the same mistakes over and over again. The basis of how I had established the principles in my life, during a low time a person is likely to base their decisions on negative feelings. If a person doesn't have those basic principles and good values they are not going to be successful in solving their problems either.

Of course there are always exceptions and personal abilities in each aspect of a person's life. Some may be adept at handling their anxieties, while others feel sorry for themselves. Others are relatively inept at getting along with someone else who has upset them. The underlying biases gives the level of ability which is no doubt an asset, or it becomes a problem for them who fail.

A lapse may come from their emotional feelings or poor judgment. This can be redeemed, to a great extent, by developing good responses to the mind-set, and developing good principles work with the right the kind of effort.

That has given me a different outlook on how I see myself in God's eyes, and how God must look at me. First of all, things happen. How I use my common sense guidelines and that gives me a bases for sound judgment. Not that emotional pull within me that says I'm a bad person.

Sound principles and values are the beginning of wisdom, and that is a big part in doing the right thing. Then a person can let their emotions kick in and trust them to bring happiness and joy.

I found that sound principles and values helped me to understand my behavior. If it didn't fit into those guidelines, I know it's probably wrong for me.

The teen years are when those principles, values, morals, and standards get tested, and it so important because each decision affects your destiny. This is when their relationship with parents is so important because of the values that were taught by their parents. This is the time for them to have fun, but some forget or ignore the morals taught them by their parents, family, church, and school teachers.

In reality, the childhood years are the best time for parents to set the right kind of principles, values, and standards. Parents can be good or bad examples. Another thing about being a teen; did you make the right kind of decisions? This is when the devil's influences can do the worst damage, because every mistake will be there for the rest of your life. The brain never forgets anything.

Each generation has basically faced some of the same challenges, but each generation has faced a new set of values that their parent's didn't have to face. I haven't gone through anything that my parents haven't faced. Each person has not faced anything or gone through anything that their kids will not face. Your influences may not be the same, but the challenges they face are going to be just as challenging. I have been open and up front, and I have looked at the good and bad points in a person's life.

I think my parents did a pretty good job of raising us kids and setting a good example of values. Like most kids I did not agree with everything they said and did, but my values are based mostly on how I was raised. They taught me to be honest and respect the other person, and have respect for myself at the same time, and that I could do anything if I put my mind to it, and they were right.

My parents did what they thought was right and I respect that I blame my problems on me.

How a person learns to deal with these treasures of the mind may very well be determined by their outlook and quality of life.

How to base self-concept on Standards and Conduct

Self-concept is also one way to base your values and in many ways it reflects on who you are and what is happening in your life. A child may have been teased a lot and they may become timid, or become aggressive in their behavior. They may develop an inferiority-complex, very determined, or they become extremely aggressive in nature. They may have been hurt as a child because of one type of teasing. If it became personal they probably felt abused, or they felt tormented by an adult. It may affect their life and attitude. And, on the other hand another child may have taken it in the spirit of fun or play.

I believe personal ethics should involve values and guidelines. The right kind of ethics begins with the way a person deals with success, while there are some that believe values have nothing to do with ethics, some believe it is measured by how much money they make or their successes in life. Being happy with one's self is the key to happiness. I can be happy or sad and still have peace in my life.

As a young boy I was taught to work. My dad was an engineer on the rail road, mom and mom and brother ran the dairy farm, plus we had Angus beef cattle for most of my young life. I got up at 4:30 in the morning and we went to bed around 9 at night. During this time dad started to build houses. This was just after WWII, and the economy was very good. We were considered upper middle class. Many of the people we knew became millionaires. Dad bought some property in Springfield, Missouri that made one of these people their first million. For several years he was very prosperous. He would often say, "I don't want a million dollars I want to live like a millionaire." He got back into the registered Angus business after getting out of the building business. He built a show place and setup Clear Creek Angus Farm and a dairy business. After that they spent six months in Florida and the other six months in Ash Grove, Missouri. There is a sad ending to this story. He became bitter, because the people he knew became richer, and he was disappointed that he did not measure up to their successes and his expectations. In his last years of his life he got into raising Fox Trotting horses and became a charter member. He trained horses and showed them for years, but that was not enough to satisfy his past accomplishments.

You may ask, "Why bring up his business experiences?" He was not able to handle his feelings of failure as a business man. His dad and brother built roads back in the 1920s. He was spoiled as a young boy. He was just fine as long as long as he was successful. He was kind and felt good about himself. He was not able to handle his failures and like a lot of people who take their frustrations out on someone else, he became abusive to mom. When things went bad I did not respect him for that.

That brings me to some of my personal experiences. I grew up with the ideal of a successful father. My goal was to be more successful than my father. When I was in high school I had one of the best cars in town. I had everything a young boy and teen would want. I played football, basketball, and baseball. As an adult I played fast pitch softball. I played until I was 35, and my last game was slow pitch softball at 65. I was successful in three businesses and at everything I did, but not at having a good marriage. That was a problem for me. I could not handle the failed marriages. The first failure wasn't so bad. Nothing really changed. I was still in a youth ministry, but the fourth divorce devastated my life and everything seemed to fall apart. I have all kinds of fears about an- other relationship. I have been able to turn my life around that is what our life enhancement studies are about. I go into to a lot more details in my family biography "Facing the real me and my real cry for help." The simple facts are that everybody has different kinds of problems and failures.

The society we live in has standards and rules of acceptance. There are laws to live by, and even religion sets standards and rules to live by. People need standards, rules and laws. The world would be in chaos without laws to govern people and society.

Society has always set standards, the family usually sets the values, and religious beliefs reinforce these sets of values according to standards.

My self-image has changed, and I have learned to control my life, whether anyone else agrees with me. All three factors are very important when I evaluate my life. I have to deal with the real me. I have to live with my decisions and actions. Plus, what is best for me may not be what is best for someone else. I have tried so hard to fit into society's standards and I think at one point I wanted to please everybody. I was so concerned about what everybody else thought of me. It created a monster I could never live up to and I was disappointed because of those standards others had set for me, and even in the ones I had set for myself. My life was changed because of all of these experiences and feelings.

A person needs to set tough standards. I believe there are so many people in the world who would like to lower the standards. Also, I approve of the need for rules and laws set by society:

- Standards of Conduct.
- Parenting and Family ties.
- Society and, or Ethnic background.
- Religious preference.

I am talking about the rules of the heart and conscience, the inside of a man or woman. This is the heart and soul of a person, the standards they live with every day, and what makes them who they are. May I say one more thing? Some don't believe we need all of these rules, laws, and standards set forth. The problem is how do we apply them? When a person sets standards in their own life, they should live by them. Some believe standards are for others. The battle begins when you are fighting so hard to live up to those standards set by family and society. Then there are problems on the job, finances to worry about, and a person may have a tendency to compromise their standards to get ahead or get a job.

Another thing is when people are so busy they don't see the real problems like setting good standards in their marriage and life. How do you set real standards? A person needs to stop and look at their goals in the marriage, and life. This may solve some of their personal problems by living up to those standards, rather than lowering them.

When I found success did not make me any happier, I still wanted to be successful. There is a difference!

It is a pity how society defines success, but for the most part standards and rules are helpful in how a person lives the problem comes from the unwritten laws in their heart. A person needs to grow and set the right kind of standards and rules.

Society has so many laws, because there are so many different views in the world. Also, may I say these standards and the rules of laws are not lived up to? The rich seem to be able to buy their way out of trouble.

It is important to understand what I mean when I say some people believe it is okay to compromise, and break the law.

Now I am going to talk about the rules of the heart and conscience. What a person believes is important because that is the heart and soul of a person, and they are governed by what they believe.

The rules of the heart should be governed by good moral standards set forth by society and religious beliefs. The Biblical principles are to help guide and comfort. I believe it is a good way of knowing if it is of God. If that is the case, how does a person know what God wants or expects, and what are the true guidelines for them? It is probably your moral guidelines more than anything else that guides your life. Let me say, I know God in a personal way, but these studies are in line with psychology. I have several books that are "faith based" self-help studies, and books on how my faith works. It takes in a lot, so I feel to do it justice to my beliefs, I do it in other studies. If you want any of my books you may contact me and I will get them to you.

What kind of personal values do you have? Log on to our website: www.sosselfhelpbooks.info

Proper balance and control

Let's say that all emotions are good when they are in a proper balance. Let's see if proper balance has to do with the emotional level in a person's life. Now I have introduced a new equation that you may not be familiar with, but I want you to equate it with the emotional level and balance. What does it mean when there is an over emotional response, or an under reaction to a particular situation?

It is also difficult to understand what is happening when a person feels down or depressed. There are likely some excessive feelings. This can be particularly true in young adults and teenagers' lives, but children face their own set of problems too. How can a person keep a proper balance when something is bothering them?

It can be like a person who walks a tightrope. They have to keep their balance and focus to keep from falling. I have seen tight- rope acts, and they usually have a safety net to catch them. But this is not always true in life. When a person falls they don't always go back up there and do it over again, and that is why our studies work. We want a person to get up and try again.

I believe a person's life can be hard. Others can be too easy on themselves, and that is not the way to balance things. I think of balance as a starting point, or at least it was in my life. The first thing is to get the human spirit under control, and deal with the behaviors that have taken over your life. Next, is by getting a proper balance in your life.

I don't think my life was ever completely out-of-control, and yet I was not in-control either. That contributed to my demise in some of my own problems. So you see you are not the only one dealing with a bad situation or problem, but in your case there is help on the way. There is a saying. "Control the things you can, leave the things alone that you can't control, and have the wisdom to know the difference."

I am thankful for the personal tragedy of a disability, and a near death situation that changed my life.

How about you?

Is there a power guiding your life and destiny? This is an interesting thought. I believe people have power within their own being. There are some interesting thoughts along this line and there is probably a lot more to the power of mind over matter. If you want to explore them, there is some truth in that statement, and I really realize there is a need for God.

How are you doing with your problems? I believe if a person places their life in the hands of God, the journey can be changed by faith. If a person is totally bent on destruction, nothing is going to alter that course unless there is a change of heart and mind in some way. There are certain eventualities to be sure, but when a person is self- destructing they need help.

Certainly a person's genetics relates to the body and mind-set, and their environment will influence the nature of a person. Such as "apple trees grow apples." When a person makes their own choices it will set the course for their life. But what about those choices a person doesn't make? Can they influence a person's life? The choices they don't make are just as important because they can hurt just as bad. But, how does proper balance fit into the picture? You have to learn to live with what happens. My dad once said, "You made your bed and you will have sleep in it" and you have to live with what happens. But what if you don't? The important thing is how you deal with the circumstances. What if my life had gone in a different direction?

Does a person really have control over what happens? Did fate play a hand or not? Was it destiny? Can anything be changed? I truly believe things can be changed with the right determination and the will of a man or woman to do things.

I would not have chosen this course in my life, nor do I believe I was destined to go through these health problems and divorces. I have always chosen a more physical way of life, and that may have helped in causing my health problems.

One thing I have learned, don't say, "I won't do something." That was the very thing I had to go through. I ended up doing things I said I would not do, like getting a divorce. Facing up to those situations was a great challenge. I hope that nothing like that ever happens to another person.

I know some people will look at my life and say what in the world are you doing writing about what happened. I have a perception of God like a lot of people. I am like the prodigal son, and the woman at the well. I know what it is like to live a wild life, and come back to God. Oh what a difference in my life after I found Him the second time. I was never a bad person, nor did I fall into great or grievous sins as you might think I just rebelled against what I believed and blamed God.

How did I find the proper balance in my life after all that happened?

Identifying with your Success and failure

Success or failure, life goes on. The important thing is what leads to the success and what caused the failures. The turning point is when a failure turns into success.

I know what you may be thinking, how can a person turn a failure into a success. How does a person achieve success and overcome failure? Can a person prevent things from happening? Maybe, or maybe not, in some cases after a person gets a victory over a problem there is a time of relief. A person is likely to feel invincible when that happens, but studies show that a person is likely to fail as many times as they succeed. When confidence takes control and a person looks at their problems or situations, old patterns can come back and take control.

The real truth I didn't understand why things were happening, but I didn't know how to control my expectations. It took time for me to control my confidence. I believed I could do anything I put my mind too. How does a person control those kinds of feelings?

This is one of the methods I used in the healing process. I had to be able to understand how to deal with my personal problems in a situation, but how did I get victory and control over my problems? One way was by taking control of them through the first 10 steps of cognitive behaviors identification, and then dealing with them was my problem not someone else's.

One of the questions a person must ask themselves is why me? I think I must have asked that question a hundred times. This is one of the ways God gets a person's attention. At least God got my attention.

If a person can find out the reason or why something happens, that makes it easier to live with and deal with it. When I look back on my problems, I understand why they happened, because now I can help someone else. Now I have a better idea of how to help others deal with their problems. Even if something turns out bad there is something to be learned from it. There is some good if a person looks for it as I did.

Thomas Edison, in his search for the perfect filament for the incandescent light bulb, tried anything he could think of, including whiskers from a friend's beard. In all, he tried about 1800 things. After about 1000 attempts, someone asked him if he was frustrated at his lack of success. He said, "I've gained a lot of knowledge, I know a thousand things that won't work."

Fear of failure is one of the major obstacles to creativity and problem solving. The cure is to change fear and turn failures in to success. A person should start with changing their attitude about failure. Failures should be expected and challenged. They are simply learning tools that help a person focus on the way toward success. Not only is there nothing wrong with failing, but failing is a sign of action, a struggle, an attempt to do something. A person who never fails is a person who does nothing. It is much better to fail than do nothing. The "Go-with-the-flow" type may never fail because they don't challenge themselves. There are essentials for success, and un- less you take advantage of those opportunities, your needs or desire to succeed, you will not enjoy the feeling of accomplishment that comes after overcoming a long struggle.

Suppose you let fear of failure guide your risk taking and your attempts to succeed. What if you try only three things in a year, and at the end of the year the score is three successful tries? Now, suppose the next year you don't worry about failing, so you try a hundred things. You fail at 70 of them. At the end of the year the score is thirty successes, and seventy failures. Which would you rather have, three successes, or thirty successes? Remember, you have to deal with seventy failures as I did. Another way to look at it is to imagine what seventy failures have taught you. If you take them as lessons learned you have never really failed. If you feel defeated, then the risk was not worth the thirty successes. A proverb: "Mistakes aren't fun, but they sure are educational." What if Thomas Edison had taken to heart his failures and stopped after a thousand attempts?

You might ask, "What is the difference between success and failure?" The difference is what it means to you.

My life had some failures. I wanted to be successful. The one thing I wanted was a successful marriage. That was the driving force in each attempt at marriage. I always felt this was going to be the right one. Sometimes the more you fail the harder you try the next time.

There is the status quo, or being moderately successful I couldn't handle being moderately successful. That is another way of making an excuse for mediocrity. I look at success as not believing I'm a failure. I overcame my own disbelief, but success is usually based on the monetary things, how big of a house or how many houses, a new car, boat, or how much money and investments, and so on. Any of these so called successes have merit, and are common denominators to judge success. This is the American dream for some. But, what if you are not successful? Is that not another aspect of failing? Of course it isn't!

Most people usually think of people who are on skid row, the alcoholic, drug addiction, those that cannot conquer their addictions or bad habits, the poor and desolate as failures.

Most people deal with success according to the way they feel about success. To some degree, success is being socially accepted, and when it is all said and done, most people believe the amount of successes should outweigh the bad things. Most people think of their life in that way, regardless of social classification. That can be a good sign, because a person is looking at who they are or what they are doing, but some people are not honest with who they are. When a person fails at something they tend to minimize their failures and build up their successes in their own mind. Some successful business people have been broke or bankrupt at least one time or more than once, and they were able to overcome their failures. J C Penny went broke and yet his business is still going today.

It does not mean everything a person does has to be counted as a success, but over the long haul a person needs to feel good about themselves. Having some success is a part of that feeling.

I believe success or failure is a variable not necessarily in the eye of the beholder. Another type of failure is when a person harms or hurts someone.

I went to church as a young person, and to the age of forty, church was a big part of my life, and that wasn't wrong. Then, I went in the opposite direction for a while. I was always looking for something, not knowing what it was. Maybe I was running away from whatever it was in my life. I'm not completely sure. I do think of myself as a rebel at heart in some ways, out of one cause into another, that pretty well describes me. I do have a cause now. All of these things that happened had an influence on me, and that is what I am trying to share with you.

One thing, I have learned everyone goes through their own kind of pain and suffering in some way. No one is exempt from having problems. To put life in a nutshell, life is not perfect. That was hard for me to accept, because I am a perfectionist at heart. My dreams did not come true, and I had to learn to live with who I was. I still deal with those feelings on a daily bases.

When did my life change? I am the same old me. I have tried to create changes in my life to help me live with who I am. I'm not so hard on myself any more. I call this leveling the playing field.

Rich, middle-class, or poor, every one faces life one day at a time. I put on my clothes and take on the day. I know some people have more to deal with than others. One of mine is dealing with a de- generating arthritis in my fingers and toes. Some of my days are filled with discomfort and some days are filled with pain, and yet my life is just like everybody else. How well I do each day depends a lot on my attitude, commitment and determination.

When I found that success was not the key to happiness, I found that more success only made me want more success. I can be happy or sad depending on my state-of-mind, and being able to have peace from within.

"Why do most people fail?" They get so tired of facing the same old problems, and they feel like they are losing the battle a person may say, "What is the use," I am going to live with my situation, and that can be a part of the solution, but there is more to it than that.

I found that a good idea is to build on a good foundation. It doesn't make any difference what a person is doing or going through! I knew I could not keep making the same mistakes in dealing with my health. If a person doesn't believe they are making mistakes, there is something wrong with their way of thinking! With that attitude nothing is going to change?

At one point I realized I needed help! But, I was not ready for God. Still I knew that I was a Christian. You may feel the same way. It is okay to feel like that, but you need to deal with who you are. Some things are going to make you feel like a failure. I had to deal with myself first, and what was happening to me. Then the other things will come if a person is willing to work on what they can accomplish.

This can be a time of trying different things in your life. That can take some time and effort, but don't give up too soon. You have to decide what you think of yourself and the direction your life is going and deal with it. These principles can work in your life regardless of the choices you have made, but they have to be applied in the right way.

If you are actually hiding things you will develop a bad attitude. When that happens people won't be able to disguise between the good and bad. The problem here is that they are just covering up their problems and feelings, but they are still there, and they will be there tomorrow. How can a person find a better way to deal with their problems?

I am applying what I learned and how I was able to separate the primary and secondary problems. Next, I started to learn how to cope with my problems. Certainly there are some other factors. It starts with whether a person is concerned or if they don't care. There are different things that went wrong, and how those influences controlled my personal thinking. You may be happy with your life as it is, and you may say you don't want any changes in your life. There are many reasons for concern with that kind of thinking, and that may be one of the reasons you fail. I tried a lot of different counseling methods and most of them had some elements that helped me.

It usually takes a crisis to shake up a person or something major to get their attention.

I finally understood why I needed the right kind of help and guidance in my life. I have learned how to take control of my inner feelings and deal with the outside influences. I think all of us are like children, a bit childish at times, and we don't look for the treasures in life.

I have been dealing with how success and failure affected me. I discussed the idealism of this world and in a person's life, next I want to discuss how life creates stress in a person's life.

The real problem is how a person lives and handles their failure. If it is according to societies standards, they are going down the wrong path. They may not have failed or want to admit it. What do I mean? For instance, when successes overrule the failures may not apply to someone who is in a bad marriage relationship. A person may say what do you mean? Personal successes don't always relate to a job or business, but a failed marriage brings down the meaning of successes when it costs someone a marriage in the process.

I have not accomplished a lot. Does that mean I'm a failure? I think it is true in a lot of cases, but it is important to realize, when parents or society says a person has failed, have they really failed?

A person is responsible for what happens, and how they are influenced by others. This is not like an insurance policy a person buys, that says, "No fault." Life is not without its faults!

Down-hill-spiral

My life was going down-hill! These things we have just studied fit into a down-hill-spiral. I keep building on the previous studies. For me, there were at least three other contributing factors. One, personally I created for myself, two others were created, or someone else had created some of the situations. The third were those that I couldn't control, when my spouse wanted a divorce, an illness, and many other kinds of things fell under that category, including an act of God.

The wisdom and the enlistment of life may have come from the perils and pit falls that I had faced along the way. How do you know if it is a down-hill-spiral? In my case I went through divorces and remarriages? This brought about some pretty extreme situations when settling these divorces and the experiences put a lot of stress in my life at the time. There will always be those specials times and places that came out of those bad times, especially the kids, people, family members that have meant so much to me, and made life better for knowing them.

What is a down-hill-spiral? It is a downward set of events. When you look at my life it may not seem so bad to you. It is usually much easier to look and laugh at my calamities, and that is okay by me. That is why I am writing about myself. I want to show you the basic differences between who I am today, and how I dealt with the different influences. The problem was how the divorces had created a down-hill-spiral. When bad things follow it is a good definition of a down-hill-spiral you keep falling into the same trap, but good also brings about good things, is that a true statement?

Let's see if that remains true, I have discussed some of my personal problems in regard to failure, but some were brought on by someone else and led to a bad relationship. It is not all one sided in a divorce, job, or many other numerous problems in a situation. The list can go on and on, but I kept on trying, and that is why I relate it in terms of a down-hill-spiral, and how the down-ward-spiral was changed in my life.

It is going to be difficult to balance things when there is a down-hill-spiral. Another good example is my health, it has left me with some disabilities and crippled fingers to deal with, but it could be much worse. I could have had a heart attack. It also left its mark in my body, which is a reminder every day. It got to where I walked with a limp at one point. This happened by overdoing physical work. But my arthritis and heart problems were not the real problem. I was the real problem. Because my lifestyle had gone into a down-ward-spiral, all these things were contributing factors.

My well to be successful would over load my body's physical capabilities. I had a problem in expecting too much of myself and how I got over these obstacles and problems was an asset. The crippling of my fingers was symbolic of a crippled life. It was in a down-hill-spiral, and it turns out that I had to deal with my personal life style in the same way. That brought on the high blood pressure, erratic heartbeat, and a degenerating arthritis from 1981 to 1997.

In 1997 there were personal pitfalls which were contributing factors to my heart problems. If you add up all of the setbacks in my health during those years, how was I ever going to get ahead of the degenerating heart and arthritis problems? All of these problems and obstacles were not just about the physical body, but also of the mind-set. Some of the circumstances were more than I could handle at different times, but the worst heart problems came because of the divorce in 1992 that took almost a year and a half to settle $25,000 in lawyer fees. She left me for another man, and she wanted the business too.

Something had changed my life, because running a business and the pressure of a divorce had almost wrecked my health and personal well-being. I thought at the time I was going to be a cripple for the rest of my life. I have overcome my heart problems, but I am physically crippled to a certain degree. I am sure of one thing I have turned my erratic heartbeat around and do not have to take any medications any more. My ambition almost cost me my health. At the time I wanted the sporting good business more than anything. I also went back to a cardiovascular workout that I had created years before during my first heart problems.

During this time I had gotten control of what was happening by going to support groups and recovery classes for about two years. I wanted to do something about the physical circumstances as well. I got into a good healthy diet and exercise program that helped my arthritis, and the exercise workout solved my heart problems. Most of my health problems can be traced to the genetics in my family, and in that case it made it much harder to deal with because it was in the genes. I studied up on the case history and learned a lot about my arthritis during those two years.

There was a bigger question in the back of my mind, and that was, "Will I ever be able to complete a life changing curriculum that will change lives? In spite of that question, I had a vision and insight as to how these studies would be formed, plus I now had a purpose in life. If this works I'm on track in my life, and I can help others.

The thing that amazed me was that I knew what needed to be done to get my health back. The real problem was not the disability it was sticking with the workout program. Stick with the program, whatever that may be in your life.

Contrary to what some might believe there is reverse order. Let me illustrate. The body actually tells the brain what needs to be done and then the brain goes into action. In the meantime the message goes though the different alarm systems set up in the brain, like fear, or wanting to overcome. I understood the fear part, because I thought I was going to die at one time in my life. Over the years my health has brought about a stronger force in my body. The arthritis is still there, and it is slowly progressing, and I cannot do a lot about it. But, I am learning to live with it. All of the other personal influences have gotten better because of a change in my mind-set.

Because there are so many different influences that you can control, you may not think of your life as a down-hill-spiral in the way I did. A person is more likely to think in terms of their problems, and when that happens problems don't get resolved. There are alternatives.

I thought I had tried everything, but I did not realize I was dealing with a down-hill-spiral. That is when I began to take responsibly for getting control again. The point is, when a person gets to the bottom they either look up or stay down.

Flashbacks

Another way to identify problems within the person is called a flashback something that happened years ago, things can lay dormant, all it needs is a flash back to remind them of something that had happened yesterday or years ago, it brings back the unpleasant memories.

The return to an earlier event which recalls a vivid memory without thinking is called a flashback the brain is able to make a narrative without you thinking, it fills in the information chronological or an emotional experience that relates to the present situation.

These flashbacks are handled differently when it relates to a fantasy, daydream, to recall, or rethink.

Such voluntary replays of a trauma, they may go in different directions, or inflame the present situation, the need to deal with flashbacks, and it should be in proportion to the memories that add to the outcome or thought known as flashbacks.

When a situation overwhelms a person with needless repetitions or by replaying of a trauma over and over again that is another kind of flashback.

And if it becomes a grim or a monotonous flashback, something needs to be done about it.

Even sounds in the night need not compel a flashback.

Some people are haunted by nightmares also they are apparent flashbacks.

In 1988 there was a terrible time in my life when I thought I was going die. It was kind of like a flashback. In my case it was a flash forward. I felt God telling me to write down what He was going to show me. To my delight that is happening.

I wanted to be successful in dealing with my life more than having personal possessions, and again, to do this a person needs to look at the total picture in their life. This may be where a person is going to see the real need for Support outreach Services and it may make a difference! A person may feel the need for Support, and guidance. The key is in helping one another. I am not trying to sell a person on some kind of products, or some fancy programs. Support outreach Services offers "HELP," not "GIMMICKS."

I think up to this point you should know all I want to do is help you know more about yourself. I want people to help others in return and get their life back on track, and find the best way for them to live a happy fulfilled life. This is what I've done in my life, and it has really helped me.

There are three methods I have used in trying to help people. One is by sharing my personal experiences, Life Enhancement studies, and Support outreach programs. I feel that it is very important for a person to be able to see what is going on in their life. I want a person to keep going on with our SOS Life Enhancement.

Our Motto: is to Inspire – Encourage – Strengthen = Success

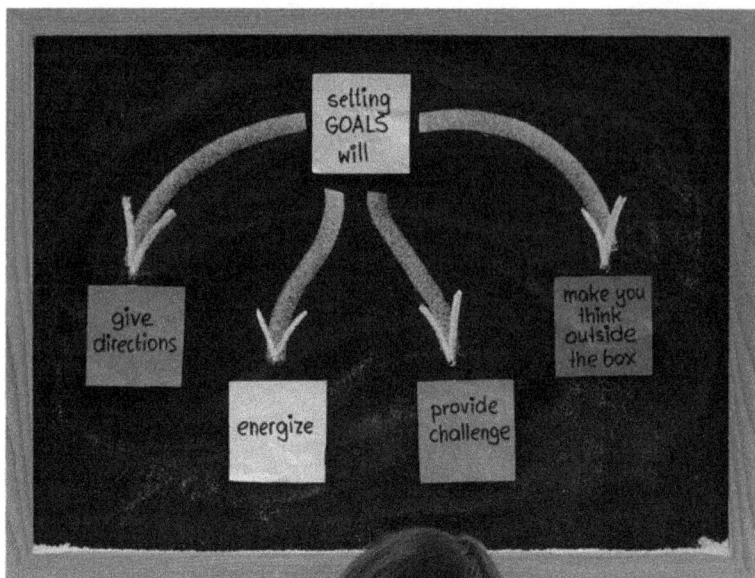

Chapter 8

Step 8
FINDING SOLUTIONS and SETTING GOALS

I think you are ready to find some solutions to your problems? Please consider all aspects of these 10 steps in our studies, but now let's see how important it is to set and reach goals. I challenge you first to try and find a solution to your problems. We have looked at how a person relates to the situation, rather than asking how to fix the situation. My goal up to this point is to get you to understand what is happening.

Door 3: opens to finding new solutions

Now I want to help you solve your problems and I want you to do something. Realize you don't have all the answers, but you must come up with some plan of your own! I want you to start by trying to fit some of the pieces of the puzzle together, and that is going to be exciting. A person needs to look at both sides of the coin if they are going to be honest with themselves.

When a person makes a decision or a promise in their own heart and mind, they may do one of two things. They may think all it takes to solve a problem is wait and see if it will go away; maybe they won't have to deal with the situation either.

There is a honeymoon stage in a solution it may last a few days or a few weeks, and then a person may find themselves right back where they started and that is OK. The decision part of any change maybe the hardest step a person takes. Here is a clue when it doesn't get easier to deal with, it may become more important to deal with the under lying problems first, that will provide some avenues to solve your problems. When it is an up-hill battle, and sometimes when a person begins to see the light at the end of the tunnel, they think everything is going to be all right, but there are some who never to see the end of their battle. WHY?

The most important factor is wanting a solution, the next is dealing with personal problems on a daily basis, don't ignore them.

It is important how it affects a person, and maybe that is the most important factor,

How a person sees themselves dealing with the solution in relation to their problems. Sometimes a person can't control what happens, or why it happened, and sometimes a person is his or her own worst enemy.

That has given me a different perspective on how I see the solution, and how I looked at the problems in my life. There are several important factors to consider are you giving into your problems, are you overlooking the possible ways there are in solving the situation. It may show up in a person's attitude toward problem solving. This can be a very important step, because it comes down to how you face each day. Are you positive about finding a solution to your problems?

I found myself getting better day by day and I hope a person will take on the daily task of getting better, as they go through this session. The thing I wanted was to help enhance the quality of my life, and in my case it was not a complete over haul job.

This part of the study guide will help make the journey easier, and add a dimension of joy and happiness to your life. I have been there, and that is the reason I can help you. I hope some of the things I have talked about up to now really sound good to you.

Now I want to bring you back to these three axioms that played a big part in helping me, they are still relevant in problem solving, the 3 D's Dedication, Determination, and Discipline in how a person sets out to tackle their problems.

I believe this is a simple case of mind over matter. Why do I say it takes time and effort? Review these qualities as a person works on problem solving, wanting a change, but be constant, start with realistic goals. There are different phases and stages that a person will go through in solving problems. It will be better to start with the low goal that can be reached, take it slow that indicates dedication. Then maintain your determination, the hardest part is discipline, and then changes will happen. Those three will increase a person's will power.

Now there are three sound principles to go by:
1. Creative thinking
2. Positive thinking
3. Problem solving

DISCOVERING THE REAL YOU?

Failure at this point is not an option when a person looks at their passions they must see some happiness in where they are going, because the total picture is very important in a person's well-being, being happy with a person's life is one of those key elements in life. The key ingredients are dedication, determination and discipline.

It is ironic when people have developed a high degree of success to do that a person should use some form of dedication to achieve their goals.

The way to overcome is by dedication to the task, each time I got a victory there was a set-back because I did something to cause the break-down, sometimes the second set-back was even worse, than the last. The task was facing the same problems over and over again. I found the situation wasn't any easier because I had not dealt with the on-set of the problem. Remember at any time a person stops "they are more likely to fall back into that old pattern," and they usually feel defeated. I found that I can do the impossible if I am dedicated and put my mind to it.

Determination is like setting goals and wanting to reach your goals. The main thing is to be constant and set realistic goals. It would be better to start with a very low goal, and build from there. Don't over do it at first! Set goals that are reachable, and a person is more likely to reach their goals. Getting started off on the right foot is very important a good indication is when a person starts to feel good mentally and physically.

I think I was going in the wrong direction to accomplish the goals for a while. After 10 years I had to set new goals and refine some old goals. It is not only setting goals, but the determination to reach those goals.

I set goals of six months to a year as a start, now it has been years of work and preparation for my writing. Over the years I have had to remind myself of the goals I had set, but I also had to redefine my goals from time to time. I knew in the back of my mind what needed to be done, but I would not have guessed it would have taken years; don't get discouraged "go for your goal." I have never been sorry that I started my writing, and would not have been able to accomplish what I have done over the years without a determination to finish my writing and put it in books. It will get done.

I certainly don't think of my life as a handicapped person any more, I think of my health as a challenge. The harder things got the more it formed my character. I thought that failure was not reaching some of my goals.

Did I set the goals too high, and was I realistic in my evaluation of my life and health. The thing that kept me going was the determination to meet the challenges, and win the battles in my life. Then it takes determination and perseverance to see anything through, but what if a person is reaching their goals, remember one thing about determination you never give up, a person can be determined, but what if they are going in the wrong direction they make excuses for what is happening, or feel it is someone else's fault.

The main thing about discipline is learning how to struggle and overcome the barriers and problems. When a person or child learns how to overcome their fears, make good decisions, plan and work hard toward achieving uncertain goals. They have learned a great lesson in how to take good care of themselves. How to be successful in reaching your goals despite the negative influences that come your way? A person has learned how to take control of those influences, and now I want to teach you discipline skills.

However, if a person wants to reach more difficult goals such as achieving success, by using discipline skills, they have to control the inner direction instead of being so dependent on others, and then a person needs to develop more discipline and motivation.

To that degree you must have the ability to be "creative in your thinking" and planning is a part of discipline, to the point of training the mind for reaching a goal. The ability to define a person's limitations and the capacity to use their innate physical and mental abilities to the degree of motivation plays in discipline. Being enthusiastic to an optimal degree is controlling your anxiety. In this sense discipline has to be mastered in an aptitude that affects a person's abilities. Discipline is a factor in reaching your goals.

But, anxiety can bring about apathy or too little motivation and discipline, a person will not have enough motivation and discipline to finish the task, while too much anxiety will over rule any attempt to do well.

To some degree a person can enhance their ability by "thinking positive thoughts" and planning to reach goals they must be pursued. The ability to define a person's limits of capacity to use their innate physical and mental abilities also is determined by how well they accomplish small goals. The degree that motivation and enthusiasm helps a person use their optimal thinking in pursuit of a goal and no matter how bad a person wants to accomplish the goals they set.

Discipline is another aspect of the person's life that has to be worked on. This is probably the most difficult of the attributes and axioms I have been dealing with, discipline. Some people are more disciplined in one area than another and some seem to have no discipline at all. They usually think of themselves as a free spirit in manner of speaking.

Finding ways to solve problems

Most people think of themselves as being able to get out of a jam, and finding ways to solve their problems, while others do not have the energy, ability, or means to solve problems. The thing a person has to do is find ways to deal with their problems, and that will help them in finding a solution in a situation. If the problems are too great a person will not be able to find a solution, and their ability to solve problems is a part of discipline. That is what I want you to see next.

Creative Thinking?

Virtual Salt Copyright - Robert Harris Version Date: July 1, 1998

"There seems to be connections between the heart of man and the eye, but also there is a connection between the heart of man and the way men and women think. The actual processing of in- formation comes through several different avenues of the mind and mind-set/heart.

However, there is another kind of thinking, one that focuses on exploring ideas, generating possibilities, looking for many right answers rather than just one. Both of these kinds of thinking are vital to a successful working life, yet the latter one tends to be ignored as a person gets older, not always wiser. A person might differentiate between these two kinds of thinking:

In sum, as Vergil once said, 'They can who think they can.'

Having the proper positive attitude about generating new and useful ideas, and solving problems is really a large part of the whole process.

Much of the thinking done in formal education emphasizes the skills of analysis--teaching how to understand claims, follow or create a logical argument, figure out the answer, eliminate the incorrect paths and focus on the correct one.

Critical Thinking	Creative Thinking
Analytic	Generative
Convergent	Divergent
Vertical	Lateral
Probability	Possibility
Judgment	Suspended judgment
Focused	Diffuse
Objective	Subjective
Answer	An answer
Left brain	right brain
Verbal	Visual
Linear	Associative
Reasoning	Richness, novelty
Yes but	Yes and

In an activity like problem solving, both kinds of thinking are creative and critical and important. First, we must analyze the problem; then we must generate possible solutions; next we must choose and implement the best solution; and finally, we must evaluate the effectiveness of the solution. As you can see, this process reveals an alternation between the two kinds of thinking, creative and critical. In practice, both kinds of thinking operate together much of the time and are not really independent of each other.

What is Creative Problem Solving?
  1. **It is an Ability**

A simple definition is that creativity is the ability to imagine or invent something new. As we will see below, creativity is not the ability to create out of nothing (only God can do that), but the ability to generate new ideas by combining, changing, or reapplying existing ideas. Some creative ideas are astonishing and brilliant, while others are just simple, good, practical ideas that no one seems to have thought of yet.

Believe it or not, everyone has substantial creative ability. Just look at how creative children are. In adults, creativity has too often been suppressed through education, but it is still there and can be reawakened. Often all that's needed to be creative is to make a commitment to creativity and to take the time for it.

2. It is An Attitude

Creativity is also an attitude: the ability to accept change and newness, a willingness to play with ideas and possibilities, a flexibility of outlook, the habit of enjoying the good, while looking for ways to improve it. We are socialized into accepting only a small number of permitted or normal things, like chocolate-covered strawberries, for example. The creative person realizes that there are other possibilities, like peanut butter and banana sandwiches, or chocolate-covered prunes.

3. It is A Process

Creative people work hard and continually improve ideas and solutions, by making gradual alterations and refinements to their works. Contrary to the mythology surrounding creativity, very, few works of creative excellence are produced with a single stroke of brilliance or in a frenzy of rapid activity. Much closer to the real truth are the stories of companies who had to take the invention away from the inventor in order to market it because the inventor would have kept on tweaking it and fiddling with it, always trying to make it a little better.

The creative person knows that there is always room for improvement.

Creative Methods

Several methods have been identified for producing creative results. Here are the five classic ones:

1. Evolution

This is the method of incremental improvement. New ideas stem from other ideas, new solutions from previous ones, the new ones slightly improved over the old ones. Many of the very sophisticated things we enjoy today developed through a long period of constant incrimination. Making something a little better, a little better gradually makes something a lot better--even entirely different from the original.

For example, look at the history of the automobile or any product of technological progress. With each new model, improvements are made. Each new model builds upon the collective creativity of previous models, so that over time, improvements in economy, comfort, and durability take place. Here the creativity lies in the refinement, the step-by-step improvement, rather than in something completely new.

Another example would be the improvement of the common wood screw by what are now commonly called drywall screws. They have sharper threads which are angled more steeply for faster penetration and better holding. The shanks are now threaded all the way up on lengths up to two inches. The screws are so much better that they can often be driven in without pilot holes, using a power drill.

The evolutionary method of creativity also reminds us of that critical principle: Every problem that has been solved can be solved again in a better way. Creative thinkers do not subscribe to the idea that once a problem has been solved, it can be forgotten, or to the notion that 'if it isn't broke, don't fix it.' A creative thinker's philosophy is that 'there is no such thing as an insignificant improvement.'

2. Synthesis

With this method, two or more existing ideas are combined into a third, new idea. Combining the ideas of a magazine and an audio tape gives the idea of a magazine you can listen to, one useful for blind people or freeway commuters.

For example, someone noticed that a lot of people on dates went first to dinner and then to the theater. Why not combine these two events into one? Thus, the dinner theater, where people go first to eat and then to see a play or other entertainment.

3. Resolution

Sometimes the best new idea is a completely different one, an marked change from the previous ones. While an evolutionary improvement philosophy might cause a professor to ask, 'How can I make my lectures better and better?' a revolutionary idea might be, 'Why not stop lecturing and have the students teach each other, working as teams or presenting reports?'

For example, the evolutionary technology in fighting termites eating away at houses has been to develop safer and faster pesticides and gasses to kill them. A somewhat revolutionary change has been to abandon gasses altogether in favor of liquid nitrogen, which freezes them to death or microwaves, which bake them. A truly revolutionary creative idea would be to ask, 'How can we prevent them from eating houses in the first place?' A new termite bait that is placed in the ground in a perimeter around a house provides one answer to this question.

4. Reapplication

Look at something old in a new way. Go beyond labels. Remove prejudices, expectations and assumptions and discover how something can be reapplied. One creative person might go to the junkyard and see art in an old model T transmission. He paints it up and puts it in his living room. Another creative person might see in the same transmission the necessary gears for a multi-speed hot walker for his horse. He hooks it to some poles and a motor and puts it in his corral. The key is to see beyond the previous or stated applications for some idea, solution, or thing and to see what other application is possible.

For example, a paperclip can be used as a tiny screwdriver if filed down; paint can be used as a kind of glue to prevent screws from loosening in machinery; dishwashing detergents can be used to remove the DNA from bacteria in a lab; general purpose spray cleaners can be used to kill ants.

5. Changing Direction

Many creative breakthroughs occur when attention is shifted from one angle of a problem to another. This is sometimes called creative insight.

A classic example is that of the highway department trying to keep kids from skateboarding in a concrete-lined drainage ditch. The highway department put up a fence to keep the kids out; the kids went around it. The department then put up a longer fence; the kids cut a hole in it. The department then put up a stronger fence; it, too, was cut. The department then put a threatening sign on the fence; it was ignored. Finally, someone decided to change direction, and asked, 'What really is the problem here? It's not that the kids keep getting through the barrier, but that they want to skateboard in the ditch. So how can we keep them from skate- boarding in the ditch?' The solution was to remove their desire by pouring some concrete in the bottom of the ditch to remove the smooth curve. The sharp angle created by the concrete made skateboarding impossible and the activity stopped. No more skate- boarding problems, no more fence problems.

This example reveals a critical truth in problem solving: the goal is to solve the problem, not to implement a particular solution. When one solution path is not working, shift to another. There is no commitment to a particular path, only to a particular goal. Path fixation can sometimes be a problem for those who do not understand this; they become over-committed to a path that does not work and only frustration results.

Negative Attitudes That Block Creative or Critical Thinking and Problem Solving

1. Oh no, a problem!

The reaction to a problem is often bigger than the problem itself. Many people avoid or deny problems until it's too late, largely because these people have never learned the appropriate emotional, psychological, and practical responses. A problem is an opportunity. The happiest people welcome and even seek out problems, meeting them as challenges and opportunities to improve things:

(1) seeing the difference between what you have and what you want or

(2) an opportunity for a positive act. Seeking problems aggressively will build confidence, increase happiness, and give you a better sense of control over your life (creative thinking)

(3) recognizing or believing that there is something better than the current situation by using positive thinking.

2. It can't be done.

This attitude is, in effect, surrendering before the battle begins. By assuming that something cannot be done or a problem cannot be solved, a person gives the problem a power or strength it didn't have before. And giving up before starting is of course self-fulfilling. But, look at the history of solutions and the accompanying skeptics: man will never fly, diseases will never be conquered, and rockets will never leave the atmosphere. Again, the appropriate attitude is summed up by the statement, 'The difficult we do immediately; the impossible takes a little longer.'

3. I can't do it. Or there's nothing I can do.

Some people think, well maybe the problem can be solved by some expert, but not by me because I'm not:

(1) smart enough,

(2) an engineer, or

(3) a blank (whether educated, expert, etc.)

Again, let's look at the history of problem solving. Who were the Wright brothers that they could invent an airplane? Aviation engineers? No, they were bicycle mechanics. The ball point pen was invented by a printer's proofreader, Ladislao Biro, not a mechanical engineer. Major advances in submarine design were made by English clergyman G. W. Garrett and by Irish schoolmaster John P. Holland. The cotton gin was invented by that well known attorney and tutor, Eli Whitney. The fire extinguisher was invented by a captain of militia, George Manby.

In fact, a major point made by recent writers about corporate excellence is that innovations in industry almost always come from individuals, not research groups, outside of the area of the invention. General Motors invented Freon, the refrigeration chemical, and tetra ethyl lead, the gasoline additive. Kodachrome was invented by two musicians. The continuous steel casting process was invented by a watchmaker fooling around with brass casting. Soap making chemists turned down the problem of inventing synthetic detergents: those detergents were invented by dye making chemists.

In a nutshell, a good mind with a positive attitude and some good problem solving skills will go far in solving any problem. Interest in and commitment to the problem are the keys. Motivation--a willingness to expend the effort--is more important than laboratory apparatus. And remember that you can always do some- thing. Even if you cannot totally eradicate the problem from the face of the earth, you can always do something to make the situation better.

4. But I'm not creative.

Everyone is creative to some extent. Most people are capable of very high levels of creativity; just look at young children when they play and imagine. The problem is that this creativity has been sup- pressed by education. All you need to do is let it come back to the surface. You will soon discover that you are surprisingly creative.

5. That's childish.

In our effort to appear always mature and sophisticated, we often ridicule the creative, playful attitudes that marked our younger years. But if you solve a problem that saves your marriage or gets you promoted or keeps your friend from suicide, do you care whether other people describe your route to the solution as 'childish?' Besides, isn't play a lot of fun? Remember that sometimes people laugh when something is actually funny, but often they laugh when they lack the imagination to understand the situation.

6. What will people think?

There is strong social pressure to conform and to be ordinary and not creative.

So, what will people think? Well, they're already talking about you, saying that your nose is too big or your shoes are funny or you date weird people. So, since others are going to talk about you in unflattering ways anyway, you might as well relax and let your creativity and individualism flow.

Almost every famous contributor to the betterment of civilization was ridiculed and sometimes even jailed. Think about Galileo. And look what happened to Jesus. Quotation: 'Progress is made only by those who are strong enough to endure being laughed at.' Solutions are often new ideas, and new ideas, are usually greeted with laughter, contempt, or both. That's just a fact of life, so make up your mind not to let it bother you. Ridicule should be viewed as a badge of real innovative thinking.

Myths about Creative Thinking – Critical Thinking and Problem Solving

1.   Every problem has only one solution.

The goal of problem solving is to solve the problem, and most problems can be solved in any number of ways. If you discover a solution that works, it is a good solution. There may be other solutions thought of by other people, but that doesn't make your solution wrong. What is THE solution to putting words on paper? Fountain pen, ball point, pencil, marker, typewriter, printer, Xerox machine, printing press?

2. The best answer/solution/method has already been found.

On a more everyday level, many solutions now seen as best or at least entrenched were put in place hastily and without much thought--such as the use of drivers' licenses for ID cards or social security numbers for taxpayer ID numbers. Other solutions are entrenched simply for historical reasons: they've always been done that way. Why do shoe laces still exist, when technology has produced several other better ways to attach shoes to the feet (like Velcro, elastic, snap buttons, and so on)?

3. Creative answers are complex.

Only a few problems require complex technological solutions. Most problems you'll meet with require only a thoughtful solution requiring personal action and perhaps a few simple tools. Even many problems that seem to require a technological solution can be addressed in other ways.

For example, what is the solution to the large percentage of packages ruined by the Post Office? Look at the Post Office pack- age handling method. Packages are tossed into bins when you send them. For the solution, look at United Parcel. When you send a package, it is put on a shelf. The change from bin to shelf is not a complex or technological solution; it's just a good idea, using commonly available materials.

As another example, when hot dogs were first invented, they were served to customers with gloves to hold them. Unfortunately, the customers kept walking off with the gloves. The solution was not at all complex: serve the hot dog on a roll so that the customer's fingers were still insulated from the heat. The roll could be eaten along with the dog. No more worries about disappearing gloves. This is a good example of changing direction. Instead of asking, "How can I keep the gloves from being taken?" the hot dog server stopped thinking about gloves altogether.

Mental Blocks to Creative Thinking and Problem Solving
1. Prejudice.

The older we get, the more preconceived ideas we have about things. These preconceptions often prevent us from seeing beyond what we already know or believe to be possible.

How to connect sections of airplanes with more ease and strength than using rivets. A modern solution is to use glue—glue the sections together. We probably wouldn't think of this solution because of our prejudice about the word and idea of glue. But there are many kinds of glue, and the kind used to stick plane parts together makes a bond stronger than the metal of the parts them- selves.

How can we make lighter weight bullet proof windows? Thicker glass is too heavy. Answer: Use plastic. Again, we are prejudiced against plastic. But some plastics are not flimsy at all and are used in place of steel and in bullet proof windows.

Another problem: Make a ship's hull that won't rust or rot like steel or wood. Solution: Use concrete. Our prejudice is that concrete is too heavy. Why not make lightweight concrete? That's what's done.

2.   Functional fixation.

Sometimes we begin to see an object only in terms of its name rather in terms of what it can do. Thus, we see a mop only as a de- vice for cleaning a floor, and do not think that it might be useful for clearing cobwebs from the ceiling, washing the car, doing aerobic exercise, propping a door open or closed, and so on.

There is also a functional fixation of businesses. In the late nineteenth and early twentieth century the railroads saw themselves as railroads. When automobiles and later airplanes began to come in, the railroads didn't change with advancements. 'That's not our business,' they said. But if they had seen themselves as in the people transportation business rather than in the railroad business, they could have capitalized on a great opportunity.

Similarly, when the telephone began its rise, some of the telegraph companies said, 'That's not our business; we're telegraph companies.' But if they had said, 'Hey, we're in the communication business, and here's a new way to communicate,' they would have grown rather than died. Compare Western Union to AT&T.

And have you heard of those big calculator companies Dietzgen or Pickett? No? Well, they were among the biggest makers of slide rules. But when electronic calculators began to rise, they didn't know what business they were in. They thought they were in the slide rule business, when they were really in the calculator business. They didn't adapt, they didn't accept the challenge of change and opportunity, and they fell.

And there's a functional fixation that has to do with people. Think a minute how you react when you see your pastor mowing his lawn, or your auto mechanic on a television show promoting a book. Stereotyping can even be a form of functional fixation--how many people would laugh at a blonde quoting Aristotle? Too often we permit only a narrow range of attitudes and behaviors in other people, based on bias, prejudice, hasty generalization, or limited past experience. Think of those statements, 'I can't believe he said that,' or 'imagine her doing that,' and so on. But recall the proverb, 'The goal of my life is not to live down to your expectations.'

3.   Feeling helpless.

This is the feeling that you don't have the tools, knowledge, materials, ability, to do anything, so you might as well not try. We are trained to rely on other people for almost everything. We think small and limit ourselves. But the world can be interacted with.

If you are in need of information, there are libraries, book-stores, web sites, friends, professors, and, of course, the Internet. And there are also city, county, and state government agencies with addresses and phone numbers and web sites. There are thousands of government agencies that really exist and that will talk to you. Contact the EPA if you're working on air pollution or pesticides. Get some government publications. Call your state senator or federal congressman for help on bills, information, problems. Contact the manufacturer of a product to find out what you want to know about it.

If you are technologically poor, you can learn. Learn how to cook, use tools, make clothes, and use a computer. You can learn to do anything you really want to do. All you need is the motivation and commitment. You can learn to fly an airplane, drive a truck, scuba dive, fix a car—you name it.

4. Mental blocks.

Mental blocks prevent you from doing something just because it doesn't sound good or right, which is a pretty ridiculous thing. Overcoming such blocks can be really beneficial. Navy commandos in Vietnam overcame their blocks and put on women's pantyhose when they marched through the swamps and jungle. The pantyhose cut down on the friction and rubbing from the plants and aided in removing the dozens of leeches after a mission.

Positive Attitudes for Critical Thinking and Problem Solving

1. Curiosity.

Creative people want to know things--all kinds of things-- just to know them. Knowledge does not require a reason. The question, 'Why do you want to know that?' seems strange to the creative person, who is likely to respond, 'Because I don't know the answer.' Knowledge is enjoyable and often useful in strange and unexpected ways.

For example, I was once attempting to repair something, without apparent success, when an onlooker asked testily, 'Do you know what you're doing?' I replied calmly, 'No, that's why I'm doing it.'

Next, knowledge is wide ranging, it is necessary for creativity to flourish to its fullest. Much creativity arises from variations of a known or combinations of two nos. The best ideas flow from a well-equipped mind. To prove this point nothing can come from nothing.

In addition to knowing yourself, creative people want to know why. What are the reasons behind decisions, problems, events, facts, and so forth? Why this way and not another?

The curious person's questions their attitude toward life is it a positive one, not a destructive one reflecting skepticism or negativism. It often seems threatening because too often there is no good reason behind many of the things that are taken for granted, there is no 'why' behind the status quo.

So ask everyone the same question just to be able to compare the answers. Look into areas of knowledge you've never before explored, weather forecasting, food additives, ship building, the U.S. budget, or the toxicity of laundry detergents.

2. Challenge.

Curious people like to identify and challenge the assumptions behind ideas, proposals, problems, beliefs, and statements. Many assumptions, of course, turn out to be quite necessary, but many others have been assumed unnecessarily, and in breaking out of those assumptions often come before a new idea, a new path, and a new solution.

For example, when we think of a college, we traditionally think of a physical campus with classrooms, a library, and some nice trees. But why must college be a place (with congregated students and faculty) at all? Thus, the electronic college now exists, where students 'go' to college right at home, and online. Correspondence courses have existed for years, too, beginning with the challenging of the school-as-centralized-place idea.

When we think of an electric motor, we automatically think of a rotating shaft machine. But why assume that? Why can't an electric motor have a linear output, moving in a straight line rather than a circle? With such a challenged assumption came the linear motor, able to power trains, elevators, slide locks, and so on.

3. A belief that most problems can be solved.

By faith at first and by experience later on, the creative thinker believes that something can always be done to eliminate or help alleviate almost every problem. Problems are solved by a commitment of time and energy, and where this commitment is present, few things are impossible.

The belief in the solvability of problems is especially useful early on in attacking any problem, because many problems at first seem utterly impossible and scare off the fainthearted. Those who take on the problem with confidence will be the ones most likely to think through or around the impossibility of the problem.

4. Seeing the good in the bad.

Creative thinkers, when faced with poor solutions, don't cast them away. Instead, they ask, 'What's good about it?' because there may be something useful even in the worst ideas. And however little that good may be, it might be turned to good or made greater. We easily fall into either/or thinking; or believe that a bad solution is bad in every aspect, when in fact, it may have some good parts we can borrow and use in the solution, or it may do inappropriately something that's worth doing appropriately. And often, the bad solution has just one really glaring bad part, when remedied, leaves quite a good solution.

5.   A problem can also be a solution.

A fact that one person describes a problem can sometimes be a solution for someone else. Above we noted that creative thinkers can find good ideas in bad solutions. Creative thinkers also look at problems and ask, 'Is there something good about this problem?'

For example, soon after the advent of cyanoacrylate adhesives (super glue), it was noted that if you weren't careful, you could glue your fingers together with it. This problem--a permanent skin bond-- was soon seen as a solution, also. Surgeons in Viet Nam began to use super glue to glue wounds together.

Another example involving glue: 3M chemists were experimenting with adhesives and accidentally came up with one that was so weak you could peel it right back off. Hold strength, shear strength, all were way below the minimum standards for any self-respecting adhesive. A glue that won't hold? Quite a problem! But this problem was also a solution, as you now see in Post-It Notes.

6.   Problems are interesting and emotionally acceptable.

Many people confront every problem with a shudder and a turn of the head. They don't even want to admit that a problem exists--with their car, their spouse, their child, their job, house, whatever. As a result, often the problem persists and drives them crazy or rises to a crisis and drives them crazy.

Creative people see problems as interesting challenges worth tackling. Problems are not fearful beasts to be feared or loathed; they are worthy opponents to be jousted with and unhorsed. Problem solving is fun, educational, rewarding, ego building, and helpful to society.

Critical Thinking and Motivation
1.   Perseverance

Most people fail because they spend only nine minutes on a problem that requires ten minutes to solve. Creativity and problem solving are hard work and require fierce application of time and energy. There is no quick and easy secret. You need knowledge gained by study and research and you must put your knowledge to work by thinking and protracted experimentation. You've surely read of the difficulties and setbacks faced by most of the famous inventors--how many filaments Edison tried before he found a working one, how many aircraft designs failed in the attempt to break the sound barrier. But planning to persevere is planning to succeed.

2. A flexible imagination

Creative people are comfortable with imagination and with thinking so-called weird, wild, or unthinkable thoughts, just for the sake of stimulation. During brainstorming or just mental playfulness, all kinds of strange thoughts and ideas can be entertained. And the mind, pragmatist that it is, will probably find something useful in it all. We will look at several examples of this later on.

3. A belief that mistakes are welcome

Modern society has for some reason conceived the idea that the only unforgivable thing is to fail or make a mistake. Actually failure is an opportunity; mistakes show that something is being done. So creative people have come to realize and accept emotionally that making mistakes is no negative biggie. One chief executive of a big American corporation warns all his newly hired managers, 'Make sure you make a reasonable number of mistakes.' Mistakes are educational and can lead to success--because they mean you are doing something.

Sir Francis Pettit Smith, one of the early developers of the screw propeller, tried one design in 1836. During the test, half of it broke off--what a failure--but then the boat increased in speed substantially, revealing the efficiency of a new design, formed from a mistake.

Having the proper positive attitude about generating new and useful ideas and solving problems is really a large part of the whole process.

A few years ago, the pipes in my mom's house had finally rusted through and I was faced with the task of finding a plumber to get a bid. Knowing how much they charge for small repairs, I knew that doing a whole house would cost a fortune. I thought, 'You know, I'd really like to do this job myself, but I wonder if I can.' My neighbor happened to be around once when I said this, and he said, 'Oh, you can do it.' Just that simple expression gave me the positive attitude I needed to do it. So I did.

Characteristics of a Person's Critical Thinking
- curious
- seeks problems
- enjoy the challenge
- optimistic
- able to suspend judgment
- comfortable with imagination
- sees problems as opportunities
- sees problems as interesting

- problems are emotionally acceptable
- challenges assumptions
- doesn't give up easily: perseveres, works hard"

Virtual Salt Home. Copyright 1998 by Robert Harris | How to cite this page www.virtualsalt.com. About the author: Robert Harris is a writer and educator with more than 25 years of teaching experience at the college and university level. Harris at virtualsalt.com Virtual Salt Copyright Copied: 1/1/05 Checked again: Version up Dated: July 27, 2005. http://www.virtualsalt.com/ 6/13/07

Processing the problem
        The first thing anyone should do is recognize and separate their problem for themselves, and find out who or what is causing the problems. They may be inner linked to both. There are always problems in the resolution of a situation, that make it hard to go about solving the situation because within a person are unresolved problems. This may include dealing with old ideas or past abuses, trying out new ideas and new solutions to the quandaries involved. The solution takes on new

thinking and how a person is taking on the conflict may see more than one route to solving disagreements.

Think about options for solving the problem before tackling the situation, look at the consequences if a person doesn't solve the problems, and what might be the outcome when solving the problems. Pick a solution and execute it to the best of your ability, get a vision of what needs to be done, and focus on the method of solving the problem first. Then pick the best way to deal with your problems, with the least amount of stress or hurt feelings, the easy way may not be the best way to deal with a problem.

Alternative actions, and anticipating the consequences

I can teach problem solving, but unless a person practices solving problems it will not help them. The basic difference is how much a person relies on their own determination to change patterns and routines, relating to their own characteristics or personality. On the other hand they may rely more on the psychological aspects of problem solving, ideally speaking. Having a proper balance is the goal in problem solving.

That is why this study works, I have gotten down to what makes a person tick, and knowing how to fix or mend the broken pieces is the way I like to put it. This agenda includes "The 1st door is mental-awareness" on how you are able to modify the problems, and use the most effective ways possible in solving problems.

Because you need the ability to think things through, hear and communicate speaks volumes with clarity as to the ability to solve problems. The need to clear your mind as to what may have created the obstacles, then be able to hear what the other person has to say and being able to communicate with a person is the bases for solving problems.

Engaged in solitary efforts, working on your own problems relating to the situation and admit you have faults as you work on fitting the pieces of the puzzle together.

Then slowly start to work collectively and assemble the pieces, resolve disagreement and resentment before going on, cool down the heated exchanges, next continue to work as a unit until all the pieces of the puzzles are solved.

Again that reminds me, when I was a child I liked playing games, but this is no game you are playing. When I got tired playing I would find something else to do, but as an adult you can't do that. There are times when playing helps. Life is not a game when it comes to solving problems. Life is filled with temptations, trials and tribulations.

I have had people say the same thing to me "everything is going to be all right" and then give me some advice on what they think is going to happen, and it did most of the time.

After listening to all the advice, a person will try to sort things out. It is hard to solve personal problems, especially when nothing seems to work. What then? This is the most dangerous time when people are saying their life is a wreck. I am really dealing with my problems the best way I can, and there is nothing to worry about. People can be blinded when it comes to their own problems, and yet they have many unsolved problems, but the failure to deal with the unsolvable problems can cause personal grief and create a bad relationship. This is like a fighter saying, "I'm okay," just about the t i m e he gets knocked out! Remember my life was like a fighter who was almost knocked out. I was down for the count 7 times and I was able to pick up the pieces in my life and turn my health around. I got tired of picking myself up off the floor, but every time I would get up and start fighting again. I was really fighting myself and my health problems at the same time.

There was a period when I was fighting to stay alive. I could not walk across the room without getting dizzy and had to hold on to the wall to make it to the bathroom. I didn't have a clue as to what I was doing or if I was going to live through the heart problems. I didn't know if I was winning or losing in those days, but I knew I was fighting for my life. I was trying hard not to get knocked out, or even die.

I thought my life may have needed some fine tuning, I was thinking everything was going to be all right, and I thought if I could only make it through the day without having a heart attack. But, there were bigger problems inside and there was the turmoil of just living with the heart problems, and my health was getting worse with each personal set back in my life. Why should I change my life? What was wrong with my thinking? Maybe I am supposed to die young. I felt I deserved to die because I had created all of these situations.

As I look back I have 20/20 vision, but there are some of those decisions and choices I made that reflect 40/40 vision, because they did not change who I am.

At the age of 39 I went through a divorce. After the divorce I decided to go in a different direction with my life. At that point I turned my back on the things I had believed as a Christian. I was very hurt and even angry because things had not turned out like I thought they would. I had tried and failed. I was a defeated person. I certainly don't want to present myself as a failure, I had failed.

I think the most revealing thing is my being human. Some will see the other side of me. I certainly don't want to judge or be judged because I went down the wrong path.

I went through some valleys and there was a time of low self-esteem. Any one of these experiences can bring about a devastating effect on a person's life and how they deal with a situation. There were certainly a lot of different emotions to deal with.

As I look back over my life, there were some special times, but there is no doubt in my mind they were the toughest times. I had to dig down deep inside and face the storms in my life. As I look back at those obstacles and health problems, it brought out the best in me. I stopped and took a look at myself, and listened to what was going on inside. In those days there was the agony of defeat in my life.

Summary

After years of failure I decided on these three things to guide me
1. Dedication,
2. Determination,
3. Discipline,

I also applied those principles in my health. I decided to use them in other areas of my life, and counseling. I was not going to give up on myself, and it has paid off. I did not let the guilt destroy me, and pull me down. I kept facing the everyday problems and I would not let myself go back to those old thoughts and feelings of hate and bitterness. I would say to myself, "I am bigger than that; I want to be a better person." I kept rising to the occasion each day, and looking forward to the time of healing.

DISCOVERING THE REAL YOU?

I was dedicated to getting stronger as a person, and as the days and weeks rolled into years, I am a much better person. I felt I could do it. I'm always mindful of how many times I slip back into those old feelings and let an evil spirit control my feelings. If I had not been determined to change how I felt I would still be enslaved by those old feelings. The discipline created a new way of thinking; I am thankful for these principles and guidelines. I have used them to help me in solving and dealing with my problems.

There is a lot more to be covered in applying these axioms and developing the healing process. Next is how to evaluate the problems.

You may choose other methods of help in your life, and that is okay. We have gone through the 8th step. The next step is how you can learn to evaluate your life and problems. I have a fresh new approach and concept in how to deal with your personal problems and behaviors. I want you to look at a personal check-up and how it will help you. You can decide for yourself how these check-ups can help you.

DR BARRETT

Chapter 9

Step 9
STRESS MANAGEMENT

By Anthony Fiore, Ph.D., the Anger Coach

I it seems that anger is everywhere in our society. One just has to read the newspaper daily or watch the evening news to conclude that controlling one's angry feelings is a major challenge for many adults, teens, and children.

Uncontrolled anger is a major factor in domestic violence and spousal abuse, in aggressive driving violations, in workplace rudeness and disruption, in marital conflicts and family fights. Several large and respected studies have shown that one-third of couples studied had at least one incident of domestic violence during the course of their marriage. The same study found that about 1,500,000 children per year are severely assaulted (kicked, punched, beaten up, burned) in their homes.

Managing angry feelings requires mastering specific thoughts and action skills and then practicing these skills on a daily basis. The costs to persons who do not learn how to regulate their negative emotions are high and include increased risk of relapse, loss of relationships, conflicts at work, loss of respect in the eyes of loved ones, and lowering of self-esteem.

A particularly high cost of anger is on your children. The effect of children witnessing extreme conflict in the home can be devastating— more harmful most of the time than a parental divorce. It is estimated that between 2.3 million and 10 million children are exposed to intimate partner violence each year in the United States alone.

Although many adults believe that they have protected their children from exposure to domestic violence, 80-90% of children in those homes can give detailed descriptions of the violence experienced in their families.

What is Anger Management?

We view angry feelings as a normal emotional reaction to frustration in our everyday world. It is natural to become angry when we have a goal and this goal is blocked in some way. Anger isn't just one emotion, but a family of emotions that are related to each other both in our brains and in our behavior. People often give a variety of names to their angry feelings, which range from mild irritation to rage.

Once anger begins it generates changes in our expressions, our faces, our voice, and changes in the way we think. It also creates impulses to action. In fact, the purpose of emotions such as anger is to organize and mobilize all of our bodily systems to respond to our environment in some way.

Anger, like all emotions, is regulated by that section of our brain called the 'limbic system' located in our mid brain beyond our inner ear. Emotional memories are stored in the 'amygdala' and other structures which are located in this limbic system.

You may experience anger now in your life which may actually be caused by a mixture of what is triggering the experiences you have had in the past—even if you don't remember them. This 'old anger' is activated by your brain in its attempt to protect you— even though the original danger is no longer present.

It is up to the thinking part of the brain, our frontal lobes, to find a way to deal with the angry feelings the amygdala and other brain structures have set in motion. Fortunately, as thinking human beings we have the unique ability to have choices regarding how we will deal with our feelings.

Our Model of Anger Management

In our view, anger management is NOT about never getting angry—that would be impossible and ridiculous goal because angry feelings are 'hard-wired' in your brain and probably serve as a protective and survival function.

Rather, anger management is about learning how to regulate and express those natural angry feelings in a way that makes you a more effective person. Persons who manage their anger well have better relationships, better health, and more occupational success than those who manage their anger poorly. They also get more of their needs met without antagonizing loved ones or colleagues.

Learning to manage anger involves mastering the eight tools of anger control that we have found to be highly effective in our local anger management classes. This model of anger management is not therapy and does not dwell on the past or the underlying reasons for anger. Rather, our approach is psycho-educational, skill-building, and practical drawing on recent research and findings in neuroscience, marriage/relationships, stress management, and the emerging science of happiness and optimism.

The Eight Tools of Anger Control
Tool 1 - Recognize Stress

Stress and anger tend to go hand and hand. The higher   one's stress level, the easier it is to allow our anger to get out of control. It is a challenge for most of us to manage our stress levels in a complex world with many demands and expectations. Learning stress management techniques is an effective way to reduce the physical, behavioral, and emotional problems caused by too much stress.

Stress is often the trigger that takes us from feeling peaceful to experiencing uncomfortable angry feelings in many common life situations. Whether the stressor is external or internal, scientists have discovered that the major systems of the body work together to provide one of the human organism's most powerful and sophisticated defenses; the stress response which you may know better as 'fight-or-flight'. Before your stress response turns into anger or aggression, use stress management strategies to get it under control.

Tool 2 - Develop Empathy

Have you ever been in a restaurant and noticed that the customers at the table next to you were speaking louder than anyone else? It was as if they had no idea that they were being so loud and intrusive to the rest of the patrons. This lack of awareness is often a sign of not being emotionally or socially alert; or have you ever been in a situation where you tried to express your feelings and it backfired in some way? Some of us are very good at knowing how we feel and expressing it, while others struggle to do so. It is crucial to express emotions in order to relate to those around us. Our ability to know how we are feeling as well as our ability to accurately sense the feelings of those around us and help us make positive connections with others. This characteristic is often called 'empathy.'

To empathize is to see with the eyes of another, to hear with the ears of another, and to feel the heart of another. A lack of empathy leads to poor communication and a failure to understand others. To manage anger, it often helps to see our anger as a combination of other people's behavior and our lack of empathy toward them or their situation.

Tool 3 - Respond Instead of React

Many times we become angry because we find people and situations that literally 'push our buttons,' and we react just like a juke box that automatically pulls down a record and starts playing when you make a selection. Rather than reacting to anger triggers in this fashion, you can learn to choose how to deal with frustrating situations — to respond rather than automatically react like that juke box.

There are many advantages to learning to how be more flexible in dealing with the stresses and frustrations of life. At the top of the list is a sense of empowerment. It just feels good and powerful to know that you are in charge of your response, rather than being con- trolled by other people or circumstances. Many people notice their anger level going down as their feeling of empowerment goes up.

Tool 4 - Change That Conversation with Yourself

'For some reason whenever I get upset I am always putting my- self down' said one woman in an anger management class. 'Even my friends tell me I am just too hard on myself', she said. When

I get upset, I will often say things like, 'I'm such a loser', or, 'if I don't make it on time, everyone will think I'm a jerk', the woman explained. 'Sometimes I even tell myself that I am worthless and stupid when I make mistakes.'

A crucial tool in dealing with angry feelings is that of challenging that conversation with yourself. Like the woman described above, you are constantly telling yourself all kinds of things which cause you to have certain feelings or emotions—even though you may not realize it. Learning to change that 'self-talk' empowers you to deal with anger more effectively in terms of how strongly you feel the anger, how long you hold onto your anger, and how you express your anger.

Tool 5 - Communicate Assertively

Good communication skills are an essential ingredient to anger management because poor communication causes untold emotional hurt, misunderstandings, and conflict. Words are powerful, but the message we convey to others is even more powerful and often determines how people respond to us and how we feel toward them.

Anger expressed toward others is often a misguided way of communicating a feeling we have or a need that is not being satisfied by other people or situations. Assertive communication—as distinct from aggressive communication— is a set of skills to honestly and effectively communicate how you feel and how you are responding to things—without getting angry or hostile about it.

Tool 6 - Adjust Expectations

Have you ever been told your expectations are too high? Anger and stress can often be caused when our expectations are too far apart from what is realistic to achieve. In other words, anger is often triggered by a discrepancy between what we expect and what we get.

Learning to adjust those expectations—sometimes upward and other times downward—can help us cope with difficult situations or people, or even cope with ourselves. In marriage, research shows that much anger is caused by trying to solve problems which are unsolvable and perpetual. Successful couples learn to live with each other and deal with these issues rather than getting angry about them.

Tool 7 - Forgive But Don't Forget!

Anger is often the result of grievances we hold toward other people or situations, usually because of our perception and feeling of having been wronged by them in some way. Resentment is a form of anger that does more damage to the holder than the offender. Holding a grudge is letting the offender live rent free in your head. Making the decision to 'let go' (while still protecting ourselves) is often a process of forgiveness – or at least acceptance – and is a major step toward anger control.

Tool 8 - Retreat and Think Things Over!

Jim and Mary Jones loved each other deeply, but often went into horrific verbal battles over any number of issues. However, they were unable to give each other 'space' during an argument insisting they solve the issue immediately. Even worse, Mary often physically blocked Jim from leaving and would follow him from room to room demanding discussion. Needless to say, this is a dangerous practice as it can escalate levels of anger even further and cause partners to do and say things they don't really mean to say and may later regret!

Research shows that we are pretty much incapable of resolving conflicts or thinking rationally in an argument when our stress level reaches a certain point. To avoid losing control either physically or verbally, it is often best to take a temporary 'time-out' - and leave. This tool of anger management works much better if (a) you commit to return within a reasonable amount of time to work things out, and (b) you work on your 'self-talk' while trying to cool down."

Tony Fiore, PH-D, is a practicing psychologist and anger management trainer in Southern California. He can be reached at 714-771-0378, on the web at www.angercoach.com or by email: drtony@angercoach.com. He publishes a free monthly newsletter "Taming the Anger Bee," and is also co-author of "*Anger Management for the Twenty-First Century*" which explains the eight tools in much more detail. Century Anger Management (www.centuryangermanage-ment.com) provides certification training for anger-management-professionals.

http://www.angercoach.com/ARTICALES_8_tools_of_anger_control.asp 8/14/2009

Pressure-relief Concepts

A person needs to be aware of who they are and their mental state of mind is vital to a person's handling and creating pressure-relief concepts. They are vital links to a person's mental and physical-well-being.

It takes a great deal of care to understand both sides of the human spirit. The human side and spiritual side of a person is a critical point in the human make-up. Every person is made up of two characteristics: biological, and genetics that come from their mother and father as far back as three generations. I think there is a correlation of the two and both of them are related to the behavior patterns. There are two other elements, the family environment and social environment that influence their human behavior and spirit.

Say for instance if both parents have anger problems, it is likely the child will have a strong tendency to have behavior anger problems because of their genetic tie to both parents. Let me take it a step farther, if only one parent has an anger problem the child is 50% less likely to have anger problems. That is not the end; there are two other contributing factors: one, their family environment, if there is arguing and fighting in the family it is likely that the child will develop anger issues. Two: there is their social environment. The child who is brought up in the inner city is very likely to have anger and behavior problems.

There is yet another influence, alcohol and drugs. The likely hood of this is passed on from the parents, but in this case it is through the blood from one or both parents, again depending on if one or both parents are into alcohol and drugs. Again, let me bring out the point, the child will have only one blood type from one parent. If their blood type comes from the alcohol or drug parent their temptation will be stronger because of blood type. If both parents are into alcohol and drugs they will have an even stronger desire. The third and final factor is their family or social environment. In a lot of my cases when dealing with all three, the strongest is the biological and genetics in any situation.

How does God fit in and where do we get our power to overcome? I have been dealing with the human side in our study on human behavior. I will continue by dealing with the human spirit. I am going to show you how I have dealt with this aspect of the human make-up. There are many different avenues and channels that cause a person to do things as they go through a situation. A person has to deal with both sides of the coin at the same time.

The human spirit can do some funny things at times. I am of the opinion that the mind has power over matter in many cases. If the inner components of a person have power, where does it come from? How a person takes rule over what they can accomplish will either lead them toward good or evil. The human-spirit is a driving force and needs to be understood at the same time. I have come to know how to deal with the human-spirit because I was able to change and know how it played a major role in every situation and in every aspect of my life.

Now let's deal with the will, it's just as important in how it works, and how it relates to the person. Some have a tendency to inflect their will over another person, but what about a selfish will. This can become a dominating force, and is a very strong factor in relationships.

The Human will is another aspect of life that has to be dealt with. The will is the very heart and soul of the person and it affects their attitude. A person's will is also inner related to the make-up of a person's character. A person is a threefold being; the will is a primary part of survival and living. The strengths and weaknesses are to some degree, instinctive. A person's will gives credence to a situation where some people never give-up under the load, while others falter in the same crisis or situation.

The phrase "the walking wounded" came out of World War II. This came out because men had to fight wounded. It was out of necessity for many reasons, and it showed up in their will to survive and serve their country. In the early part of World War II the enemy was winning and in close pursuit. They would have to fight or be killed so they fought to the death rather than give up. Their inner power was to win the war. That is what we are talking about when I say survival. The will to live can make all the difference between living and dying in some cases.

I know of a story that was told me, it is another example of a person's will. I was going to high school at the time and one of the boys on the football team told me that two of the coaches on the team were brothers. He said, "When they were in their teens they had an accident and the younger brother was pinned under the car. Under the stress of the moment the older brother literally picked the car enough for the younger brother to get out from under it." A person never knows what they can do, but under any given situation adrenalin kicks in and they don't think of themselves at that moment and time, consequently, they can do supernatural things. I'm sure he thought it was a life or death situation.

The moral to this story is we have supernatural power within the human body.

This is a fact that may seem impossible to believe, but science has come up with this statistic that a person uses about 30% of their brain and the same is true about our physical strength. What would happen if we used more of our physical abilities and brain? Could we even do more to improve our abilities to enhance our lives if we put our mind to it? Some people give up before they start.

Every person needs to have a way to relieve the pressure from time to time. It is very important to keep the situation under control. The way to do this is by having check points set up in your life. Then, be aware of your emotional needs in your life.

This is a major step in the healing process. It takes more than just talking about relieving pressure, but dealing with the pressures in a situation at some point. A person has to do something about the stress, and that will help them in dealing with their own problems. Sometimes a person needs to get out of a rut most of the time that includes dealing with the mind, the soul and the body they go hand in hand. May I remind you the mind sets the tone in the way=a person is going to deal with their problems?

That is when a person needs some kind of pressure-relief. At this point their emotions are probably running high they may feel the need to escape that activates the mechanism needed for pressure-relief. What happens when their problems are handled in the wrong way?

Try to find a way to vent the frustration, but try to do it in a positive way. Sometimes people don't have the right kind of pressure-relief and when that happens, it only makes it harder to deal with a situation. A person must want help and a plan of action in their life.

These are some of the cross over benefits from pressure-relief, and help in the other aspects of a person's life. The purpose of pressure-relief is to take the pressure off the situation for a while, it is still there. The proper idea is to get a good balance in all aspects in a person's life.

The wrong kind of pressure relief

Now let's talk about the bad things that can happen if it is the wrong kind of pressure-relief. This can lead to over dependence on drinking, drugs, pills, smoking and any number of ways people relieve pressure in the wrong way. These are some the common social disorders in our society. There is usually some form of abuse associated with these addictions. The spouse and family need help just as bad, because they are suffering too. Let me assure you that a person can overcome addictions or anything else in their life.

It will take all the help a person can get to overcome the travesty of addictions. We don't ask any person to do this alone. In fact, the biggest mistake comes when a person thinks they can tackle this alone. A person is going to need all of the love, support, and guidance possible. This is a major step in any healing process. That is why we and other organizations go about helping people.

I think when a person needs help with addictions, it is also a sign they need help in other areas that may have caused the addiction. People look for help, but the problem may lie in not knowing where to look, or what kind of help they are looking for. In most cases they want help, but are not willing to go through the healing process.

Don't feel alone when there is despair that is when you need help the most. The real challenge is to find the right kind of help. "WHY?" There is a basic principle people need to understand, one is why group sessions work in the process of healing and getting past the addiction.

In this case, I'm talking about dealing with their feelings. There are many avenues, particularly when a person is dealing with personal feelings that are a primary factor in any situation. The problem can be finding the right way to deal with their feelings of remorse. How can a person go about not adding another problem in their life? Let me say this again, a person needs to be wise enough to know if it is good for them or not.

We all know what anger is, and we've all felt it at times: whether as a fleeting annoyance or as full-fledged rage.

Anger is completely normal, usually a healthy human emotion. But, when it gets out of control and tends to be destructive, it can lead to problems solving—solutions that work, in your personal relationships, and in the overall quality of your life. And it can make you feel as though you are at the mercy of an unpredictable and powerful emotion.

The Nature of Anger   **Pages 1-4**

"Anger is 'an emotional state that varies in intensity from mild irritation to intense fury and rage,' according to Charles Spielberger, PhD, a psychologist who specializes in the study of anger. Like other emotions, it is accompanied by physiological and biological changes; when you get angry, your heart rate and blood pressure go up, as do the levels of your energy hormones, adrenaline, and noradrenaline cause imbalances in the body and mind.

Anger can be caused by both external and internal events. You could be angry at a specific person, such as a coworker or supervisor or an event such as a traffic jam, or a canceled flight, or your anger could be caused by worrying or brooding about your personal problems. Memories of traumatic or enraging events can also trigger angry feelings.

Chapter 9

ANGER MANAGEMENT

Expressing Anger

The instinctive natural way to express anger is to respond aggressively. Anger is a natural, adaptive response to threats; it inspires powerful thinking, often aggressive behaviors, feelings and emotions, which allow a person to fight and to defend themselves when they are attacked. A certain amount of anger, therefore, is necessary to our survival.

On the other hand, we can't physically lash out at every person or object that irritates or annoys us. Laws, social norms, and common sense place limits on how far our anger can take us.

People use a variety of both conscious and unconscious processes to deal with their angry feelings. The three main approaches are expressing, suppressing, and calming. Expressing your angry feelings in an assertive—not aggressive—manner is the healthiest way to express anger. To do this, you have to learn how to make clear what your needs are, and how to get them met, without hurting others. Being assertive doesn't mean being pushy or demanding; it means being respectful of yourself and others.

Anger can be suppressed, and then converted or redirected. This happens when you hold in your anger, stop thinking about it, and focus on something positive. The aim is to inhibit or suppress your anger and convert it into more constructive behavior. The danger in this type of response if it isn't allowed an outward expression, a person's anger can turn inward. Anger turned inward may cause hypertension, high blood pressure, or depression.

Unexpressed anger can create other problems. It can lead to pathological expressions of anger, such as passive-aggressive behavior (getting back at people indirectly, without telling them why, rather than confronting them head-on) or a personality that seems perpetually cynical and hostile. People who are constantly putting others down, criticizing everything, and making cynical comments haven't learned how to constructively express their anger. Not surprisingly, they aren't likely to have many successful relationships.

Finally, you can calm down inside. This means not just con- trolling your outward behavior, but also controlling your internal responses, taking steps to lower your heart rate, calm yourself down, and let the feelings subside.

As Dr. Spielberger notes, "when none of these three techniques work, that's when someone—or something—is going to get hurt." The goal of anger management is to reduce both your emotional feelings and the physiological arousal that anger causes. You can't get rid of, or avoid, the things or the people that enrage you, nor can you change them, but you can learn to control your reactions.

Are You Too Angry?
There are psychological tests that measure the intensity of angry feelings, the important thing is to know how prone a person is to anger, and how well you handle it. But chances are the bad outweighs the good and if you do have a problem with anger, you already know it. If you find yourself acting in ways that seem out of control and frightening, you might need help finding better ways to deal with these kinds of emotions."

Why Are Some People Angrier Than Others?
American Psychological Association

"According to Jerry Deffenbacher, PhD, a psychologist who specializes in anger management, some people really are more 'hotheaded' than others are; they get angry more easily and more intensely than the average person does. There are also those who don't show their anger in loud spectacular ways but are chronically irritable and grumpy. Easily angered people don't always curse and throw things;

sometimes they withdraw socially, sulk, or get physically ill.

People who are easily angered generally have what some psychologists call a low tolerance for frustration, meaning simply that they feel that they should not have to be subjected to frustration, inconvenience, or annoyance. They can't take things in stride, and they're particularly infuriated if the situation seems somehow un- just: for example, being corrected for a minor mistake.

What makes these people this way? A number of things! One cause may be genetic or physiological: There is evidence that some children are born irritable, touchy, and easily angered, and that these signs are present from a very early age. Another may be sociocultural. Anger is often regarded as negative; we're taught that it's all right to express anxiety, depression, or other emotions but not to express anger. As a result, we don't learn how to handle it or channel it constructively.

Research has also found that family background plays a role. Typically, people who are easily angered come from families that are disruptive, chaotic, and not skilled at emotional communications.

Is it Good to "Let it All Hang Out?"

Psychologists now say that this is a dangerous myth. Some people use this theory as a license to hurt others. Research has found that "letting it rip" with anger actually escalates anger and aggression and does nothing to help you (or the person you're angry with) resolve the situation.

It's best to find out what it is that triggers your anger, and then to develop strategies to keep those triggers from tipping you over the edge.

Relaxation

Simple relaxation tools, such as deep breathing and relaxing imagery, can help calm down angry feelings. There are books and courses that can teach you relaxation techniques, and once you learn the techniques, you can call upon them in any situation. If you are involved in a relationship where both partners are hot-tempered, it might be a good idea for both of you to learn these techniques.

Some simple steps you can try:
- Breathe deeply, from your diaphragm; breathing from your chest won't relax you. Picture your breath coming up from your 'gut.'
- Slowly repeat a calm word or phrase such as 'relax,' 'take it easy.' Repeat it to yourself while breathing deeply.
- Use imagery; visualize a relaxing experience, from either your memory or your imagination.
- Non strenuous, slow yoga-like exercises can relax your muscles and make you feel much calmer.
- Practice these techniques daily. Learn to use them automatically when you're in a tense situation.

Cognitive Restructuring

Simply put, this means changing the way you think. Angry people tend to curse, swear, or speak in highly colorful terms that reflect their inner thoughts. When you are angry, your thinking can get exaggerated and overly dramatic. Try replacing these thoughts with more rational ones. For instance, instead of telling yourself, 'oh, it's awful, it's terrible, everything is ruined,' tell your- self, 'it's frustrating, and it's understandable that I'm upset about it, but it's not the end of the world and getting angry is not going to fix it anyhow.'

Be careful of words like 'never' or 'always' when talking about yourself or someone else. 'This !&*%@ machine never works,' or 'you're always forgetting things' are not just inaccurate, they also serve to make you feel that your anger is justified and that there's no way to solve the problem. They also alienate and humiliate people who might otherwise be willing to work with you on a solution.

Remind yourself that getting angry is not going to fix anything that it won't make you feel better (and it may actually make you feel worse).

Logic defeats anger, because anger, even when it's justified, can quickly become irrational. So use cold hard logic on yourself. Remind yourself that the world is "not out to get you," you're just experiencing some of the rough spots of daily life. Do this each time you feel anger getting the best of you, and it'll help you get a more balanced perspective. Angry people tend to demand things:

fairness, appreciation, agreement, willingness to do things their way.

Everyone wants these things, and we are all hurt and disappointed when we don't get them, but angry people demand them, and when their demands aren't met, their disappointment becomes anger. As part of their cognitive restructuring, angry people need to become aware of their demanding nature and translate their expectations into desires. In other words, saying, 'I would like' something is healthier than saying, 'I demand' or 'I must have' something. When you're unable to get what you want, you will experience the normal reactions—frustration, disappointment, hurt—but not anger. Some angry people use this anger as a way to avoid feeling hurt, but that doesn't mean the hurt goes away.

Problem Solving

Sometimes our anger and frustration are caused by very real and inescapable problems in our lives. Not all anger is misplaced, and often it's a healthy, natural response to these difficulties. There is also a cultural belief that every problem has a solution, and it adds to our frustration to find out that this isn't always the case. The best attitude to bring to such a situation, then, is not to focus on finding the solution, but rather on how you handle and face the problem.
Make a plan, and check your progress along the way.

Resolve to give it your best, but also do not punish yourself if an answer doesn't come right away. If you can approach it with your best intentions and efforts and make a serious attempt to face it head-on, you will be less likely to lose patience and fall into an all-or-nothing thinking, even if the problem does not get solved right away.

Better Communication Skills

Angry people tend to jump to—and act on—conclusions and some of those conclusions can be very inaccurate. The first thing to do if you're in a heated discussion is slow down and think through your responses. Don't say the first thing that comes into your head, but slow down and think carefully about what you want to say. At the same time, listen carefully to what the other person is saying and take your time before answering.

Listen to what is underlying the anger. For instance, you like a certain amount of freedom and personal space, and your "significant other" wants more connection and closeness. If he or she starts complaining about your activities, don't retaliate by painting your partner as a jailer, a warden, or an albatross around your neck.

It's natural to get defensive when you're criticized, but don't fight back. Instead, listen to what's underlying the words: the message that this person might feel neglected and unloved. It may take a lot of patient questioning on your part, and it may require some breathing space, but don't let your anger—or a partner's—let a discussion spins out of control. Keeping your cool can keep the situation from becoming a disastrous one.

Using Humor

'Silly humor' can help defuse rage in a number of ways. For one thing, it can help you get a more balanced perspective. When you get angry and call someone a name or refer to them in some imaginative phrase, stop and picture what that word would literally look like. If you are at work and you think of a coworker as a 'dirtbag' or a 'single-cell life form,' for example, picture a large bag full of dirt or an amoeba sitting at your colleague's desk, talking on the phone, going to meetings. Do this whenever a name comes into your head about another person. If you can, draw a picture of what the actual thing might look like. This will take a lot of the edge off your fury; and humor can always be relied on to help unknot a tense situation.

The underlying message of highly angry people, Dr. Deffenbacher says, is 'things ought to go my way!' Angry people tend to feel that they are morally right, that any blocking or changing of their plans is an unbearable indignity and that they should NOT have to suffer this way. Maybe other people do, but not them!

When you feel that urge, he suggests, picture yourself as a god or goddess, a supreme ruler, who owns the streets and stores and office space, striding alone and having your way in all situations while others defer to you. The more detail you can get into your imaginary scenes, the more chances you have to realize that maybe you are being unreasonable; you'll also realize how unimportant the things you're angry about really are. There are two cautions in using humor. First, don't try to just 'laugh off' your problems; rather, use humor to help yourself face them more constructively. Second, don't give in to harsh, sarcastic humor; that's just another form of unhealthy anger expression.

What these techniques have in common is a refusal to take yourself too seriously. Anger is a serious emotion, but it's often accompanied by ideas that, if examined, can make you laugh.

Changing Your Environment

Sometimes it's our immediate surroundings that give us cause for irritation and fury. Problems and responsibilities can weigh on you and make you feel angry at the 'trap' you seem to have fallen into and all the people and things that form that trap.

Give yourself a break. Make sure you have some 'personal time' scheduled for times of the day that you know are particularly stressful. One example is the working mother who has a standing rule that when she comes home from work, for the first 15 minutes 'nobody talks to Mom unless the house is on fire.' After this brief quiet time, she feels better prepared to handle demands from her kids without blowing up at them.

Some Other Tips for Easing Up on Yourself

Timing: If you and your spouse tend to fight when you discuss things at night—perhaps you're tired, or distracted, or maybe it's just habit—try changing the times when you talk about important matters so these talks don't turn into arguments.

Avoidance: If your child's chaotic room makes you furious every time you walk by it, shut the door. Don't make yourself look at what infuriates you. Don't say, 'well, my child should clean up the room so I won't have to be angry!' That's not the point keep your- self calm in any circumstance.

Finding alternatives: If your daily commute through traffic leaves you in a state of rage and frustration, find another route— use a map or GPA system to map out a different route, one that's less congested or more scenic. Or find another alternative, such as a bus or commuter train.

Do You Need Counseling?

If you feel that your anger is really out of control, if it is having an impact on your relationships and on important parts of your life, you might consider counseling to learn how to handle it better. A psychologist or other licensed mental health professional can work with you in developing a range of techniques for changing your thinking and your behavior.

When you talk to a prospective therapist, tell her or him that you have problems with anger that you want to work on, and ask about his or her approach to anger management. Make sure this isn't only a course of action designed to 'put you in touch with your feelings and express them'—that may be precisely what your problem is. With counseling, psychologists say, a highly angry person can move closer to a middle range of anger in about 8 to 10 weeks, depending on the circumstances and the techniques used.

What about Assertiveness Training?

It's true that angry people need to learn to become assertive, rather than aggressive, but most books and courses on developing assertiveness are aimed at people who don't feel enough anger. These people are more passive and acquiescent than the average person; they tend to let others walk all over them. That isn't some- thing that most angry people do. Still, these books can contain some useful tactics to use in frustrating situations.

Remember, you can't eliminate anger—and it wouldn't be a good idea if you could. In spite of all your efforts, things will hap- pen that will cause you anger; and sometimes it will be justifiable anger. Life will be filled with frustration, pain, loss, and the un- predictable actions of others. You can't change that; but you can change the way you let such events affect you. Controlling your angry responses can help you keep you from making you even unhappy in the long run."

"Understanding the Importance of Optimum Stress Levels"

Pages 1- 3

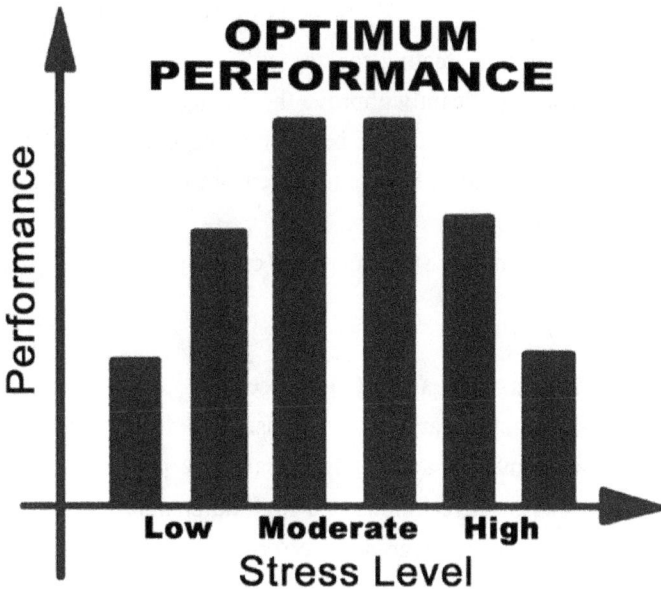

Ever wonder how some people, with incredibly busy lives and multiple responsibilities, seem to take their stress in stride while other people, with even fewer responsibilities seem to fall apart under the least bit of pressure? We can begin to understand this paradox when we begin to understand the power of control; the power to function within the optimum stress bracket.

The level of stress under which you operate is important: if you are not under enough stress, then you may find that your performance suffers because you are bored and unmotivated. If you are under too much stress, then you will find that your results suffer as stress related problems interfere with your performance.

People who feel in control of their lives are invigorated and challenged by their busy schedules. People who don't feel in control, often report being 'overwhelmed' by the stresses of life. This second group tends to see problems as unsolvable and obstacles as insurmountable. But the first group believes there is a solution to every problem and a way around any obstacle.

It is important that you recognize that you are responsible for your own stress, and often it is a product of the way you think. Learn to monitor your stress levels, and adjust them up if you need to be more alert, or down if you are feeling too tense. By managing your stress effectively you can significantly improve the quality of your life.

This section explains the linkage between being in control of stress and performance, and shows how you can ensure that you perform at your best by optimizing stress levels.

The approach to optimizing stress depends on the sort of stress being experienced:

- Short term stress such as difficult meetings, sporting or other performances, or confrontational situations. Here the emphasis is on short term management of adrenaline to maximize performance.
- Long term stress, where fatigue and high adrenaline levels over a long period can lead to degraded performances. Here optimizing stress concentrates on management of fatigue, health, energy and morale.

Naturally there is some element of overlap between these.

Short term stress

The following graph shows the relationship between stress and the quality of performance when you are in situations that impose short term stress. (Please note that this graph will be a slightly different shape for different people in different circumstances.)

Where stress is low, you may find that your performance is low because you become bored, lack concentration and motivation.

Where stress is too high, your performance can suffer from all the symptoms of short-term stress.

In the middle, at a moderate level of stress, there is a zone of best performance. If you can keep yourself within this zone, then you will be sufficiently aroused to perform well while not being over-stressed and unhappy.

This graph and this zone of optimum performance are different shapes for different people. Some people may operate most effectively at a level of stress that would leave other people either bored or in pieces. It is possible that someone who functions superbly at a low level might experience difficulties at a high level. Alternatively someone who performs only moderately at low levels might not perform exceptionally under extreme pressure.

Long term stress

Are you going great guns, with all cylinders firing?
Driving on the fast lane gives one a heady feeling, but the question arises - how long will the gas last?

However big your tank might be if you don't stop for a refill, sooner rather than later you will start running out of gas. But it's never too late, shift to a slower lane and stop over at a nearby gas station or else very soon you will be stranded without gas that too on a high speed 120 miles/hour track. Stranded to become history—a hit and run case.

DISCOVERING THE REAL YOU?

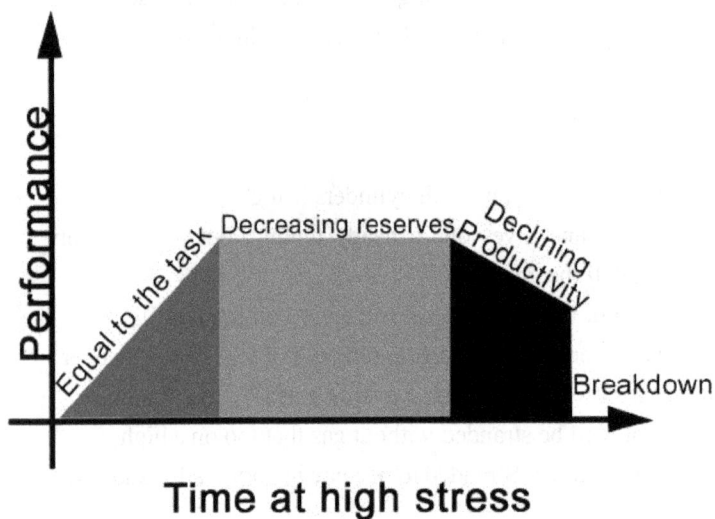

The problems of long term, sustained stress are more associated with fatigue, morale and health than with short   term adrenaline management.

The following graph shows the way in which performance can suffer when you are under excessive long term stress:

The graph shows four major stages that you may go through in response to sustained levels of excessive stress:

1.   All cylinders firing: During the first phase you will be up to the task and face challenges with plenty of energy. Your response will probably be positive and effective.

2.   Running out of gas: After a period of time as your energy re- serves decrease you may begin to feel seriously tired. You may start to feel anxious, frustrated and upset. The quality of your work may begin to suffer.

3.   Stranded without gas: As high stress continues you may begin to feel a sense of failure and may be ill more frequently. You may also begin to feel exploited by your organization. At this stage you may start to distance yourself from your employer, perhaps starting to look for a new job.

4.   A hit and run case: If high levels of stress continue without relief you may ultimately experience depression, burnout, nervous breakdown, or some other form of serious stress related illness.

Different people may move between these stages with different speeds under different stress conditions.

High performance in your job may require continued hard work in the face of high levels of sustained stress. If this is the case, it is essential that you learn to pay attention to your feelings. This ensures that you know when to relax, slacken off for a short period, get more sleep, or implement stress management strategies. If you do not take feelings of tiredness, upset or discontent seriously, then you may face failure, burn-out or breakdown.

As well as paying attention to your own stress levels, it may be worth paying attention to the stress under which people around you operate. If you are a manager seeking to improve productivity, then failing to monitor stress may mean that you drive employees into depression or burn-out. If this is a danger, then reduce stress for long enough for them to recover, and then reconsider the pace you are setting. At the other extreme it is also important to maintain some pressure or else the effects of monotony and lack of challenges will start taking a toll.

Encouraging employees to get organized, both at home and at work can also help them feel more in control. Whether that means working from a clean desk, tidying one's car, or working from a list of things to do, these techniques (which as a trainer you may take for granted) can give a person a much greater sense of control over his stress levels.

Finding your optimum stress levels

The best way of finding your optimum level of stress is to keep a stress diary for a number of weeks.

What can happen if stress gets out of control?

The long term effects of stress do not begin all of a sudden. It gives sufficient early warning for one to be able to take the necessary precautions. Where you are under excessive levels of short term stress, you may find that your performance goes to pieces. Afterwards, however, you will be able treat this as a learning experience and can adopt stress management strategies to avoid the problem in the future.

However, the effects of long term stress going out of control can be much more severe. If you do not take action to control it, this can lead to:

- Fatigue and Exhaustion
- Irritability and Agitation
- Depression
- Burn Out
- Breakdown

Fatigue and exhaustion

When getting up in the morning, one ought to feel as "fresh as a daisy." One should be able to work hard without undue haste or agitation, calmly and methodically the whole day long. In the evening one should feel tired but in a pleasant way. This is normal natural fatigue, which can be banished by a good night's sleep, and the same cycle should begin the next day.

But a person under long term stress becomes incapable of relaxing, resulting in fatigue and exhaustion. Under these circumstances the daily routine of one's work becomes a constant effort, even disagreeable and stress starts taking its toll.

Irritability and Agitation

A weary person rarely experiences the early morning freshness. On the contrary he knows clearly that from morning to evening he will have to "put up with himself," and that he will have to endure fatigue inertia and lack of willpower. He knows that he will have to make a great effort to keep a smiling face, that one tension will be added to another etc. It is therefore easy to understand that the tired person will have "had enough" of him or herself, of other people, or of everything. All this will give rise to irritability often manifesting as agitation.

Remedial Measures

Steps to remedy this can be as simple as going to bed earlier, or taking a good break. When you feel that you are getting exhausted very easily during your work hours you can try out some of the following suggestions:

- Take a stroll when you are stressed, it can help restore your perspective.
- Take a five minutes break from your work every hour or so.
- Avoid the habit of taking work home with you every night.
- Next time you feel you have too much work to do delegate at least one task.
- Learn from those who do not suffer from stress.
- Avoid routinely working late and at weekends.
- Arrange to have lunch with your partner or a close friend at least once a week.

- Learn to talk openly about your emotions and feelings with your close friends and confidants.
- Relieve pressure by discussing work problems openly.
- Spend an hour or two alone each week away from work and family.
- Learn to say 'no'. You have the right to refuse other people's excessive demand on your time.
- Do not ignore your problems acknowledge them as they arise.

Alternatively re-examine your life and check whether the things you are doing lead to you meeting your personal goals. This may show you which jobs or commitments you can drop. Implementing time management strategies may also help you to work more effectively, giving you more time to relax.

When the problem is serious, go to see your doctor.

Handling Depression

Depression may often be initiated by high levels of long term stress, by failure associated with stress-related under-performance, or by life crises.

Deep depression is a clinical illness should be treated medically. It is important that if you are depressed that you take this seriously. Severe depressions that can cause years of unhappiness and low performance can be neutralized quickly with drugs, by the appropriate form of psychotherapy, or by other forms of personal action. An important part of intelligence knows when there is a problem, and when to ask for help.

Depression may start when:
- you miss important deadlines, dates, and responsibilities
- feel like a failure
- you are passed and neglected
- you feel out of control
- you are very tired
- you are feeling inadequate while coming to grips with a new and difficult situation
- you are bored for a long period of time

The following points may help in handling depression before it gets serious:

An important way of guarding against depression is getting your attitude right: positive thinking really can help. As long as you can draw useful lessons from failure, then failure can be positive.

Similarly, talking about problems to a partner or to a respected family member, friend, or colleague can often help a lot. They may have been through a similar situation, be aware of the problem before it happens, or they may be able to gently point out that you have the wrong perspective on a situation.

When you are under stress caused by excessive demands, using effective time management can improve things. Similarly taking an enjoyable break may reduce stress.

When you are not under enough pressure, you can set personal challenges to increase stimulus.

If you are already suffering from a mild form of depression, then the following suggestions may help you to deal with it.

Self-confidence: where lack of self-confidence is a factor, there are a number of things you can do:

- Start to set personal goals. This will help you to give yourself direction in life, and will help you to acknowledge that you can achieve useful and important things.

Write down a list of your negative points. Challenge each item on the list objectively, asking yourself:

- is this fair?
- is this really serious?

You should find that many of your negative beliefs are wrong or insignificant.

When you identify serious failings, set measurable personal goals to eliminate or neutralize them.

Similarly, bring your anxiety and negative self-talk up to the surface of your consciousness. Ask yourself whether it is realistic or wrong to worry about the things you are worried about: if you have no control over them, then why worry, it does no good. When you look at them rationally, you may find that worrying is irrational or none productive.

Write down a list of the things that you can do well, and of the positive parts of your personality. Ignore 'virtues' like humility and modesty - these are not good for your self-confidence or well-being. Be proud of your good points - they can help you to contribute positively to the world.

Positive thinking: almost all apparently negative experiences have positive elements to them if you look for them. Learn to identify these positives: this will help you to draw the best from every situation. Even failing at something can be an intense and valuable learning experience.

Relationships: You may find that the root of problems lies with:
- **Assertiveness:** if you are failing to assert yourself, you may find that other people are not paying attention to your wants and needs. This can be upsetting and humiliating. Learn to express your wishes firmly and fairly, don't be confrontational unless it is absolutely necessary. Assertiveness training in self-control can be beneficial in learning to do this.
- **Social Skills:** if your relationships are difficult, then you may need to identify the difficulties in the way in which you deal with other people. In this case some form of Social Skills training may be beneficial. Alternatively if you can identify where things are going wrong, you may be able to set goals to over- come the problem.
- **Other people:** it is easy to assume (especially when you are depressed) that the fault or problems lie within the relationship or is it with you. This may or may not be the case. Examine your relationships rationally: you may find that people around you are causing the problems - there are some extremely rude, awkward, arrogant or confused people in the world. If people are making your life worse, then you may be better off without them.

- **Standards:** You may find that you have set your standards unrealistically too high. This will typically occur when you believe that a certain standard of achievement is necessary, but when you do not have either the financial, time or resources available to achieve those standards. In this case it may be realistic to assess the standards that you can reasonably achieve within the set constraints, and aim at these.

• **Fatigue and exhaustion:** If you are very tired, or have been under stress for a long period, you may find that a good break helps you to put problems into perspective.

When Depression interferes with the functioning of a person it ought to be taken seriously. Note that Major Depressive Disorder is a clinical condition; the person may need treatment by qualified psychiatrist. Delay might result in fatal occurrences, so do not neglect."

http://www.twilightbridge.ccom/stress/complete/aoverthecliff.html
8/14'2009

Drawing a Conclusion

What would happen if we extended the tradition of being thankful not only during the holiday season, but throughout the entire year? In that case gratitude would be rewarded with better health and good well.

No pill? No strict diet or an exercise regimen? Can a positive emotion such as forgiveness guarantee better health? It may be a dramatic departure from what we've been taught how to get healthier, but the connection between being able to forgive actually goes a long way in making things right.

Thousands of years of literature have talked about the benefits of cultivating gratefulness as a virtue. Throughout history, philosophers and religious leaders have extolled forgiveness as an integral link to health and psychical-well-being. Now, through a recent movement, psychology has called for positive mental health. Mental Health Professionals are taking a close look at how virtues such as being thankful can benefit your health these attributes will reap some promising results.

In some instances doctors will not do surgery because the patient is up-set or panicked about the surgery. They will change the surgery to

261

another day. People who are extremely scared do terrible in surgery. They are likely to bleed too much. They have more infections and complications, and they have a harder time recovering; it's much better if they are calm.

This a good reason for being straightforward with people when they panic or have high anxiety, it can lower their blood pressure, but it could lead to other complications and even sometimes death.

Beyond the medical anecdotes, there is mounting evidence that substantiate the need for emotional support to calm the person. Perhaps the most compelling data on emotions is the medical significance comes from a mass analysis combining the results of a 101 smaller studies into one single larger study of several thousand men and women.

To be sure, there is broad skepticism. This by no means indicates that everyone who has such chronic feelings will thus fall prey to mental health problems, heaven forbid. But the evidence for the potential role is there for other diseases to be more extensive to-say- the-least. Taking a look at the data on these three specific emotions:

- Anger
- Anxiety
- Depression

Let me make it very clear that we need to pay-attention to the potential dangers and influences in our life and life expectancy, and the quality of life. To be sure we need to know more and be specific in the ways we deal with our feelings. There is a medical significance, even if the biological mechanisms by which such emotions have their effect if they are not fully understood or under control.

Let's look what the Bible says about: Anger
Colossians 3:8-10 (KJV)

8 But now ye also put off all these; anger, wrath, malice, blasphemy, filthy communication out of your mouth.

9 Lie not one to another, seeing that ye have put off the old man with his deeds;

10 And have put on the new man, which is renewed in knowledge after the image of him that created him:

Ephesians 4:24-27 (KJV)

24 And that ye put on the new man, which after God is created in righteousness and true holiness.

25 Wherefore putting away lying, speak every man truth with his neighbour: for we are members one of another.

26 Be ye angry, and sin not: let not the sun go down upon your wrath:

27 Neither give place to the devil.

Anxiety

Philippians 4:4-9 (KJV)

4 Rejoice in the Lord alway: and again I say, Rejoice.

5 Let your moderation be known unto all men. The Lord is at hand.

6 Be careful for nothing; but in every thing by prayer and supplication with thanksgiving let your requests be made known unto God.

7 And the peace of God, which passeth all understanding, shall keep your hearts and minds through Christ Jesus.

8 Finally, brethren, whatsoever things are true, whatsoever things are honest, whatsoever things are just, whatsoever things are pure, whatsoever things are lovely, whatsoever things are of good report; if there be any virtue, and if there be any praise, think on these things.

9 Those things, which ye have both learned, and received, and heard, and seen in me, do: and the God of peace shall be with you.

Depression

Romans 7:15-21 (KJV)

15 For that which I do I allow not: for what I would, that do I not; but what I hate, that do I.

16 If then I do that which I would not, I consent unto the law that it is good.

17 Now then it is no more I that do it, but sin that dwelleth in me. 18 For I know that in me (that is, in my flesh,) dwelleth no good thing: for to will is present with me; but how to perform that which is good I find not.

19 For the good that I would I do not: but the evil which I would not, that I do.

20 Now if I do that I would not, it is no more I that do it, but sin that dwelleth in me.

21 I find then a law, that, when I would do good, evil is present with me.

Romans 12:16-19 (KJV)

16 Be of the same mind one toward another. Mind not high things, but condescend to men of low estate. Be not wise in your own conceits.

17 Recompense to no man evil for evil. Provide things honest in the sight of all men.

18 If it be possible, as much as lieth in you, live peaceably with all men.

19 Dearly beloved, avenge not yourselves, but rather give place unto wrath: for it is written, Vengeance is mine; I will repay, saith the Lord.

The power over the mind
Ephesians 6:10-18 (KJV)

10 Finally, my brethren, be strong in the Lord, and in the power of his might.

11 Put on the whole armour of God, that ye may be able to stand against the wiles of the devil.

12 For we wrestle not against flesh and blood, but against principalities, against powers, against the rulers of the darkness of this world, against spiritual wickedness in high places.

13 Wherefore take unto you the whole armour of God, that ye may be able to withstand in the evil day, and having done all, to stand.

14 Stand therefore, having your loins girt about with truth, and having on the breastplate of righteousness;

15 And your feet shod with the preparation of the gospel of peace; 16 Above all, taking the shield of faith, wherewith ye shall be able to quench all the fiery darts of the wicked.

17 And take the helmet of salvation, and the sword of the Spirit, which is the word of God:

18 Praying always with all prayer and supplication in the Spirit, and watching thereunto with all perseverance and supplication for all saints;

Excusive Stress Levels

It's no secret that stress can make a person sick, particularly when they cannot cope with their emotions. It's linked to several leading causes of death, including heart disease and cancer, and those are some of the ailments. Gratitude and good will can help a person in their career by managing their stress. Gratitude research is beginning to suggest that thankfulness has a tremendous positive value in helping people cope with their daily problems, especially stress.

Grateful people and those who perceive gratitude as a permanent trait, rather than a person's temporary state of mind, have an edge on those who are not-so-grateful. It is a proven fact that happy people enjoy good health. A person with a healthy mind takes better care of themselves and engages in more protective health behaviors like regular exercise, a healthy diet, and regular physical examinations.

Immune Booster

Grateful people tend to be more optimistic, a characteristic that boosts the immune system. There are some very interesting studies linking optimism to a better immune function. Researchers comparing the immune system of healthy first-year law students under stress found that by midterm, students characterized as optimistic maintained a higher number of blood cells that protect the immune system, compared with their more pessimistic classmates. Optimism also has a positive health impact on people, and those preparing to undergo surgery had better health outcomes when they maintained their attitude of optimism.

Even in the face of tremendous loss or tragedy, it is possible to feel gratitude. In fact, adversity can boost gratitude.

I am going to draw a simple analysis from aggressive to passive aggressive behaviors.

I hope this will help you understand one of the ways I draw an analysis. I always look at the extremes when I show an analysis of any behavior. I want them to take a look at both ends of the spectrum, for instance aggressive behaviors. I have used several other examples in our

265

study, now I want to use a different approach to aggressive behaviors. We usually think of them as hostile in nature, but not always.

Men and women who are aggressive in nature can have positive behavior problems, suffer such things as a high blood pressure and have a higher risk of a heart-attack. My conclusion is extreme aggressive behaviors can and does cause problems. The point I have made in this study is to be able to balance things in your life.

Socially Aggressive men and women are better adjusted,
1. They are usually more popular with their kids
2. They are better liked by their peer's
3. They have fewer behavioral problems such as rudeness or aggressive behaviors
4. This is a benefits of cognitive reinforcement which I have used all the way through this study
   a) They pay attention better
   b) They are better learners.

An example of passive behavior:
"Don't bother me—I'm too busy—I've got more important things to do."

When such encounters become routine and typical in parenting and in relationships, the outlook is not favorable for learning or adapting, it will likely get worse and also the child will get worse as they get older it becomes deep seated.

The risk is greatest when children live in and with—immature parents, abuse, drugs, depression, or chronic anger, or simply aim- less living:
- They are less likely to give them adequate care
- They are neglectful
- They have little or no attachment and give little emotional sup- port.
- These simple things can do as much damage as abuse, worst of all:
- They showed more anxiety
- They were inattentive and apathetic
- They were aggressive and also withdrawn

Examples of passive-aggressive behavior

The fact of inept parents pass these behaviors on to their children, this is true whether it's either the mother or father:

- If their parents are belligerent and violent, so are their children
- If their parents were aggressive, trouble makers, (bullies) so are their children
- When parents were punished as children, they also punished their children
- When their parents took little interest in them as a child they took little interest in their children
- When patents don't finish high school for most part neither their children

Another example of passive-aggressive is in the way parents discipline their children:

- Usually it's when they are in a bad mood they take it out on the children
- But on the other hand when parents were in a good mood, they could get away with much more
- The degree of punishment is much more server when they are in a bad mood
- The punishment was more attuned to their feelings, than to the incident

These patterns usually follow generation after generation unless it is stopped, by a parent or parents by using adequate emotional guidelines. What is more disheartening in these passive and passive-aggressive behaviors, one of the ways it shows up when a person "says or thinks? I well get even for what someone has done or said." Another is how young children learn these lessons from their parents, and how grim the costs are in a child's life?

I hope these examples will help you evaluate your parenting skills and in life a reminder not to be overly aggressive or too be too passive or strict; have a happy well balanced life.

I would love to hear from you regardless of your need:
Write:
Dr. John Barrett –PH-D

Self-Help Books
1122 W Cass Ave
West Plains, MO. 65775
Here is how to access our email: drbarrettphd@yahoo.com On the
Internet: http://www.sosselfhelpbooks.info

My hope is you will find a link to us or some organization,
church, or support-group that will help you because people who take
time to evaluate their life will help themselves in the healing process.

You may want to talk with someone else and get their point of
view because of your problems or situation, and that is OK.
Remember to talk with a neutral party because friends will have a basis
opinion. It is important to talk with a friend, but you should look for
others for support help. It's your burden to carry, it's okay to share your
burden with someone else who cares, and that usually helps. I provide
that kind of support help at Support Outreach Services.
The right kind of help and support is so important.

Personal change does not come easy. It takes a minimum of 21 days
to change any characteristic, or a way of thinking, and then making the
changes.

These studies can be vital in a young person's life because they need
help in understanding what went wrong. Children are affected by the
changes in their life, and they may react differently. They can become
hostile and very angry because they don't like what has happened.

I have done my best to show you how I have dealt with these aspects
and the makeup of a person.

SUPPORT OUTREACH SERVICES LINKS

I believe there is a bridge that will fill in the gaps in a person's life.
What is a person looking for, and how do they find the missing LINKS?

1. Common Ground - A personal encounter, "One to One."
2. The Panic Button - Is Our Message Line.
3. Independent Processing Center for Materials – Self-Help Study
   Guides, Books, Booklets, and Services.

4. Decision Materials: Life Enhancement ABC's study guide, & Life Enhancement Stress Evaluations, Assessments, & Analysis My health & fitness program.

5. Support Center (A) Support Partner (B) Support Group (C) Support Information (D) Group Identities

CHECK THE LIST OF SUPPORT OUTREACH SERVICES AND PROGRAMS

(Please check which of these "Services and Programs," you will want)?

Regardless of your faith in God there is someone out there that will share your views. People have a common bond as they share their experiences, and that is what brings them closer together.

SOS Self-Help Books

My family and my life story (book) "Facing the real me, Run John Run, the real world and me, the hurt and pain, The real cry for help." (Book).

I would like to let you know something about our self-help books for an individual, family, organization or in a church library. Please contact me if you would like to set up a conference, and seminars based on our books. We have workshops and manuals and we will help you with these programs.

Books:

"SOS LIFE ENHANCEMENT" Who is that person in your mirror; the functions of the brain, 10 steps in behavior identification & modification; as we help you climb your mountain?

"SOS SELF IMPROVEMENTS" personal identity Self-Image, Self-Esteem relates to Self-Control, Self-Discipline, & Motivation – Self-Worth is your Core Identity Pride, Ego, and Vanity.

"SOS NEW BEGINNINGS" Study Guide on Premarital Relationships, Marriage and Children, Divorce, Single Parenting, Blended Families, & Addiction Treatments)

Book: "The Fundamentals of Christian Psychology" & the Modern Techniques of Psychology.

We believe churches and organizations might like workshops along with our training manuals on "Mentoring & Coaching; and another is "Leadership Training" on how to conduct group sessions.

You might ask what your credentials I have a B/S from Baptist Bible College and Seminary; and from Louisiana Baptist University an M/A Thesis on Mentoring & Coaching, my PH-D Distortion "Counseling for Results".

What is your experience, I am a Clinical Christian Psychologist & Analyst, I do counseling and testing for the Master Ranch and Christian Academe, and have been doing group sessions since 2008, and I am the facilitator of Community Outreach Group Sessions.

If you want one or all of our books we will give you a break depending on how many you want. I would love to come to your church or organization based on what you can afford for our conference, seminars, and workshops. They will not need to buy any of the books for the conference, seminars; the manuals for the workshops will be a part of the workshop.

If you or your organization would like more information or references please contact me.

To participate in any of our services are free. When you order our books, and the study materials and DVD's, there is an expense:
One book $15.00
Two Books $25.00
Three Books $35.00
Study materials$10.00
Shipping costs $ 10.00
What you do will enable us to carry out some of these programs and services.

Our information network will give you list of study guides, newsletters are on the link, and some booklets are free. There is so much information out there and there are all kinds of help.

Check out our Support Outreach Services and Processing Center.

Support outreach Services is a non-profit organization, I am not supported by any government agency, church or denomination. Support Outreach Services is supported by our directory, conferences, donations, and book sales. When you help us I will share the results of our surveys and studies, and keep you up to date with our newsletters. I hope you will want to help, but if you can't I will be glad to help you if I can. Only what you feel in your heart is all that is expected from you.

Our processing center is an independent processing center. One of the links is called: "Gems for Jams." This is a community service bulletin board, but really it is much more than that. Here you can share those special thoughts, poems, or words of wisdom that have helped you. This could be something you have written yourself, or someone else may have written. The main idea is to get people to share something personal out of their life. This will give us a chance to access a wealth of information, and this information will be shared with others. There are lots of DVD's, books, and studies out there too.

I would like to hear about the experiences in your life, and may be you would like to share your experiences with someone else. This is a wonderful program and my hope is you are going to enjoy having this as a part of your life. Support Outreach Services can do this in one of two ways, book lists, or you may choose to put it in our News Letters "SOS Life Line News."

Newsletters.

Our newsletters are a vital link with the person. The "SOS Life Line News" is on our web site www.sosselfhelpbooks.info will have information pertaining to teens and college age young people. We will have information that adults can identify with whether they are single or married, and whatever your relationship is with your children.

The next step is to get you to respond and to participate. There are no specials because all of the services are based on what a person or organization wants. Some may want to support us along with some churches, and organizations that would be greatly appreciated and help us provide these free services. I want you to be a part of our services and programs. I don't use pressure tactics.

My hope is you will want to be a part of OUR HELP NETWORK I have a wonderful Pastor in my life, church, and class that has helped me so much in many ways they gave me the support when I really needed it. You know how my life was changed and there is a real need for the right kind of help and support in a person's life. There are inspirational speakers and I have a list of programs and services in the prefix. You can pick and choose the subjects and information that are of interest to you or your organization.

There are no membership fees or meetings to attend OUR COMMUNICATION NETWORK is set up for you. I feel that the age we live in has given us some of the best avenues available to communicate. The phone, the Internet, and our news letters are ways of meeting with you. Then you can share with us and/or partner with us. There will be special meetings conferences, and seminars you can attend if you would like. Then we will present different subjects and speakers using information from our books.

The most important thing I want you to know is how Support Outreach Service works. The purpose is to bring people together from all walks of life, have them share their experiences and help each other.

Support Outreach Services links

I believe there is a bridge that will fill in the gaps in a person's life. What is a person looking for, and how do they find the missing LINKS?

1. Common Ground - A personal encounter, "One to One."
2. The Panic Button - Is Our Message Line.
3. Independent Processing Center for Materials – Self-Help Study Guides, Books, Booklets, DVD's, and Services.
4. Decision-Materials:

My Family Biography and my life story book: "Facing the real me, Run John Run, the real hurt and pain, the real cry for help, the real changes in my life."

Book: SOS LIFE ENHANCEMENT study guide, Stress Evaluations Assessments & Analysis My health & fitness program.

Book: SOS SELF IMPROVEMENT self-image, self-esteem, and self-worth.

Book: SOS NEW BEGINNINGS relationships, marriage & parenting.

Divorce, single parenting, blended families, and addictions treatment process and recover programs.

5. Support Center (A) Support Partner (B) Support Group (C) Support Information (D) Group Identities.

6. drbarrettphd.yahoo.com / email access.

Check the list of Support outreach Services and programs

(Please check which of these "Services and Programs," you will want)?

Regardless of your faith in God there is someone out there that will share your views.

People have a common bond as they share their experiences, and that is what brings them closer together.

SOS Communication Network

To get the information you want, you will need to participate in OUR SOS on line surveys, programs, and services.

www.ingramcontent.com/pod-product-compliance
Lightning Source LLC
Chambersburg PA
CBHW051816090426
42736CB00011B/1509